THE NEW DYNAMICS OF AGEING
Volume 2

Edited by Alan Walker

First published in Great Britain in 2018 by

Policy Press
University of Bristol
1-9 Old Park Hill
Bristol
BS2 8BB
UK
t: +44 (0)117 954 5940
pp-info@bristol.ac.uk
www.policypress.co.uk

North America office:
Policy Press
c/o The University of Chicago Press
1427 East 60th Street
Chicago, IL 60637, USA
t: +1 773 702 7700
f: +1 773-702-9756
sales@press.uchicago.edu
www.press.uchicago.edu

British Library Cataloguing in Publication Data
A catalogue record for this book is available from the British Library

Library of Congress Cataloging-in-Publication Data
A catalog record for this book has been requested

978-1-4473-1478-3 hardback
978-1-4473-1479-0 paperback
978-1-4473-1481-3 ePdf
978-1-4473-1483-7 ePub
978-1-4473-1482-0 Mobi

Cover design by Policy Press
Front cover image: istock
Printed and bound in Great Britain by CMP, Poole
Policy Press uses environmentally responsible print partners

Contents

List of tables and figures

Tables

Figures and photographs

List of contributors

Tim Adlam, Head of Mechanical Engineering, Designability at the Royal United Hospital, Bath

David Amigoni, Professor of Victorian Literature, Pro Vice-Chancellor, Research and Enterprise at Keele University

Sara Arber, Professor of Sociology at the University of Surrey

Arlene Astell, Professor of Neurocognitive Disorders at the University of Reading

Claire Bamford, Senior Research Associate at Newcastle University

Ruth Basten, Counsellor in private practice

Miriam Bernard, Professor of Social Gerontology at Keele University

Barry Bogin, Professor of Biological Anthropology at Loughborough University

Laura Brown, Lecturer at the University of Manchester

Deborah Cairns, Research Fellow, Scottish Learning Disabilities Observatory, Institute of Health and Wellbeing, University of Glasgow

Michael Calnan, Professor of Medical Sociology at the University of Kent

Ailsa Cameron, Senior Lecturer in Policy Studies at the University of Bristol

Jasmin Chowdhury, Partnerships Delivery Manager at Diabetes UK

Sarah Cooper, Business Development Manager at the National Institute for Health Research, Clinical Research Network

Lynne S. Cox, Associate Professor of Biochemistry at the University of Oxford

Miranda Davies, Senior Research Analyst, Nuffield Trust, London

Chadni Deb, Medical Student

Niharika Arora Duggal, Research Fellow at the University of Birmingham

Ingrid Eyers, Independent Expert at CRaNe (Care Research Network), Germany

Nigel Foreman, Professor Emeritus at Middlesex University

Vanja Garaj, Senior Lecturer in Digital Design at Brunel University London

Kenneth Gilhooly, Research Professor in Quantitative Gerontology, Institute of Environment, Health and Societies, Brunel University London

Mary Gilhooly, Professor of Gerontology and Health Studies, Department of Clinical Sciences, Brunel University London

Alan Godfrey, Senior Research Associate at Newcastle University

Anna Goulding, Research Associate at Newcastle University.

Diane Harper, Postgraduate Researcher at Loughborough University

Priscilla Harries, Head of Department, Department of Clinical Sciences, Brunel University London

Michael Heinrich, Professor of Pharmacognosy at UCL School of Pharmacy

Ann Hockey, Honorary Visiting Research Fellow at Anglia Ruskin University

Nick Hubble, Reader in English at Brunel University London

Faustina Hwang, Associate Professor Interactive Systems at the University of Reading

Hannah Jennings, Research Associate at University College London

Hassan Khadra, FM Consultant, Contract Manager, Mace Macro, London

Deborah Kinnear, Research Fellow, Scottish Learning Disabilities Observatory, Institute of Health and Wellbeing, University of Glasgow

Mike Lewis, Professor of Sport Science at Swansea University

Liz Lloyd, Professor of Social Gerontology at the University of Bristol

Janet Lord, Professor of Immune Cell Biology at the University of Birmingham

Alastair S. Macdonald, Senior Researcher at the School of Design at the Glasgow School of Art

Lin MacLean, Sackler Research Fellow at the University of Glasgow

Wendy Martin, Senior Lecturer in the Department of Clinical Sciences, Brunel University London

Penelope A. Mason, Post-Doctoral Scientist

Joy Merrell, Professor of Public Health Nursing at Swansea University

Lisa Methven, Director of FaBS at the University of Reading

Bablin Molik, Development Manager and Communications Lead at Cardiff County Council

Paula Moynihan, Professor of Nutrition & Oral Health at Newcastle University

Lucy Munro, Reader in Shakespeare and Early Modern English Literature (Drama) at King's College London

Michael Murray, Professor of Social and Health Psychology at Keele University

Andrew Newman, Professor of Cultural Gerontology at Newcastle University

Jan Oyebode, Professor of Dementia Care at the University of Bradford

Judith Phillips, Professor of Gerontology at the University of Stirling

Charanjit Randhawa, Medical Student

Jackie Reynolds, Public Engagement (with Research) Fellow at Keele University

Jill Rezzano, Head of Education at New Vic Theatre

Michelle Rickett, Freelance Researcher

Jane Seymour, Professor of Palliative and End of Life Care at the University of Sheffield

Randall Smith, Professor of Social Gerontology at the University of Bristol

Tom Smith, Director, Generic Robots at the University of Reading

Gemma Teal, Research Fellow and Innovation Designer at the Glasgow School of Art

Philip Tew, Professor of English (Post-1900 Literature) at Brunel University London

Janice L. Thompson, Professor of Public Health Nutrition and Exercise at the University of Birmingham

Claire Timon, Senior Researcher, Applied Research for Connected Health, Dublin

Jane Upton, Head of Evidence at the University of Birmingham

Susan Venn, Senior Research Fellow at the University of Surrey

Christina R. Victor, Professor of Gerontology and Public Health at Brunel University London

Nigel Walford, Professor of Applied GIS at Kingston University

Alan Walker, Professor of Social Policy & Social Gerontology at the University of Sheffield

Lorna Warren, Senior Lecturer in Social Policy at the University of Sheffield

Anna C. Whittaker, Professor in Behavioural Medicine at the University of Birmingham

Kate White, Research Assistant to the project at the University of Bristol

Elizabeth Williams, Senior Lecturer in Human Nutrition at the University of Sheffield

Maria Zubair, Research Fellow at the University of Sheffield

Preface

This volume and its companion stem from the New Dynamics of Ageing (NDA) research programme 2005–15, funded by five UK Research Councils: Arts and Humanities Research Council (AHRC), Biotechnology and Biological Sciences Research Council (BBSRC), Engineering and Physical Sciences Research Council (EPSRC), Economic and Social Research Council (ESRC) and Medical Research Council (MRC). In breaking the mould of previous inter-Council collaborations to create this single programme, the Research Councils are to be congratulated and thanked, not only for the pooled funding, but also for the enormous effort involved to fashion a single commissioning process from five different systems. The Cross-Council Committee on Ageing did the bulk of the heavy lifting, and is duly thanked most warmly. The ESRC led for the other Research Councils, and special thanks are due to it and especially to Joy Todd, for both her initial hard work and constant support over the life of the programme.

Thanks are also due also to the numerous researchers who took part in Commissioning Panels and in the extensive peer review processes. The NDA Advisory Committee, chaired by Sally Greengross, was a tremendous source of support. Other members were Alan Beazley, Alan Blackwell, Chris Carey, Mark Gorman, Tessa Harding, David Leon, Angela McCullagh, Bronagh Miskelly, Naina Patel, Chris Phillipson, Jim Soulsby and Anthea Tinker. Previous members included Keith Bright, Paul Cann, Steve Cook, Rachel Kyrs, Janet Lord and Tony Martin. Special praise must be given to Anthea Tinker, whose wise advice, clear judgement, enthusiasm and warm friendship could always be relied upon.

The Older Persons Reference Group, while rightly challenging at times, was also an essential ingredient in this programme's success. Led superbly by Mary Sinfield, its members included John Barry, Mary Brown, Cynthia Conrad, Jim Harding, Anthony Hill, John Jeffrey, Savita Katbamna, Teresa Lefort, Irene Richards, Elsie Richardson, Elizabeth Sclater, Harbhajan Singh and Brian Todd. Previous members included Diane Andrews, John Appleyard, Bob Bell, Brian Booker, Tony Carter, John Christie, Janet Cullup, Iris Dodds, Christine Hamilton, David Hart, Shirley Heselton, Pauline Richards, Norman Richards, Barbara Shillabeer, Diane Smeeton, Steve Thornett, Stephen Townsend and Urmilla Tanna.

Last, but by no means least, sincere thanks to those most closely engaged in the final production process: Sarah Howson, Adele Blinston and Vanessa Rodgers at Sheffield; and Laura Vickers, Isobel Bainton and Rebecca Tomlinson at Policy Press; together with the anonymous reader who provided helpful comments.

ONE

Introduction

Alan Walker

This book is the second of two volumes of work arising from the New Dynamics of Ageing (NDA) research programme. This 10-year multidisciplinary research endeavour comprised 35 individual projects, 29 of which are represented in the two volumes. As with Volume 1, each chapter has been specially prepared, to a standard format, to provide context, methods, findings and implications. The first book contained chapters on three broad themes – active and healthy ageing, designing for an ageing population and global ageing – as well as an overview of the implications for social care of demographic changes to 2020. This book comprises four major themes: autonomy and independence in later life, biological perspectives, nutrition in old age, and representations of old age. This section list for the two books emphasises the extraordinary multidisciplinary collaboration that the NDA programme achieved. It is, to say the least, highly unusual to embrace such a wide range of disciplines – from biology to the visual arts – within one programme of research. These two volumes were preceded by a multidisciplinary synthesis of all of the projects in the NDA programme, *The new science of ageing* (Walker, 2014), which also provides a full account of the important recent transition in the broad field of gerontology. While it is not necessary to repeat that background, a brief outline of the NDA programme will assist readers to locate the research represented in this volume within the programme as a whole.

The New Dynamics of Ageing research programme

The NDA programme was the first of its kind: a multidisciplinary collaboration between five UK Research Councils. At the beginning, in April 2005, there were four Research Councils behind the programme: the Biotechnology and Biological Sciences Research Council (BBSRC), the Engineering and Physical Sciences Research Council (EPSRC), the Economic and Social Research Council

(ESRC) and the Medical Research Council (MRC). A year later the Arts and Humanities Research Council (AHRC) joined in as a co-founder of the programme. Later, in 2008, the Canadian Institute of Aging (part of the Canadian Institutes of Health Research) also became a co-funding partner in the programme as 10 new projects were linked to existing UK ones.

The NDA programme was established with the aims of understanding the new dynamics of ageing, the various influences shaping them, and their implications for individuals and society. It had five specific objectives:

- to explore the ways in which individual ageing is subject to different influences over the life course;
- to understand the dynamic ways in which the meaning and experience of ageing are currently changing and becoming more diverse;
- to encourage and support the development of innovative interdisciplinary research groups and methods;
- to provide a sound evidence base for policy and practice (including the development of prototype systems, procedures and devices) so that research contributes to wellbeing and quality of life;
- to promote new opportunities for UK science to link with researchers in the European Union (EU) and beyond.

The NDA programme consisted of two substantive research themes – ageing well across the life course and ageing and its environments – with eight sub-themes:

- active ageing
- autonomy and independence
- later life transitions
- the oldest old
- resources for ageing
- locality, place and participation
- the built and technological environment
- the global dynamics of ageing.

The multifaceted and lengthy commissioning process produced a total of 35 projects (excluding the Canadian ones), each of which lasted anywhere between 18 months and 4 years, with the majority spanning 2 to 3 years. These projects fell into two broad groups. On the one hand there were 11 large collaborative research projects. Those multidisciplinary and multi-work package collaborations (involving disciplines under at least two of the participatory Research Councils) could be said to represent the essence of the NDA programme. On the other hand, there were 24 smaller-scale programme projects that included a few that were not multidisciplinary. The box at the end of this chapter contains a list of these projects with the names and affiliations of the principal investigators (PIs). (An asterisk marks the projects from which this volume's chapters are drawn.)

Introducing the book

The first section of the book, 'Autonomy and independence in later life', is opened by Sara Arber and her colleagues discussing the hugely important, but hardly researched, topic of sleep. (Indeed, when the NDA specification was prepared, based on extensive consultations, sleep was not considered to be a priority topic. Its presence in the final programme is a tribute to the quality of the application for the SomnIA project and the peer review process.) Sleep is central to health and wellbeing, and often deteriorates with advancing age, but is rarely placed among the major targets of health promotion, alongside a good diet, physical exercise, smoking cessation and restricting alcohol consumption. A major contribution of the research reported in Chapter Two is to switch the focus from sleep purely as a physiological process to the societal factors that influence its quality and duration. For older people living in the community, social aspects include the meaning of napping, caregiving for partners, and the strategies they use to optimise their sleep, alongside their general reluctance to take sleeping medication. In contrast, care home residents usually lack control over the night-time and their sleep, with care home routines, staffing levels and regular night-time checking by staff having a fundamental influence on the quality of residents' sleep. The SomnIA research has major policy and practice implications, outlined in the chapter, such as the need for GPs to prescribe alternatives to sleeping medications that are strongly resisted by older people.

In Chapter Three Judith Phillips and her co-authors consider the mechanisms and strategies used by older people to navigate unfamiliar spaces as pedestrians. The chapter provides rare insights into older people's perceptions of space and the landscapes they have to negotiate, including the 'unseen' one beyond the immediate vision, which forms part of their perception of an area. Key navigational features are landmarks and distinctive buildings, rather than signs, and sensory overload in an unfamiliar area is both a barrier to navigation and inhibits positive appreciation of the environment. This research emphasises the importance of not only an age-friendly environment to enable older people to 'age in place' but also of a diversity of experience. To accommodate this aspect it is essential to start from an understanding of the environment, and appreciate the agency that older people have in order to cope with unfamiliarity in their surroundings.

Another under-researched topic is the focus of Chapter Four, financial elder abuse. In fact, as Mary Gilhooly and her colleagues show, there is no agreed definition of financial abuse, nor is its prevalence known precisely. The team took the psychological phenomenon of 'bystander intervention' and applied it to the professional groups who are likely to be involved in financial elder abuse, such as health, social care, banking and financial sector professionals. They identified several significant barriers to intervening in cases of suspected financial elder abuse, such as identifying the abuse, the difficulty of reporting suspicions because of the Data Protection Act, lack of experience in identifying and dealing with cases of financial abuse as well as knowing how to deal appropriately with both victims and potential abusers, particularly family members. As the authors note, it was concerning that 'mental capacity' was identified as a key determinant of both the certainty that abuse was taking place and the likelihood of intervention.

Chapter Five considers yet another elusive topic: the perspectives of older people on dignity in care. Instead, policy-makers have focused on the ways in which care providers should 'deliver dignity'. Liz Lloyd and her team adopted a qualitative, life course approach to their investigation so that fluctuations and changes in circumstances and perspectives on these could be examined. The research shows how older people draw on the values, skills and knowledge they build up throughout their lives in order to respond to changed circumstances. They often show great ingenuity in the practical ways they adapt to impaired mobility or dexterity. The chapter demonstrates that maintaining dignity when support is needed involves more than good standards in services, although these are essential. Personal dignity depends on the recognition of individual difference. It requires support to maintain identity and self-respect.

Chapter Six ends the first section of the book with a focus on families and caring in South Asian communities. This chapter helps to address the general neglect of ethnicity in gerontological research. In the 2011 census, 16 per cent of the population of England and Wales self-defined themselves as non-White (compared with 5 per cent in 1991). While 18 per cent of the White population are aged over 65, the proportion varies among minority ethnic groups: 14 per cent of the African Caribbean group, 8 per cent of the Indian community and 4 per cent each for the Pakistani and Bangladeshi populations. As Christina Victor and her colleagues point out, a key feature of older members of the minority ethnic groups is that they are mainly first-generation migrants. The specific focus of their research was the Bangladeshi and Pakistani communities, which are characterised by profound material and health inequalities and social exclusion in comparison with both the general population and other minority groups. (Chapter Eleven also focuses on the Bangladeshi community through the lens of nutrition.)

In this NDA project Victor and her research team examined the experiences and perceptions of old age and later life among elders in the two minority ethnic communities. They found that chronological age did not carry the same connotations as a marker of ageing among these two communities as it commonly does in Western notions of ageing. Key contextual factors in the experience of ageing were weather, the socio-spatial environment, and the importance of space/place and time. Religion was also a key factor in forming a contextual framework for the experience of ageing daily life. For example, the majority of participants were Muslim and expressed a strong belief that individual life expectancy was determined by the will of God. Resources were crucial to the experience of later life, especially health, material resources and social resources including statutory services, family, friends and community. The key message from the project, for both policy and practice, is to recognise the diversity of experience within the minority ethnic communities and the dynamic nature of their notions of ageing and the resources, norms and expectations they bring to later life.

In the second section, 'Biological perspectives', the first of the chapters featuring biological scientists in the NDA programme addresses the topic of immunesenescence. As Anna Whittaker and her co-researchers identify, hip fractures are a major source of disability among the older population, with at least half of patients never regaining their previous function. Their research was focused on the close association between depression and the increased risk of infections and poor survival among hip fracture patients. Immune dysregulation, or immunesenescence, contributes to the increased risk of infection in old age. This research brought together biologists and psychologists to assess the impact of post-hip fracture depression on recovery and, specifically, to test whether it amplifies the physical stress of the hip fracture on immunity and physical frailty. They found that depressive symptoms do indeed impede recovery and exacerbate physical frailty. Moreover, they conclude that this psychological distress following a hip fracture in older adults is the main driver of immune suppression. This research implies that, in order to speed recovery of physical function, immunity and infection protection, and independence following hip fracture, patients should be routinely assessed and treated for depressive symptoms. The researchers proposed simple supplementation to correct cortisol levels and improve depressed mood – the subject of the next stage of this research.

Chapter Eight, by Lynne Cox and Penelope Mason, provides a superb introduction to cell ageing, which lies at the heart of biological ageing. The gradual loss of tissue and organ function associated with later life is thought to result from an inability of cells to divide, or cell senescence, which results in failure to repair the body. Cox and Mason's NDA project aimed at investigating what causes this senescence at the fundamental level of the genes involved and the proteins they encode, an experimentally challenging endeavour. For example, to obtain senescent cells in the laboratory takes many months of painstaking cell culture under strict sterile conditions, with regular feeding and sub-culturing. An average experiment takes about six months to complete with an additional few months to analyse the outcomes. Moreover, at least three replications are commonly performed to ensure validity. To cut a long story short, the research reported in Chapter Seven demonstrates that senescence can be studied in the laboratory, that it is associated with marked changes in protein composition, highlighting novel pathways of study for altering the onset of senescence, and that the drug rapamycin can delay the start of senescence in human cells grown in culture.

Cox and Mason conclude their chapter with a plea for an understanding of the mission of biological gerontologists to tackle the biological deficits of ageing while retaining full regard and respect for the person. They reject utterly the view that biogerontologists equate the accumulation of detrimental cells in the body to an older person being detrimental to society. Nothing could be further from the truth, they assert.

The third section, 'Nutrition in later life', opens with a chapter on the 'Novel assessment of nutrition and ageing' (NANA) project that developed a comprehensive assessment using technology to facilitate the collection of detailed dietary information, cognition, mood and physical function. This complex, multilayered and multidisciplinary project found that older people are happy to use new technology in their own homes; are comfortable recording what they eat and drink on a daily basis; are prepared to record their mood and complete cognitive measures daily; and will record their physical activity and function using new technology. The research demonstrated that the NANA technology is accessible and acceptable for a wide range of older adults. The validated toolkit measures nutrition, cognitive function, mood and physical activity among older people. This highlights the potential for early detection and intervention for older people not only at risk of malnutrition but also frailty, cognitive decline and mood disorders. This work is of importance because of the risk of nutrient deficiencies and malnutrition among older people and the link between poor nutritional status and sarcopenia, or loss of muscle mass and strength, which may reduce their capacity for independent living.

The starting point for the research reported in Chapter Ten was the risk facing two-fifths of older people of becoming malnourished while in hospital. So Paula Moynihan and her colleagues set out to both explore and define the current interactions between food, people and procedures in the elder care hospital setting, and to develop an appropriate technological response aimed at preventing malnutrition. They succeeded magnificently, starting with seven service principles that should guide a new food system for older people, such as considering food provision as treatment and considering all older patients to be at risk of malnutrition until presented with evidence to the contrary. The final prototype for a new food provision service for older patients produced by this research was the 'hospitalfoodie' system. This is a prototype for a nutritional management and food provision system that facilitates the increased engagement of all staff in the process of providing adequate nutrition to patients and embeds a chain of accountability for nutritional care.

Chapter Eleven looks at the connection between migration and nutrition, with specific reference to the Bangladeshi community in the UK. This minority ethnic community is not only one of the UK's fastest growing but also among the most deprived, with high rates of social deprivation and low levels of education relative to the majority population and some other minority ethnic groups. They also have poorer self-reported and measured health status including higher levels of disability, obesity and chronic diseases. Janice Thompson and her team set out to investigate the connections between migration, nutrition and ageing via an intergenerational and transnational project. They found that varied migration histories and changing family structures play important roles in influencing nutritional status, perceived and actual health status, and future health and social care needs among ageing Bangladeshis. Their research is of the utmost importance in attempts to raise the health status of this (and other) minority ethnic group(s), and in disease prevention. For example, they found a clear need for greater access to leisure facilities, day centres and other social opportunities that can consistently offer culturally appropriate physical and social activities. There is also a 'clear and critical' need for further culturally relevant health promotion, disease prevention and public health campaigns for the Bangladeshi community. In particular, nutrition-related health promotion messages need to focus more on portion sizes as opposed to the concept of the Eatwell plate that has limited relevance for communities that eat communally.

The final section of the book, 'Representations of old age', featuring several of the NDA arts and humanities-related projects, kicks off with Lorna Warren's path-breaking research among older women. The aim of the 'Representing self – representing ageing' project was to engage lay older women in the creation of visual images, equipping them with a novel means of critiquing and challenging persistent media stereotyping and invisibility. The essential research question of the study was how media and cultural representations framed later life, conveying ideas and expectations about age and gender. To achieve this end a team of researchers drawn from the social sciences and arts and humanities worked with 41 women, aged 43-96, using a range of qualitative visual methods to elicit knowledge and understanding of their everyday experiences. They found that participants in the third age were far more conscious of older women being stereotyped, misrepresented or absent from media images and to feel pressure to look a certain way compared to those in the fourth age, who discussed ageing in terms of health and mobility. Across all ages there was a call for images that spoke directly to them and their experiences: images of 'ordinary', 'real' or 'natural' older women. They also saw the importance of representing older women of power, independence and voice.

In Chapter Thirteen Philip Tew and Nick Hubble report on their investigation into changing narrative representations of ageing and how older people respond to and reflect on them. Of particular interest was whether either fictional representation or self-reflection in diaries mirrors and/or resists commonplace assumptions concerning ageing. What they found was that older people's capacity to control their own personal narratives was central to 'good ageing' or, more generally, for effective social agency. The research also found widespread agreement on the lack of positive older characters in fictional narratives, written or filmed, while certain stereotypes of passive dependency and an inability to manage were readily identified. Overall Tew and Hubble's research established the central importance to older people of continued control over their personal narratives in maintaining identity and agency. This NDA project developed a close collaboration with the think tank Demos and, towards the end of the chapter, some of the policy proposals arising from this work are set out. The conclusion includes a plea for re-thinking policy based on a re-imagination of current narratives of ageing.

Chapter Fourteen continues the representations of ageing theme with a focus on contemporary visual art. Andrew Newman and Anna Goulding explored how and why older people create narrative identities of the self in response to encounters with contemporary visual arts. They found that older people used the encounters with contemporary art provided by the project to negotiate identity positions in relation to meta-narratives associated with ageing. They tended to reject the characteristics they associated with the category 'old' that they had internalised in preference for a more positive counter-narrative. Thus the research demonstrated a way of understanding the social value of arts engagement for older people that is not addressed by current arts/ cultural policy. It also represents one of the ways in which art might support wellbeing in later life by providing resources through which past, current and future selves might be negotiated.

The final chapter in this section completes the programme's arts and humanities contribution to ageing research by looking at the role of theatre in representations of ageing. In another of the programme's path-breaking projects Miriam Bernard and her multidisciplinary team examined historical representations of ageing with the New Victoria Theatre's archive of documentaries and docudramas, produced between 1964 and 1995, and explored the contemporary recollections and experiences of older people who are, or had been, associated with the theatre in different ways. Archival and interview material were combined to create an exhibition and an hour-long documentary drama, 'Our age, our stage'. The project on which the chapter is based aimed to explore how age and ageing have been constructed, represented and understood in North Staffordshire's Victoria/New Victoria Theatre's social documentaries; the part theatre has played in constructing individual and community identities and creating and preserving community memory; and the relationship between older people's involvement in the theatre and their continuing social engagement. The chapter provides a comprehensive account of the 'Ages and Stages' project, with rich insights into the ways in which theatre constitutes a pivotal point of reference in some older people's lives. The chapter reinforces the importance of continuing to challenge the false stereotype that creativity declines or ceases in old age.

The concluding chapter summarises the key findings from the selection of NDA projects represented in this volume, and reflects on the contributions made by the programme to ageing research.

Box 1.1: The New Dynamics of Ageing projects

(* denotes those projects included in this volume)

Collaborative research projects

- SomnIA: Sleep in Ageing, Optimising sleep among older people in the community and care homes: An integrated approach – Sara Arber, University of Surrey (May 2011)*
- NANA: Novel assessment of nutrition and ageing – Arlene Astell, St Andrews University (March 2013)*
- SUS-IT: Sustaining IT use by older people to promote autonomy and independence – Leela Damodaran, Loughborough University (September 2012)
- Working Late: Strategies to enhance productive and healthy environments for the older workers – Cheryl Haslam, Loughborough University (March 2013)
- Rural Ageing: Grey and pleasant land? An interdisciplinary exploration of the connectivity of older people in rural civic society – Catherine Hennessey, University of Plymouth (March 2012)
- HALCyon Project: Healthy Ageing across the Life Course – Diana Kuh, MRC (December 2013)
- Design for Ageing Well: Improving quality of life for the ageing population using a technology enabled garment system – Jane McCann, Newport School of Art, Media & Design (April 2012)
- mappmal: Multidisciplinary approaches to develop prototype for the prevention of malnutrition in older people: Products, people, places and procedures – Paula Moynihan, Newcastle University (April 2012)*
- MAP2030: Modelling ageing populations to 2030 – Michael Murphy, London School of Economics (MAP2030), (June 2010)
- MINA: Migration, nutrition and ageing across the life course in Bangladeshi families: A transnational perspective – Janice Thompson, University of Bristol (November 2011)*
- TACT3: Tackling ageing continence through theory, tools and technology – Eleanor van den Heuvel, Brunel University London (April 2012)

Programme projects
- Ageing and Biology: A combined genetic and small molecule approach to studying the role of the p38/MK2 stress signalling pathway in a human premature ageing syndrome – Mark C. Bagley, Cardiff University (December 2012).
- BRAZZA2: Ageing, well-being and development: A comparative study of Brazil and South Africa – Armando Barrientos, University of Manchester (June 2011)
- Ages and Stages: The place of theatre in representations and recollections of ageing – Miriam Bernard, Keele University (July 2012) (follow-on funding August 2012–July 2013)*
- Longitudinal data: Transitions, choices and health at older ages: Life course analyses of longitudinal data – David Blane, Imperial University (December 2009)
- Quality of life: Psychometric testing of the multidimensional older people's quality of life (OPQOL) questionnaire and the causal model of QoL under-pinning it – Ann Bowling, University College London (March 2009) (follow-on funding October 2010–September 2011)
- Cell Ageing: Towards understanding the biological drivers of cellular ageing – Lynne Cox, University of Oxford (September 2012)*
- Detecting and preventing financial abuse of older adults: An examination of decision-making by managers and professionals – Mary Gilhooly, Brunel University London (March 2011) (follow-on Knowledge Transfer Grant September 2011–August 2012)*
- Music for life: Promoting social engagement and well-being in older people through community supported participation in musical activities – Susan Hallam, Institute of Education (January 2011) (follow-on funding September 2011–December 2012)
- Dignity in Care: Maintaining dignity in later life: A longitudinal qualitative study of older people's experiences of supportive care – Liz Lloyd, University of Bristol (June 2011)
- Stress and Immunity: Synergistic effects of physical and psychological stress upon immunesenescence – Janet Lord, University of Birmingham (December 2012)*
- Envision: Innovation in envisioning dynamic biomechanical data to inform healthcare and design practice – Alastair Macdonald, Glasgow School of Art and Design (January 2009)
- Safety on Stairs: Biomechanical and Sensory Constraints of Step and Stair Negotiation in Old Age – Constantinos Maganaris, Manchester Metropolitan University (February 2013)
- Mobility and Ageing: New metrics for exploring the relationship between mobility and successful ageing – Lynn McInnes, Northumbria University (December 2009)

- CALL-ME Project: Promoting independence and social engagement among older people in disadvantaged communities – Michael Murray, Keele University (February 2011)
- Art and Identity: Contemporary visual art and identity construction – Wellbeing amongst older people – Andrew Newman, Newcastle University (October 2011) (follow-on funding January 2012–January 2013)*
- Kitchen Living: Transitions in kitchen living – Sheila Peace, Open University (November 2011)
- OPUS: Older people's use of unfamiliar space – Judith Phillips, University of Wales (April 2010)*
- Cardiovascular Ageing: Dynamics of cardiovascular ageing – Aneta Stefanovska, Lancaster University (March 2012)
- Longitudinal Ageing Model: Trajectories of senescence through Markov Models – David Steinsaltz, University of Oxford (June 2012)
- Ageing and Fiction: Fiction and the cultural mediation of ageing – Philip Tew, Brunel University London (May 2012) (follow-on funding September 2012–July 2013)*
- Poverty in India: Ageing, poverty and neoliberalism in urban South India – Penny Vera-Sanso, Birkbeck College (April 2010)
- South Asian Communities: Families and caring in South Asian communities – Christina Victor, University of Reading (June 2011)*
- Look At Me!: Representing self – representing ageing – Lorna Warren, University of Sheffield (November 2011)*
- Landscapes: Landscapes of cross-generational engagement – Peter Wright, Sheffield Hallam University (December 2010).

The Canadian New Dynamics of Ageing

As mentioned above, a partnership was formed with the Canadian Institutes of Health Research (CIHR) that enabled Canadian researchers to bid for funds to link themselves to NDA research teams. Two commissioning rounds were carried out, in 2008 and 2009, which produced the 10 linked projects shown below:

- Health and Creative Ageing: Theatre as a pathway to healthy ageing – Janet Fast, University of Alberta. This is linked to the NDA project 'Ages and Stages: The place of theatre in representations and recollections of ageing' led by Miriam Bernard, Keele University (2012).
- How do catastrophic events by modulating the immune response lead to frailty? – Tamos Fulop, Universite de Sherbrooke. This is linked to the NDA project 'Synergistic effects of physical and psychological stress upon immunesenescence' led by Janet Lord, University of Birmingham (2012).
- Working Late: Strategies to enhance productive and healthy environments for the older workforce – the Canadian context – Lan Gien, Memorial University

of Newfoundland. This is linked to the NDA project 'Working Late: Strategies to enhance productive and healthy environments for the older workers' led by Cheryl Haslam, Loughborough University (2013).

- Interactive Analysis of Functional and Cognitive Change across the IALSA (Interactive Analysis of Longitudinal Studies of Aging) (Canada) and HALCyon (UK) Longitudinal Research Networks – Scot Hofer, University of Victoria. This is linked to the NDA project 'HALCyon Project: Healthy Ageing across the Life Course' led by Diana Kuh, MRC (2013).
- Developing and Validation of a Questionnaire to Measure the Psychological Impact of Assistive Technologies for Continence in Elderly Individuals – Jeffrey Jutai, University of Ottawa. This is linked to the NDA project 'TACT3: Tackling ageing continence through theory, tools and technology' led by Eleanor van den Heuvel, Brunel University London (2012).
- Connectivity of Older Adults in Rural Communities: Health in Context – Norah Keating, University of Alberta. This is linked to the NDA project 'Rural Ageing: Grey and pleasant land? An interdisciplinary exploration of the connectivity of older people in rural civic society' led by Catherine Hennessey, University of Plymouth (2012).
- Effects of normal and impaired cognitive function on stair descent mobility for older adults – Bradford McFadyen, Université Laval. This is linked to the NDA project 'Safety on Stairs: Biomechanical and sensory constraints of step and stair negotiation in old age' led by Costantinos Maganaris, Manchester Metropolitan University (2013).
- The extension of the COACH prompting system to nutrition-related activities among older adults – Alex Mihailidis, University of Toronto. This is linked to the NDA project 'NANA: Novel assessment of nutrition and ageing' led by Arlene Astell, St Andrews University (2013).*
- Sustaining Information Technology Use by Older Adults to Promote Autonomy and Independence: Newfoundland and Labrador Cohort – Wendy Young, Memorial University. This project is linked to the NDA project 'SUS-IT: Sustaining IT use by older people to promote autonomy and independence' led by Leela Damodaran, Loughborough University (2012).
- Improving Continence across Continents, an RCT of Continence Promotion Intervention for Older Women in the Community – Cara Tannenbaum, University of Montreal. This is linked to the NDA project 'TACT3: Tackling ageing continence through theory, tools and technology' led by Eleanor van den Heuvel, Brunel University London (2012).

Reference

Walker, A. (2014) *The new science of ageing*, Bristol: Policy Press.

Part One:
Autonomy and independence
in later life

TWO

Sleep and autonomy in later life: the SomnIA project

Sara Arber, Susan Venn and Ingrid Eyers

Introduction

Sleep is central to health and wellbeing, yet sleep is likely to deteriorate with advancing age. Health promotion over the last two decades has emphasised the importance for health and wellbeing of the 'big four' – a good diet, physical exercise, not smoking, and restricting alcohol consumption. A fifth health promotion message is also essential for good health and wellbeing, namely, sleep. Sleep of a sufficient duration and quality is important for older people's wellbeing and ability to engage fully in daytime activities, whether living in their own homes or in a care home.

While many sleep researchers view sleep purely as a physiological process, social scientists have increasingly shown how a range of societal factors associated with individuals' roles, relationships, family circumstances, daytime activities and environmental factors have an impact on sleep quality and duration (Hislop and Arber, 2006; Williams et al, 2010; Arber et al, 2012). While not denying that sleep has some physiological basis, this chapter examines some of the social aspects of sleep that are critical in influencing the autonomy and independence of older adults. As Williams (2005) reminds us, *how, when* and *where* we sleep are all societally, historically and culturally contingent.

Prospective epidemiological studies show a link between short sleep duration (under 6 hours) and elevated mortality, especially from cardiovascular disease (Ferrie et al, 2010; Grandner et al, 2012). Sleep is also important for cognitive functioning and memory consolidation (Busto et al, 2001), and sleep problems have an impact on quality of life, on daytime functioning and on recovery from illness (Haimov and Vadas, 2009).

It is well known that depression is associated with sleep problems, although recent research has shown that sleep problems often predate depression, and may therefore be a causal factor in the development of depression (Ferrie et al, 2011). During sleep, various physiological mechanisms take place associated with repair of the immune and other biological systems. Thus, sleep problems have detrimental effects on health in later life, with those who suffer from poor sleep being more likely to be at risk of heart attacks, falls, stroke, obesity and depression (Ancoli-Israel, 2005; Harrington and Lee-Chiong, 2007).

Not only are poor quality and short sleep associated with adverse health outcomes, but also chronic physical health problems and pain at night lead to poorer sleep. A major reason for poorer sleep with increasing age is because chronic ill health causes pain and discomfort at night (Vitiello et al, 2002; Arber and Venn, 2011). People with dementia have poor sleep quality, because of disruption of sleep–wake patterns resulting in fragmented night-time sleep and more sleep during the day (Bliwise, 1993; van Someren, 2000).

Physiological research on sleep in later life has found that changes take place to sleep as we age, particularly greater difficulty initiating sleep and an increased likelihood of awakening during the night (Dijk et al, 2010; Maglione and Ancoli-Israel, 2012). Also, other physiological changes to the ageing body affect sleep, including an increased propensity to daytime sleep and nocturia (going to the toilet at night) (Venn and Arber, 2011).

Light is known to be the major factor influencing the body's biological clock and sleep–wake patterns, however, changes in the eye with increasing age reduce the amount of light reaching the body clock (Revell and Skene, 2010). These ocular changes as well as other consequences of ageing (for example, nerve degeneration) result in older people requiring three to five times more light than younger people. Lack of light can also lead to poor differentiation between day and night, which may result in poor sleep and poor daytime functioning.

The most common form of treatment for chronic sleep problems in older people has been hypnotic drugs (Whalley, 2001), which are themselves associated with risks of impaired cognitive function and falls (Martin, 2002; Morgan, 2008). Hypnotics in the form of benzodiazepines were widely prescribed for sleep problems from the 1960s onwards, until reports in the late 1970s highlighted potential problems with their usage, such as physical and psychological dependence (Authier et al, 2009). More recently, alternative non-benzodiazepine hypnotics, known as 'z' drugs, have become available for the treatment of poor sleep, anxiety and depression. UK policy has focused on reducing hypnotic prescribing by general practitioners, on encouraging older people who have been on sleeping medication for long periods of time to reduce their reliance, and on offering effective non-pharmacological approaches to sleep management, such as cognitive behaviour therapy (CBT) (Sivertsen and Nordhus, 2007; Morgan et al, 2012; Venn and Arber, 2012).

Older people, whether living at home or in care home settings, remain the most *likely* and most *vulnerable* recipients of hypnotic drugs which, in this age group, are associated with risks of impaired daytime functioning, falls and dependence (Whalley, 2001; Morgan, 2008). Among the very old, poor sleep quality *and* hypnotic drug use have been shown to exacerbate frailty and cognitive impairment (Whalley, 2001; Glass et al, 2005). The need to reduce hypnotic drug prescribing and to provide effective non-pharmacological approaches to sleep management are recognised policy and practice objectives (Sonnenberg et al, 2012). In summary, among older people, untreated chronic sleep disturbance degrades their quality of life, inhibits recovery and rehabilitation following illness, and is an independent risk factor for falls and depression. The SomnIA research project was designed to examine these issues.

Aims of the SomnIA research project

The SomnIA (Sleep in Ageing) interdisciplinary research project[1] was funded by the New Dynamics of Ageing (NDA) programme and aimed to:

- understand the meanings and determinants of poor quality sleep among older people living in the community and in care homes – by assessing social, psychological and environmental factors, medication use and health status, and identifying potential solutions;
- develop a cost-effective approach to non-pharmacological self-management of insomnia among older people with chronic disease;
- develop and evaluate 'blue-enriched' light in improving the sleep of older people in the community and in care homes;
- develop sensor-based products to enhance sleep among frail older people at home and in care homes.

These aims were addressed through eight interlinked research studies in the form of work packages, as illustrated in Figure 2.1.

The first three work packages focused on understanding the meanings and determinants of poor quality sleep through (1) epidemiological analysis of large-scale survey data (WP1), (2) qualitative research with older people who had poor sleep living in the community (WP2)

Figure 2.1: The SomnIA work packages

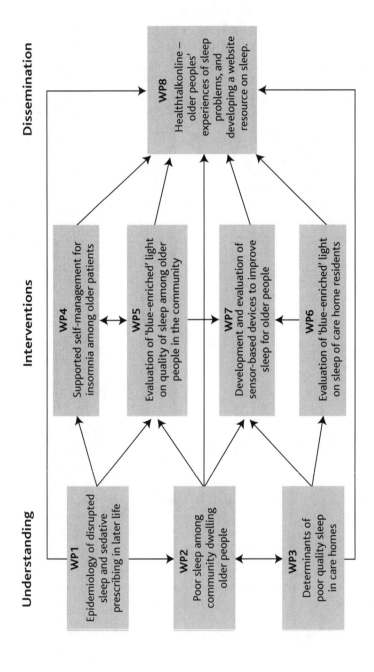

and (3) qualitative research among older people living in care homes (WP3). A range of nationally representative large-scale surveys were analysed in WP1 to examine the determinants of poor sleep quality and short sleep duration in the UK and European countries (Dregan and Armstrong, 2009, 2010, 2011; Lallukka et al, 2011; Dregan et al, 2013). This chapter focuses on social scientific factors influencing the sleep quality and sleep management strategies of older people living in the community (WP2) and older care home residents (WP3).

Four intervention studies examined various non-pharmacological ways of optimising sleep among older people, but will not be discussed in this chapter. They were a randomised controlled trial of the self-management of insomnia (CBT-I) among older people with chronic illness (WP4) (Morgan et al, 2011, 2012; Gregory et al, 2012); two studies that evaluated the impact of bright light and 'blue-enriched' light on sleep – among older people living in the community (WP5) and a 12-week trial with older residents living in seven care homes (WP6) (Skene, 2008, 2009; Revell and Skene, 2010); and finally, four novel sensor-based products were developed to optimise sleep for frail older people living in care homes (WP7) (Carey-Smith et al, 2013; Eyers et al, 2013).

Understanding social aspects of sleep among older people in the community

This section discusses some of the social factors associated with sleep quality and the strategies used by older people living in the community to manage their poor sleep (WP2). Several methods of data collection were used in this work package. A self-completion survey questionnaire was completed by 1,158 people aged 65 and over from 10 general practices in South East England. This included the Pittsburgh Sleep Quality Index (PSQI) (Buysse et al, 1989), which asks questions about sleep in the previous month. A PSQI sleep score of 6 or more represents a threshold for 'clinically poor sleep'. From survey respondents with 'clinically poor sleep' (PSQI score of 6+), 30 men and 30 women were selected for in-depth semi-structured interviews in their own home. Interview questions included perceptions of their patterns of sleep, sleep quality and attitudes to sleep disturbance, as well as their strategies to improve sleep, and any medications taken to aid sleep (prescribed or over the counter). All interviews were transcribed and analysed thematically.

Thirty-nine of the respondents gave consent for their interviews to be recorded (33 video recorded and 6 audio recorded) for inclusion in a module on 'Sleep Problems in Later Life' for the healthtalk.org website (WP8). This web module contains extracts from the interviews where participants talk about their experiences of poor sleep, how they cope with different aspects of poor sleep and the strategies they use to improve their sleep. These personal stories enable older people, family members and friends, doctors, nurses and other health professionals to better understand the experiences of older people who have poor sleep.

For 14 days, audio-sleep diaries (Hislop et al, 2005) were completed by the 60 interviewees. Each morning soon after waking up, participants were asked to talk into a small audio-recorder about their previous night's sleep, any sleep disturbances they experienced and how they dealt with them. These audio-sleep diaries provided qualitative data about older people's perceptions of their sleep and factors influencing their sleep on a nightly basis. Participants (and their partners) also wore an Actiwatch on their wrist continuously for the same two-week period. Actiwatches include small movement and light sensors and can be used to show activity and rest patterns and light exposure over 24-hour periods, enabling the estimation of sleep duration and sleep fragmentation (Meadows et al, 2010).

The following three subsections present analysis of WP2 interview data to highlight findings relevant to understanding how sleep is related to autonomy and independence in later life.

Sleep, napping and active ageing

Increased napping or dozing in later life may result from a combination of factors, some being physiological changes and the effects of poor night-time sleep, others related to release from institutional structures (of getting up to go to work), and lack of stimulating activities or boredom. The goal of 'active ageing' is to empower older people to be independent and autonomous in later life. Success in later life often links ageing with activity, productivity and health. Failing to be active and productive in retirement is seen as equating to 'unsuccessful ageing' (Katz, 2005; Bowling, 2008). However, the premise of 'active ageing' assumes that older people have the capacity to be active and productive in later life (Walker, 2002; Bowling, 2008). There is also a need to acknowledge that some bodily changes that accompany ageing, such as poor night-time sleep, may have an impact on energy levels during the day, and therefore constrain the number and duration of activities that older people may wish to undertake.

Maintaining an active lifestyle was regarded as very important by all older participants in WP2 with great emphasis placed on the desirability of undertaking physical exercise, such as walking, swimming or cycling; leisure activities, such as socialising and attending clubs or church; and mental activities, such as using the computer and reading (Venn and Arber, 2011). While it was acknowledged that activity levels had diminished to a degree in later life, and adjustments therefore had to be made to the type and amount of activities undertaken, being active was universally regarded as desirable and even essential.

For many older people, daytime sleep, whether as planned naps or as unplanned 'dozing', can be integral to remaining 'active' in later life. Our study participants who accepted daytime sleep reported that their ability to undertake daily routines and activities was adversely affected by poor night-time sleep, so that having a nap, or dozing off during the daytime or early evening were valuable in order to maintain their desired activity levels (Venn and Arber, 2011). They linked the need to nap, or justified unplanned napping, with the desire to have sufficient energy to undertake household jobs or tasks. Napping was therefore sometimes planned before a proposed leisure activity, such as playing bowls, or going out for an evening, in order to be refreshed and have sufficient energy to enjoy the activity. Planned or unplanned napping was also seen as acceptable compensation for a poor night's sleep, or a series of poor nights, so that productivity could be re-established. By accepting napping as part of their everyday routines, these poor sleepers were able to continue to be active and maintain independent and 'busy' lives.

While many older people regarded napping as beneficial in our study, some resisted it at all costs because of its implication of time wasting or laziness, and yet others regarded it as a 'necessary evil', to enable them to carry on with their daily activities.

Seeking medical help and using other strategies for poor sleep

In our qualitative interviews, older people's decisions about whether to seek help for poor sleep were influenced by the perceived impact of taking prescribed sleeping medications on their ability to maintain their daily routines (Venn and Arber, 2012; Venn et al, 2013). Men and women were concerned that if they visited their doctor for help with poor sleep, they would be prescribed some form of sleeping medication or tranquiliser, which they identified as being harmful and addictive. Beliefs that *only* sleeping medication would be prescribed by their doctors for poor sleep prevented many participants from seeking professional help, as did their perceptions of the moral inappropriateness of being reliant on such medication were it prescribed and taken (Venn and Arber, 2012). Fear of the side effects of taking sleeping medication, such as feeling drowsy the following day, also prevented older people seeking medical help for their poor sleep, and those who had been prescribed sleeping medication and had experienced these side effects declined to return to the doctor for further treatment.

Our research demonstrates that control is of paramount importance in influencing older people's decisions about seeking medical help for poor sleep, manifested in their desire to remain independent and in control of the way they live their lives, and to continue to be active, productive members of society, albeit within the limitations of their physical health and ageing bodies (Venn and Arber, 2011, 2012). Therefore lack of sleep only became important to participants when their ability to be autonomous and in control of their daily activities was severely compromised (Venn and Arber, 2012).

Advice for coping with sleep disturbance is often focused on improving sleep through addressing sleep 'hygiene' or habits, such as maintaining routines of going to bed and getting up at the same time every day, avoiding caffeinated drinks and alcohol near to bedtime, and not eating or exercising too late. Pharmaceutical companies and manufacturers of sleep aids also offer a plethora of readily available medications, remedies and solutions for poor sleep (Williams, 2005).

Although both older men and women included sleep in discussions of health behaviours, such as diet and exercise, there were gender differences in the use of self-help strategies for poor sleep (Venn and Arber, 2013). Women were more likely to seek out information from the media, friends and family and to draw on their own experiences to find the most appropriate and effective ways to cope with their poor sleep. Men, on the other hand, relied on their own 'body' to indicate when sleep was needed (Meadows et al, 2008), and rarely tried any particular sleep 'hygiene' strategies or over-the-counter medications. Therefore in coping with poor sleep, women were more likely to experiment with self-help behavioural practices such as relaxation techniques, lavender pillows and avoiding going to bed on a full stomach after eating (Venn et al, 2013). Older women were also much more likely than men to try a range of over-the-counter remedies and treatments for poor sleep, such as herbal tablets and antihistamines.

Caregiving and sleep

Among older people, not only is their own sleep likely to be disrupted by their ill health and disability, but also by the ill health of their partner or other family caregivers. Caregiving for a partner or other household member often has an impact on the independence, wellbeing and daytime activities of the carer. Although numerous studies have examined the burdens of caregiving and how caregiving can lead to stress, reduced psychological wellbeing, reduced quality of life and higher levels of depression (Beaudreau et al, 2008), little research has examined how caregiving impacts on a carer's sleep. Caregiving at night, resulting in reduced sleep quality/duration, may have an adverse impact on a carer's ability to function during the day, and may contribute to caregiver stress (Arber and Venn, 2011).

Many older people are caregivers. Our qualitative WP2 research found that older people caring for partners or other relatives could have their own sleep profoundly disturbed by caregiving (Arber and Venn, 2011). These sleep disturbances included the anticipation and actual provision of physical care, as well as worries and anxieties about the care-recipient. In particular, caring for a person with dementia led to 'light' non-restorative sleep, partly because of needing to monitor the care-recipient during the night. Therefore, ill health, disability or dementia may lead to disrupted sleep of *both* the older person and their caregivers. Since caregiving is more likely to be undertaken by women than men (Arber and Venn, 2011), night-time care provision is more likely to affect women's sleep quality, continuity and duration, and thus their ability to be independent and active during the day.

Researching sleep in care homes

Discussions of autonomy and independence among older people focus almost exclusively on the community, with little attention paid to those resident in institutional contexts. This section considers the night time in care homes, focusing on how aspects of the structural environment and staff routines within care homes have an impact on both the night-time sleep of residents and their ability to be autonomous and engaged during the daytime.

Care homes should be seen as 24-hour environments, in which aspects of residents' night-time influence their daytime activities and ability to engage in 'active ageing' (Eyers et al, 2012a, b; Ellmers et al, 2013). In the UK, care home residents generally have their own 'private' bedroom, which is also the workplace of care staff.

Sleep not only takes place in a social context, but may be constrained and influenced by the actions of others or constraints of that context. Privacy, autonomy and personal control are fundamental normative dimensions of adult sleep, but often compromised in a residential or institutional context, such as a care home. Goffman (1961) reminds us that in 'normal' adult life an individual 'sleeps, works and plays' in different places with different sets of other social actors. However, in 'total institutions', these activities all tend to occur in the same setting, with the same group of others, operating according to an institutional time schedule as opposed to that of the individual. Sleep is more likely to be highly controlled and consequently disturbed within 'total institutions'. To the extent that care homes have analogies with 'total institutions', this will reduce a resident's autonomy and power over many aspects of their everyday lives, including the temporal and spatial aspects of their sleep (Williams, 2005).

The SomnIA research was conducted in 10 care homes in South East England (WP3) using multi-methods. Daily sleep and activities diaries were collected for 14 days from 125 care home residents aged over 60. Few residents were able to complete these diaries alone, so for the majority a researcher visited each day to collect information about their activities the previous day, including times at which they went to bed, fell asleep, woke up and got up, any disturbances during the night, and so on. Residents also wore an Actiwatch on their wrist continuously over the 14-day period to measure movement and provide an estimate of rest–activity periods.

Semi-structured audio-taped interviews were conducted with the manager of each care home, with 50 staff working day or night shifts, and 38 care home residents (Eyers et al, 2012a, 2012b). Observational data were collected in each care home, totalling 250 hours, covering dawn, dusk and night time. Analysis of observational data and the accompanying field notes enabled the researchers to evaluate the validity of the daily information provided in residents' diaries.

Many studies have found that nursing home residents have poor sleep quality (Maglione and Ancoli-Israel, 2012). This was substantiated in the SomnIA research by comparing the actigraphic recordings of sleep–wake patterns of older care home residents (WP3) with those of poor sleepers in the community (WP2); Meadows et al (2010) show that after adjusting for age, gender and dependency level, care home residents' sleep was substantially more fragmented and of poorer quality than that of older people with 'poor sleep' living in the community.

The following subsections focus on two aspects of WP3 research findings related to the night time in care homes that highlight what factors contribute to the poor sleep of care home residents.

Monitoring care home residents at night

Our observational data and qualitative interviews with staff and residents show that the everyday matter of sleep represents an area over which residents have little basic control, either over their sleeping environment or their sleeping bodies. Care homes adopt regular and routine monitoring and observation of residents' sleeping bodies during the night time (Luff et al, 2011; Eyers et al, 2012a, b). This contrasts with the normative expectations of most adults that sleep is a time of privacy. The notion of 'observed sleep' and control of the sleep environment by care home staff, rather than by the residents themselves, demonstrates unequal power relations, and undermines resident choice and independence in the most basic aspects of residents' everyday lives.

When night-time sleep is disturbed, residents are more likely to sleep during the day and have less energy to undertake organised and other social or leisure activities. Care home residents experience sleep disruptions by staff coming into their room at frequent intervals during the night to perform care tasks (Luff et al, 2011; Eyers et al, 2012b; Ellmers et al, 2013). Care homes are 'risk-averse' environments, with staff concerned about possible falls, incontinence, and ill health at night. One of the practices staff employ to 'reduce risk' is the routine checking of residents at night, which involves staff going into bedrooms at set hourly intervals, but this restricts residents' experience of restorative sleep, and impacts on their cognitive and physical abilities during the day (Eyers et al, 2012b).

Time in bed and control of bedtimes

One fundamental aspect of personal autonomy should be that older people can decide themselves when to go to bed and to get up, and therefore the length of time spent in bed. Our WP3 research found that care home residents frequently lack control over when they go to bed or wake up in the mornings (Luff et al, 2011). The routines of the care home and timing of staff shifts take precedence in determining residents' sleep timing, especially for residents who are more physically disabled. Thus, residents lack control and agency over this critical aspect of their everyday life. The mean length of time care home residents spent in bed at night was 10 hours 50 minutes, and more than half of the residents spent over two hours awake in bed each night (Luff et al, 2011). Residents with high dependency, requiring assistance from staff to go to bed and get up in the morning, tended to spend longer in bed than those able to do so independently. From 14-day diaries, residents with high dependency reported spending on average 2 hours 50 minutes in bed awake at night, some 50 minutes longer than the more independent residents.

The more physically able residents, who could 'choose' their sleep timing, were still constrained by care home routines (Luff et al, 2011). Some residents described going to bed earlier than previously accustomed, citing a sense that they *ought* to, or *should* fit in with what other care home residents were seen to be doing, or that there was nothing else to do in the evening in the care home. Therefore, independent residents were also influenced by the limited choices within the care environment, and so tended to adapt to the institutional routine.

Policy and practice implications

This section highlights some policy and practice implications of SomnIA findings discussed in this chapter. Hitherto the main intervention to improve older people's sleep has been prescribed sleeping medications, but these have adverse consequences, increasing the risk of falls and confusion. Most older people (in WP2) were reluctant to seek help from general practitioners to improve their poor night-time sleep, and did not want to take prescribed sleeping medication (Venn and Arber, 2012).

Difficulty sleeping and frequent waking in the night were regarded as a normal and expected indicator of 'old age', along with napping and dozing during the day, and going to the toilet in the night (Venn and Arber, 2011, 2012). Seeking medical help for poor sleep was consequently not seen as a priority. However, if older people felt their ability to continue to be active during the day was compromised by poor sleep, and impinged on their ability to maintain control over their daily routines and activities, they would consider seeking medical help. A current difficulty is that general practitioners are perceived to only offer sleeping medication, which is strongly resisted by most older people.

One of the non-pharmacological interventions to improve sleep evaluated in the SomnIA research that could be provided by general practitioners was cognitive behavioural therapy for insomnia (CBT-I). A randomised clinical trial (WP4) evaluated the effectiveness of CBT-I delivered through a programme of six self-help booklets sent weekly to chronically ill patients (Morgan et al, 2011, 2012). This structured psycho-educational programme addressed the key components of treatment and health education typically included in therapist-delivered CBT-I, such as the basic 'do's' and 'don'ts' for optimal sleep, the importance of establishing and keeping to routines, setting realistic expectations for sleep, and strategies for 'winding down'. The trial found that self-help CBT-I significantly improved sleep quality over a six-month follow-up period, suggesting that weekly self-help books can make a major difference in improving sleep, and that their use should be more widespread for patients consulting general practitioners about problematic sleep. It represents a cost-effective alternative to sleeping medication, which has no longer-term adverse effects.

Our WP2 research found that older men and women providing care for partners or other elderly relatives often experienced disturbed sleep that had an impact on their own health and wellbeing during the day (Arber and Venn, 2011). There should be greater recognition that the demands of family caregiving often continue throughout the night, and may adversely hamper the sleep of caregivers, which, in turn, can cause stress and precipitate care home admission (Pollak and Perlick, 1991). Therefore, use of CBT-I by general practitioners, as well as promotion of other non-pharmacological ways of reducing sleep problems of older people with chronic illnesses, and providing greater support for caregivers at night, should be policy objectives.

Many of the 'oldest old' spend the final period of their lives in a care home, therefore ensuring that care home residents can retain autonomy and independence for as long as possible. Policy attention needs to be paid to the delivery of night time care in care homes, so that staff can fulfil their duty of care without disturbing residents' sleep through frequent checking. Other policy concerns include low night-time staffing levels and the length and timing of night shifts, which are often of 12 hours duration. Both factors are implicated in residents spending long hours in bed, and having little choice about time of going to bed and getting up (Luff et al, 2011). It is equally important to value the positive impact of good sleep on a resident's physical and cognitive abilities during the day, and therefore their ability to engage in 'active ageing'. A good night's sleep for residents could improve both residents' and care staffs' daytime experiences.

Key findings

- Good sleep is a pre-requisite for older people's wellbeing and ability to engage fully in daytime activities, whether living in their own homes or in a care home.
- Older men and women would rather not go to their doctor for help with poor sleep because they expect to sleep less well as they age and believe they may be prescribed sleeping medication.
- Planned napping can enable older people to be active and maintain independent and busy lives.

- Older people caring for partners or other relatives often have their own sleep disturbed by caregiving which could adversely impact on their health and wellbeing during the day.
- Care home routines, staffing levels and care practices influence both the sleep and night-time experience of care home residents.

Conclusions

By adopting a sociological approach to studying sleep, the research discussed in this chapter shows how sleep-related practices, embedded within the daily lives of older people both at home and in care homes, influence their independence and autonomy in later life. Exploring the social context of sleep reveals diverse influences, over and above the physical impact of ageing, on the quality, quantity, timing and expectations for sleep in later life.

For older people living in the community, social aspects include the meaning of napping, caregiving for partners, and the strategies older people use to optimise their sleep, alongside their general reluctance to take sleeping medication. In contrast, care home residents generally lack control over the night time and their sleep, with care home routines, staffing levels and regular night-time checking by staff having a fundamental influence on the quality of residents' sleep.

Poor sleep is often ignored by both the medical profession and the general public, yet it is fundamental in terms of optimising health and wellbeing in later life, and in enabling older people to achieve independent and active lives.

Acknowledgements

The SomnIA (Sleep in Ageing) project was grateful for funding from the NDA initiative, a multidisciplinary research programme supported by AHRC, BBSRC, EPSRC, ESRC and MRC (RES-339-25-0009).

Note

[1] The SomnIA project was undertaken by a multidisciplinary team of researchers from four universities led by Sara Arber (WP2/WP8, University of Surrey). The co-investigators were David Armstrong (WP1, King's College London), Ingrid Eyers (WP3, University of Surrey/University of Vechta, Germany), Kevin Morgan (WP4, Loughborough University), Roger Orpwood (WP7, University of Bath) and Debra Skene (WP5/WP6, University of Surrey). Other researchers and staff who made key contributions to the project are indicated on the project website at www.somnia.surrey.ac.uk

References

Ancoli-Israel, S. (2005) 'Sleep and aging: Prevalence of disturbed sleep and treatment considerations in older adults', *Journal of Clinical Psychiatry*, vol 66, no 9, pp 42-3.

Arber, S. and Venn, S. (2011) 'Caregiving at night: Understanding the impact on carers', *Journal of Aging Studies*, vol 25, pp 155-65.

Arber, S., Meadows, R. and Venn, S. (2012) 'Sleep and society', in C.M. Morin and C.A. Espie (eds) *The Oxford handbook of sleep disorders*, Oxford: Oxford University Press., pp 223-47

Authier, N., Balayssac, D., Sautereau, M., Zangarelli, A., Courty, P., Somogyi, A.A., et al (2009) 'Benzodiazepine dependence: Focus on withdrawal syndrome', *Annales Pharmaceutique Françaises*, vol 67, no 6, pp 408-13.

Beaudreau, S.A., Spira, A.P., Gray, H.L., Depp, C.A., Long, J., Rothkopf, M. and Gallagher-Thompson, D. (2008) 'The relationship between objectively measured sleep disturbance and dementia family caregiver distress and burden', *Journal of Geriatric Psychiatry and Neurology*, vol 21, no 3, pp 159-65.

Bliwise, D.L. (1993) 'Sleep in normal aging and dementia – A review', *Sleep*, vol 16, pp 40-81.

Bowling, A. (2008) 'Enhancing later life: How older people perceive active ageing?', *Aging and Mental Health*, vol 12, no 3, pp 293-301.

Busto, U.E., Sproule, B.A., Knight, K. and Herrmann, N. (2001) 'Use of prescription and non-prescription hypnotics in a Canadian elderly population', *Canadian Journal of Clinical Pharmacology*, vol 8, no 4, pp 213-21.

Buysse, D.J., Reynolds, C.F. 3rd, Monk, T.H., Berman, S.R. and Kupfer, D.J. (1998) 'The Pittsburgh Sleep Quality Index: A new instrument for psychiatric practice and research', *Journal of Psychiatry Research*, vol 282, pp 193-213.

Carey-Smith, B.E., Evans, N.M. and Orpwood, R.D. (2013) 'A user-centred design process to develop technology to improve sleep quality in residential care homes', *Technology and Disability*, vol 25, no 1, pp 49-58.

Dijk, D.J., Groeger, J.A., Stanley, N. and Deacon, S. (2010) 'Age-related reduction in daytime sleep propensity and nocturnal slow wave sleep', *Sleep*, vol 33, no 2, pp 211-23.

Dregan, A. and Armstrong, D. (2009) 'Age, cohort and period effects in the prevalence of sleep disturbances among older people: The impact of economic downturn', *Social Science & Medicine*, vol 69, pp 1432-38.

Dregan, A. and Armstrong, D. (2010) 'Adolescence sleep disturbances as predictors of adulthood sleep problems – A cohort study', *Journal of Adolescent Health*, vol 26, no 5, pp 482-7.

Dregan, A. and Armstrong, D. (2011) 'Cross-country variation in sleep disturbance among working and older age groups: An analysis based on the European Social Survey', *International Psychogeriatrics*, vol 23, no 9, pp 1413-20.

Dregan, A., Armstrong, D. and Lallukka, T. (2013) 'Potential pathways from biopsychosocial risk factors to sleep loss due to worry: A population based investigation', *Journal of Public Mental Health*, vol 12, no 1, pp 43-50.

Ellmers, T., Arber, S., Luff, R., Eyers, I. and Young, E. (2013) 'Factors affecting residents' sleep in care homes', *Nursing Older People*, vol 25, no 8, pp 29-32.

Eyers, I., Carey-Smith, B.E., Evans, N.M. and Orpwood, R.D. (2013) 'Safe and sound? Night-time checking in care homes', *British Journal of Nursing*, vol 22, no 14, pp 827-30.

Eyers, I., Young, E., Luff, R. and Arber, S. (2012b) 'Striking the balance: Night care versus the facilitation of good sleep', *British Journal of Nursing*, vol 21, no 5, pp 303-7.

Eyers, I., Young, E., Luff, R., Ellmers, T. and Arber, S. (2012a) 'Rhetoric and reality in daily life in English care homes', *International Journal of Ageing and Later Life*, vol 7, no 1, pp 53-78.

Ferrie, J.E., Kivimaki, M. and Shipley, C. (2010) 'Sleep and death', in F.P. Cappuccio, M.A. Miller and S.W. Lockley (eds) *Sleep, health and society: From aetiology to public health*, Oxford: Oxford University Press, pp 50-82.

Ferrie, J.E., Kumari, M., Salo, P., Singh-Manoux, A. and Kivimaki, M. (2011) 'Sleep epidemiology – A rapidly growing field', *International Journal of Epidemiology*, vol 40, pp 1431-7.

Glass, J., Lanctot, K.L., Herrmann, N., Sproule, B.A. and Busto, U.E. (2005) 'Sedative hypnotics in older people with insomnia: Meta-analysis of risks and benefits', *British Medical Journal*, vol 331, pp 1164-9.

Goffman, E. (1961) *Asylums: Essays on the social situation of mental patients and other inmates*, New York: Doubleday.

Grandner, M.A., Jackson, N.J., Pak, V.M. and Gehrman, P.R. (2012) 'Sleep disturbance is associated with cardiovascular and metabolic disorders', *Journal of Sleep Research*, vol 21, pp 427-33.

Gregory, P., Morgan, K. and Lynall, A. (2012) 'Improving sleep management in people with Parkinson's', *British Journal of Community Nursing*, vol 17, no 1, pp 14-20.

Haimov, I. and Vadas, L. (2009) 'Sleep in older adults: Association between chronic insomnia and cognitive functioning', *Harefuah*, vol 148, no 5, pp 310-14.

Harrington, J.J. and Lee-Chiong, T. Jr (2007) 'Sleep and older patients', *Clinics in Chest Medicine*, vol 28, no 4, pp 673-84.

Hislop, J. and Arber, S. (2006) 'Sleep, gender and ageing: Temporal perspectives in the mid-to-later life transition', in T. Calasanti and K. Slevin (eds) *Age matters: Realigning feminist thinking*, London: Routledge, pp 225-45.

Hislop, J., Arber, S., Meadows, R. and Venn, S. (2005) 'Narratives of the night: The use of audio diaries in researching sleep', *Sociological Research Online*, vol 10, no 4. Available at www.socresonline.org.uk/10/4/hislop.html

Katz, S. (2005) 'Busy bodies: Activity, aging and the management of everyday life', in S. Katz (ed) *Cultural aging, life courses, lifestyle and senior worlds*, Peterborough, ON: Broadview, pp 121-39.

Lallukka, T., Dregan, A. and Armstrong, D. (2011) 'Comparison of a sleep item from the GHQ-12 with the Jenkins sleep questionnaire as measures of sleep disturbances', *Journal of Epidemiology*, vol 21, no 6, pp 474-80.

Luff, R., Ellmers, T., Eyers, I., Young, E. and Arber, S. (2011) 'Time spent in bed at night by care homes residents: Choice or compromise?', *Ageing and Society*, vol 31, no 7, pp 1229-50.

Maglione, J.E. and Ancoli-Israel, S. (2012) 'Sleep disorders in the elderly', in C.M. Morin and C.A. Espie (eds) *The Oxford handbook of sleep disorders*, Oxford: Oxford University Press, pp 769-86.

Martin, P. (2002) *Counting sheep*, London: HarperCollins.

Meadows, R., Hislop, J., Venn, S. and Arber, S. (2008) 'Engaging with sleep: Male definitions, understandings and attitudes', *Sociology of Health and Illness*, vol 30, no 5, pp 696-710.

Meadows, R., Luff, R., Eyers, I., Venn, S., Cope, E. and Arber, S. (2010) 'An actigraphic study comparing community dwelling poor sleepers with non-demented care home residents', *Chronobiology International*, vol 27, no 4, pp 842-54.

Morgan, K. (2008) 'Sleep and insomnia in later life', in B. Woods and L. Clare (eds) *Handbook of the clinical psychology of ageing* (2nd edn), New York: Wiley, Chapter 14.

Morgan, K., Kucharczyk, E. and Gregory, P. (2011) 'Insomnia: Evidence-based approaches to assessment and management', *Clinical Medicine*, vol 11, no 3, pp 278-81.

Morgan, K., Gregory, P., Tomeny, M., David, B.M. and Gascoigne, C. (2012) 'Self-help treatment for insomnia symptoms associated with chronic conditions in older adults: A randomised controlled trial', *Journal of the American Geriatrics Society*, vol 60, pp 1803-10.

Pollak, C.P. and Perlick, D. (1991) 'Sleep problems and the institutionalization of the elderly', *Journal of Geriatric Psychiatry and Neurology*, vol 4, no 4, pp 204-10.

Revell, V. and Skene, D.J. (2010) 'Impact of age on human non-visual responses to light', *Sleep and Biological Rhythms*, vol 8, pp 84-94.

Sivertsen, B. and Nordhus, I.H. (2007) 'Management of insomnia in older adults', *The British Journal of Psychiatry*, vol 190, pp 285-6.

Skene, D.J. (2008) 'Blue light and sleep', *Cataract and Refractive Surgery Today*, March supplement, pp 9-10.

Skene D.J. (2009) 'Testing blue light with the elderly', *Lighting Journal*, vol 74, no 3, pp 15-18.

Sonnenberg, C.M., Bierman, E.J., Deeg, D.J. and Comlis, H.C. (2012) 'Ten year trends in benzodiazepine use in the Dutch population', *Social Psychiatry and Psychiatric Epidemiology*, vol 47, no 2, pp 293-301.

van Someren, E.J.W. (2000) 'Circadian sleep disturbances in the elderly', *Experimental Gerontology*, vol 35, pp 1229-37.

Venn, S. and Arber, S. (2011) 'Daytime sleep and active ageing in later life', *Ageing and Society*, vol 31, no 2, pp 197-216.

Venn, S. and Arber, S. (2012) 'Understanding older people's decisions about the use of sleeping medication: Issues of control and autonomy', *Sociology of Health and Illness*, vol 34, no 8, pp 1215-29.

Venn, S., Meadows, R. and Arber, S. (2013) 'Gender differences in approaches to self-management of poor sleep in later life', *Social Science & Medicine*, Special Issue on 'Sleep, Culture and Health', vol 79, no 1, pp 117-23.

Vitiello, M.V., Moe, K.E. and Prinz, P.N. (2002) 'Sleep complaints cosegregate with illness in older adults', *Journal of Psychosomatic Research*, vol 53, pp 555-9.

Walker, A. (2002) 'The evolving meaning of retirement: A strategy for active ageing', *International Social Security Review*, vol 5, no 5, pp 121-39.

Whalley, L. (2001) *The ageing brain*, London: Phoenix.

Williams, S.J. (2005) *Sleep and society: Sociological ventures into the (un)known*, Abingdon: Routledge.

Williams, S.J., Meadows, R. and Arber, S. (2010) 'Sociology of sleep', in F. Cappaccio, M. Miller and S. Lockley (eds) *Sleep epidemiology*, Oxford: Oxford University Press, pp 275-99.

THREE

Negotiating unfamiliar environments

Judith Phillips, Nigel Walford, Ann Hockey,
Mike Lewis and Nigel Foreman

Introduction

'Active and healthy ageing', with the goal of staying as independent as possible for as long as possible, has continued to be the policy focus in many countries (WHO, 2015). 'Ageing in place' and individual responsibility have also become enshrined in policy, reinforcing the importance of designing age-friendly communities that support independent living. To feel safe and comfortable in one's local neighbourhood with access to a variety of activities are crucial factors in retaining independence in later life. 'Ageing in place' and 'place attachment', another concept well used in ageing research (Smith, 2009), however, assumes some familiarity over time with that place.

Age-friendly cities are viewed as sensitive to age from the perspective of older residents living there. Although this is a critical component, which should be at the heart of all considerations of town planning, increasingly there is a need to assess the environment from the perspective of a visitor or someone who is unfamiliar with the environment. There are three major reasons that older people are increasingly experiencing environments that can be unfamiliar to them. This may be because of travelling as tourists to new areas; urban regeneration; or as a result of cognitive decline, where the familiar becomes unfamiliar.

The central aim of the project was to determine the mechanisms and strategies used by older people to navigate unfamiliar spaces as pedestrians ('unfamiliar' defined as new spaces to the older person or spaces that have become unfamiliar). Although there are many studies on accessibility (Granborn et al, 2016; I'DGO, no date), there is less research on the impact and effects of architecture and town design on older people's walkability, usability or their perception of the unfamiliar built environment.

The effects of the built environment and use of space on older people's self-perception and identity are being increasingly recognised (Peace et al, 2006). As people go through the life course, their use of space changes (Rowles, 1978). The drivers potentially altering or affecting people's use of and 'comfort' in different spaces as they grow older come from two directions: first, changes in their personal circumstances and physical/mental wellbeing – with changes in cognitive functioning, some older people will experience unfamiliarity in their previously recognisable household surroundings; and second, as urban landscapes change through regeneration or decline, the use of space changes and previously familiar places may become unfamiliar. Unfamiliarity with one's location also occurs when the built environment is new – an experience encountered by increasing numbers of older people as they travel the world as tourists or must relocate due to necessity or choice in later life. Unfamiliarity can lead to insecurity, disorientation, fear over personal safety, social exclusion and loss of independence. Enabling navigation and orientation in built environments is therefore essential to 'ageing in place'.

Use of space and mobility may be restricted through disability, dependency and care needs, or expanded through travel and leisure interests, migration and relocation (Wu et al, 2015). Social factors such as population density, crime rate and ethnic mix may also influence people's use and perception of space and their radius of activity (Scharf et al, 2003). The meaning and use of space will vary between older people depending on their biography and past experiences, and the extent to which they encounter new spaces alone or in the company of friends and family (Diehl and Willis, 2004; Rubinstein and de Medeiros, 2004). They may also adjust their use of space because of changes that occur in the environment, for example, changes in the physical features and users of public spaces. While most people will be aware of changes in the form and nature of the spaces they experience over time, there is little understanding of how reproduction of this background space affects older people in particular ways.

Brain changes in later life may predispose older participants to use different spatial strategies from younger people. Zhong and Moffat (2016) examined the differences between younger, middle-aged and older adults with regards to their navigation performance in a virtual maze and subsequent performance in landmark recognition memory, landmark-direction associative learning and visuospatial ability. Overall, younger adults outperformed older adults in all the tasks except in critical landmark recognition. On the other hand, older individuals may have enjoyed spatial competence for most of their lives and may have developed and will be familiar with the use of map-like representations of space. This can enable them to utilise inferential strategies, based on what is usual and expected based on prior experience (cf Beck and Wood, 1976), for example, using their knowledge of the likely design features of a building, a factor that may mask spatial learning deficits (Kirasic, 2000). While older participants may be seriously impaired when making spatial judgements about a house having an atypical layout, their performance is as good as younger participants for typical layouts (Arbuckle et al, 1994). The same is likely to apply to road and town layouts.

A further body of literature on the built environment comes from a planning perspective. The use of space and unfamiliarity are prominent issues for spatial planners considering the changing age profile of local areas because it has an impact on existing residents, new residents and visitors to the area, as indicated above. There is increasing recognition and consideration in the UK among spatial planners at national, regional and local levels of the needs of an older population (Royal Town Planning Institute, 2007, 2017). While previously much attention has been given to the housing needs of the older population, more recently attention has also turned to the neighbourhood level with a focus on building sustainable communities for all sectors of the population (Welsh Government, 2017). There are a variety of mechanisms available to spatial planners to ensure that the needs of the older population are considered, including, at a broad level, statutory duties under Section 149(1) of the Equality Act 2010 and Disability Discrimination Act 1995 to consult with and provide equality of opportunity to all sectors of the population. Specific measures include policies in regional and local development documents relating to older people and the built environment, local area agreements involving local authorities and other key partners, and community plans. The Planning Advisory Service (2009), which supports planning professionals and elected representatives on councils through consultancy, peer support learning and online resources to help planners working in local government to respond to planning reform, has identified six exemplar local authorities' planning for an ageing population. However, there is little research into the extent to which these mechanisms have achieved solutions tailored to the needs of older people.

Taking these areas of literature together, the research to date has concentrated on older people's use of familiar places, often their own 'home' (Rowles and Bernard, 2013). We know that 'ageing in place' and familiarity with environment can hide deterioration in cognitive and physical functioning; it can also lead to increased engagement and confidence and maintaining one's integrity and identity (Oswald and Wahl, 2013). In contrast, we know little about older people's responses to public spaces and the changes that may occur there (Holland et al, 2007; Peace, 2013). Imposing buildings, poor street layout and expanses of empty space can intimidate people with dementia (Ward Thompson et al, 2013). There is less understanding of the triggers that may be involved in leading people to feel less comfortable with experiencing unfamiliar spaces as they grow older, which may, in turn, lead to a retreat into familiar spaces (Blackman et al, 2007), and the factors producing differential responses to these triggers.

Aims and methods

The central aim of the OPUS study (Older people's use of unfamiliar space) was to determine the mechanisms and strategies employed by older people when experiencing unfamiliar spaces (defined as new spaces to the older person or spaces that have become unfamiliar). The central aim of the project was to determine the mechanisms and strategies used by older people to navigate unfamiliar spaces as pedestrians. There were five specific objectives:

- Investigate the influences on someone's ability to cope with unfamiliar environments.
- Examine the extent to which unfamiliar environments curtail autonomy and independence, and lead to social (and environmental) exclusion.
- Identify the environmental triggers that older people respond to, for example, to determine the characteristics of places that make them threatening or worrisome.
- Explore how technologies can assist in enabling older people to adapt to or ameliorate change in their environment.
- Engage with spatial planners in discussing forms of environmental design that facilitate older people's use of space.

Forty-eight older volunteers were recruited into the study, and 42 were interviewed to collect both quantitative and qualitative data (of the 48, one was a wheelchair user, one withdrew, one was younger than 60 and in three cases, there were technical difficulties that led to incomplete interviews). A qualitative interview explored the extent to which older people encountered unfamiliar environments, the issues that arose and interventions that might assist them in navigation.

Participants were asked to complete a questionnaire detailing demographic information; cognitive functioning (Cognitive Abilities Screening Instrument, CASI); sense of direction (Santa Barbara[1]); and travel networks and social network measures, among other measures. The survey included questions about visits to familiar and unfamiliar towns, dealt with the frequency of visits and modes of transport used, open-ended themes about why they visit, how they prepare, what they do, how they navigate and avoid getting 'lost', the usefulness of signage and presence of obstacles, situations and areas to be avoided as well as general impressions and experiences of familiar areas.

Following this, 2D images and routes in a familiar (Swansea in Wales) and unfamiliar town (Colchester in eastern England) were displayed in a 'reality cave' (a room with a wraparound virtual image projected of Colchester), and participants were asked to comment on general impressions and distinctive features, such as the use of signage, confusing and helpful cues, colour, lighting and their confidence –on the assigned (30-minute walking) route. The participants' electrocardiograms were monitored while in the reality cave, to facilitate calculation of cardiac stress–related indices that reflect cardiac regulation via the autonomic nervous system. People's physical and perceptual response to using the reality cave were calibrated with films of familiar spaces within their localities as pedestrians.

To compliment the project, we undertook street audits and focus group discussions relating to the design and ambience of both the familiar and unfamiliar town centres. The tools used included the Senior Walking Environment Assessment Tool – Revised (SWEAT-R) (Michael and McGregor, 2005) and the Urban Design Quality (UDQ) index (Ewing et al, 2006). The first of these has been developed as a quantitative measure of the 'walkability' of urban environments recording information about such physical characteristics as pavement width, curb height and the presence of controlled crossing facilities. The second captures information about the quality of urban spaces including such items as the range of building uses, the presence of amenity areas and planting. The UDQ in particular captures emotional responses to the aesthetics and structure of the built environment. One section of the UDQ relates to the memorability of a locality and covers features such as historic buildings and landmarks that can make a lasting impression and evoke feelings (imageability), and the visual richness of places covering items related to the diversity of the physical, built and social environments (complexity). Other sections cover a sense of enclosed space (enclosure and transparency) such as observable sky, and items that match the sizes and dimensions of people (human scale), such as the presence of potted plants and street furniture. Using this measure in conjunction with the SWEAT-R and the oral narratives from the reality cave enabled us to look at what key features created meaning for older people in the unfamiliar town landscape in comparison with a familiar landscape. Together these provided a quasi-objective assessment of the condition and ambience of the urban environment along the route screened in the reality cave.

Finally, a site visit by Swansea participants in the research to an unfamiliar town centre allowed the opportunity for a smaller group (10) to follow the route 'for real' with a 'walk around town' with older residents, to meet as a focus group with some older residents and spatial planners of the 'unfamiliar' town. Qualitative data were collected through participants recording their experiences in notes and through discussions with a group of local residents (10) and local planners (who had suggested the assigned route for viewing in the cave). Consequently, the research led to the identification of policy and practice implications for making unfamiliar environments safe and accessible for older adults.

Findings

Landmarks and distinctive buildings

Landmarks and distinctive buildings were more important than signage in navigating unfamiliar areas; however, the meaning of space and memories attached to places was significant, particularly in familiar spaces.

The hidden 'unseen' landscape beyond the immediate vision forms part of people's perception of the area. When viewing images of the local, familiar area in the reality cave, participants conveyed a sense of history behind the scenes, describing the former and current usage and history of a building, and consequently providing greater detail of the image. In a similar way, the hidden 'unseen' landscape beyond the immediate vision formed part of people's perception of the area. Older people were taking a much wider spatial lens describing the view beyond the scene. When questioned on what landmarks people used in navigating and orientating in a familiar landscape through the series of still images, they talked of the 'dangers of the street behind', the difficulty of walking down the road because of the (unseen) bollards, or described the ambience of the setting as 'a popular leisure area'. Even areas that are familiar can potentially have unseen 'dangers' behind what appears on view.

Buildings and landmarks were important and helpful markers in unfamiliar environments. Participants relied on landmarks to avoid getting lost in both familiar and unfamiliar towns; this, however, was a more prominent strategy in navigating unfamiliar than familiar places. In unfamiliar towns this was supplemented by the use of signs (by one-fifth rather than one-tenth of respondents) and by using a town map. Participants were less likely to rely on remembering a route, and very few (3 per cent) took notes. The types of landmark found most useful in both familiar and unfamiliar settings were mostly architectural, historic buildings, particularly churches and church spires. In unfamiliar areas, shops provided useful cues, both in terms of their colours and branding.

Landmarks were important navigational aids, but people had difficulty keeping them in view, particularly if these were upward cues, requiring constant adjustment between looking at higher elevations to keep the landmark in sight and at street level to negotiate their immediate environment and attend to lower-level cues such as broken pavements and street furniture.

> 'It's interesting to look up, but you can't when you've got all this furniture, and you have to be watching where you are walking.... If you start by looking up at all this beautiful decoration on the town hall or looking ahead towards the water tower, you could walk into something; there is too much cluttering the pavements that you can't walk straight.' (Jean, 69)

Signage

Signs are an explicit attempt by the local authority and other organisations to guide people through spaces, and participants in the study generally perceived the utility of such devices. Half of the respondents said that street signs were useful directional aids in unfamiliar areas.

Signs, however, were seen as of limited use, even in unfamiliar new areas – they were often too high, positioned incorrectly in the street and without any indication of distance to the feature they were signposting. The issue of distance between locations within an unfamiliar environment is crucially connected with people's willingness to venture 'into the unknown'. Signs may guide people towards an objective, but if information about distance is not included, there remains some uncertainty over the length of walk to which people are committing themselves. Some participants made a connection between signage for pedestrians and drivers, and commented on the inappropriateness of signs intended for the former being used by the latter.

> 'You could be driving for hours looking for a toilet and you would have no chance of reading those signs.' (Brian, 76)

> 'It's not easy to find tourist information offices, even though there is a sign post and I walk in the direction of the sign post, very often the sign post is out of date and the tourist office has moved to a different location – I then get quite cross as I have wasted time as I am on a time limit as I have to catch a bus to get back home.' (Janice, 68)

Preparation is important to overcome such confusion for visits to unfamiliar areas, and most respondents spent time 'Googling' or accessing atlases and maps, scoping guide books and checking out places of interest. In many ways, our respondents described themselves as 'tourists' or visitors when in unfamiliar areas. In a social network analysis, participants who followed directions (to the reality cave, without difficulty) were more 'adventurous', travelling to more unfamiliar towns using different modes of transport and travel arrangements. This group had a larger radius of movement and travelled for a variety of reasons.

Public spaces

The *meaning of space* is important. Despite the barriers and complexity of the environment to our older visitors, many could create a sense of meaning in spaces and places that were unfamiliar to them. Unfamiliarity does not necessarily mean people do not use spaces or that places are meaningless and emotionless. Unfamiliar urban environments can have meaning (even negative). The key issue to positive aspects of attachment is whether they are usable; this is based not just on the functional ability of an older person in the environment, but also on their psychological attachment and assessment of the usability of that space.

Familiar places are imbued with memories, histories and identities that enable people to navigate their environments. Memories are often used as 'shortcuts' in giving directions.

Stressful areas

Sensory overload in an unfamiliar area is a barrier to navigation and positive appreciation of the environment. Similarity existed in what people experienced as troublesome or worrying in both familiar and unfamiliar areas. Whether people could follow directions or not, both groups expressed concern with visiting town centres, and in particular, poorly lit areas in the evening. During the day poorly lit areas, derelict, dirty and run-down streets, alleyways, underpasses and crowded areas, particularly where there were numbers of young people, led to anxiety and avoidance. For some participants, sensory overload, particularly in an unfamiliar area, was difficult. Such sensory and informational overload can provoke negative appreciation of the physical setting.

> INTERVIEWER: 'Was there anything that surprised you?'
> PAM: 'I think the first thing is the noise. When you come out of the station it was quite noisy and walk[ing] up past all the buses and all that way, it was very busy. It looked on the film a quiet town, but when you actually come into that area and there are buses coming from everywhere ... buses seem to have priority.'

Sensory overload goes beyond just sight, noise and colour; it extends to ambience, perception and smell. These became barriers to some people, but were easier to avoid in familiar rather than unfamiliar areas.

Participants expressed mixed views when asked about what they thought about other obstacles in both familiar and unfamiliar areas. Most commented on such barriers from a pedestrian perspective:

> 'I noticed particularly the seats, tables, sticking out in the pavement, making it so narrow to get by – their swinging signs, so any blind person would be lucky if they hit those studs. They are more likely to walk straight into the tables or that swinging sign.' (Alice, 70)

Shared space is often not segregated, and for the visitor is seen as negotiated space. The 'taken for granted' in the familiar had to be negotiated and 'guessed at' in the unfamiliar environment. Assumed 'rules' applied in the familiar, such as the priority given to traffic over pedestrians or safe places to cross, but there is uncertainty over whether these assumptions can be transferred to an unfamiliar space. In unfamiliar areas, such 'shared space' is often not segregated between cars and pedestrians, and for the visitor, is seen as negotiated space. This can be difficult, however, with street design being the same in two areas yet operating in different ways, for example, raised 'humps' in the road taken as 'informal' pedestrian crossings in one area and seen as speed humps with priorities for bus use in another unfamiliar town.

Designing outdoor spaces that are pleasant and easily walkable as well as routes that are navigable is important in making the environment less worrisome. Forty of our participants undertook physiological assessments. Older people's observation of environmental images was associated with significantly more stress than during adjacent rest periods.

Our results prompt us to tentatively suggest that potentially worrisome environmental triggers do have a measurable influence on an individual's cardiac function. This information might be useful in future assessments of optimal strategies for environmental planning when considering the needs of older people. These results were found irrespective of gender.

In a piece of work additional to the main study (but linked to navigational tools use), 29 older people were compared with 40 younger people for their ability to navigate using either a map or a hand-held navigation device. In healthy older people, age per se is clearly not a barrier to navigation; indeed, after a 10-minute walk along a predefined route in a nondescript residential environment, when asked to point back to the starting location, older individuals (both male and female, using a map or navigation device) could do so with greater accuracy than the younger age group.

As part of the main study the perspective of planners was sought, asking, To what extent are older people's voices heard and taken into account when planning and regenerating areas? What processes are necessary to engage older people in a meaningful way? Are specific areas of the town planned with older people in mind? Are there older people spaces, and do planners factor age into the design, spatial layout, signage etc? How can space be redesigned to make them more older person-friendly? How can we improve the ambience of spaces and the experiences of older people?

The process of consultation with older people as a 'singled-out' focus of the process is relatively recent and carried out through older people's fora or groups such as Age UK. In some cases consultations were tailored to specific groups; older people were not generally felt to be a 'hard-to-reach' group, and appeared as a group under the UK Equality Impact Assessment (Equality Act 2010), a requirement placed on local authorities. Planners considered older people today had greater political awareness and power, and could engage with the process.

Efforts were made to make public spaces 'older person-friendly' following lifetime places guidelines (Bevan and Croucher, 2011); this specifically related to the location of bus shelters, seats, pavement clutter and the number and location of public toilets. They did consider older people in relation to housing issues – around the land use requirements of specialist housing, such as bungalows and care homes and the mechanisms of how to encourage older people to downsize into smaller properties. Planners were also conscious of intergenerational issues, for example, the citing of a play area next to specialist housing, which could be viewed by some as positive and others negative. The special consideration of age and older people also extended to the location of special housing, particularly the growing space requirements of retirement communities. Some consideration was factored in regarding community facilities, but few planners mentioned land use planning and the design of areas with 'ageing' in mind, other than those above.

Planners were conscious of different stakeholders and interests in taking forward an ageing agenda in the planning process. This was expressed through the trade-off between designing for an eco-friendly environment versus building bungalows with large land footprints, or the question of how to preserve a historic city with narrow streets while accommodating the use of mobility scooters and wheelchairs.

Policy and practice implications

Such experiences can contribute to policy and practice implications for planners, architects, urban designers, and community development, tourism and regeneration managers in designing for an ageing population.

As independence and mobility become important features in later life, walking routes as well as public spaces need the attention of spatial planners. It is important to take a 'travel chain perspective' (Iwarsson et al, 2000) to ensure a smooth transition between walking, driving and using public transport. Rules are different in different places, and people need to have an appreciation and understanding of transition points, that is, where it is safe to cross a road, without any ambiguity through design. Liminal spaces need attention by planners where negotiation takes place in relation to rules in familiar and unfamiliar areas. This leads us to a bigger question of who controls and owns public urban spaces and pedestrianised areas, and how older people can exert influence over an environment that enhances their sense of independence and confidence, which is crucial.

Memories are applicable in creating meaning in the wider environment, which can be used to sustain independence for those older people 'ageing in place'. Attachment to place is tied into such collective memories (Burholt, 2006). A biographical life course record of a 'walk around town' would be useful to help capture key memories and histories of the location. Older people come with a variety of experiences and knowledge of areas, which planners need to pay attention to if areas are to become attractive, safe and walkable. Developing the meaning of space and place is also a spatial skill, one that older people as a subset of the general population possess to varying degrees, in relation to familiar areas.

Key findings

- The meaning of space is important: cognitive maps are constructed through more than just physical and built environments. Emotional spaces are pertinent for older people.
- The hidden 'unseen' landscape beyond the immediate vision forms part of people's perception of the area.
- Neighbourhood environment walkability (how pedestrian-friendly the environment) is a significant determinant of 'ageing in place'.
- Buildings and landmarks are important and helpful markers in unfamiliar environments.
- Designing outdoor spaces that are pleasant and easily walkable as well as routes that are navigable is important in making the environment less worrisome.

Conclusions

Unfamiliarity can be exciting and challenging as well as creating unpredictability, risk and uncertainty for older people. The diversity of experience needs to be accommodated in policy and planning practice for older people as tourists as well as for older people challenged with mobility, sensory, visual or spatial issues. Treating 'age' as a single category can therefore be unhelpful for planners in designing urban space. The immediate town environment needs to be as accommodating as possible if older people are to 'age in place' and retain independence. However, for the diversity of experience to be accommodated, it is useful to start from an understanding of the environment and to appreciate the agency that older people have to cope with unfamiliarity in the surroundings. This also provides us with a framework to move from the individual to societal level.

Further research is needed to explore other specific unfamiliar environments that might be challenging for older people – spaces and places of unfamiliarity such as supermarkets and airports. What navigational aids are most useful and for what type of older person and in what circumstances are further questions to develop to enhance mobility, independence and wellbeing. How do we enable (older) people to grow and enrich their narratives of unfamiliar areas? How can they be encouraged/enabled to see beyond the immediate physical features of the environment?

Note
[1]   The Santa Barbara Sense of Direction scale is a self-report measure of environmental spatial ability.

References

Arbuckle, T., Cooney, R., Milne, J. and Melchouir, A. (1994) 'Memory for spatial layouts in relation to age and schema typicality', *Psychology and Aging*, vol 9, no 3, pp 467-80.

Beck, R. and Wood, D. (1976) 'Cognitive transformations from urban geographic fields to mental maps', *Environment and Behaviour*, vol 8, pp 199-238.

Bevan, M. and Croucher, K. (2011) *Lifetime neighbourhoods*, London: Department for Communities and Local Government.

Blackman, T., van Schaik, P. and Martyr, A. (2007) 'Outdoor environments for people with dementia: An exploratory study using virtual reality', *Ageing and Society*, vol 27, no 1, pp 811-25.

Burholt, V. (2006) '"Adref": Theoretical contexts of attachment to place for mature and older people in rural North Wales', *Environment and Planning A*, vol 38, pp 1095-114.

Diehl, M. and Willis, S. (2004) 'Everyday competence and everyday problem solving in aging adults: The role of physical and social context', in H. Wahl, R. Scheidt and P. Windley (eds) *Aging in context: Socio-physical environments*, New York: Springer, pp 130-66.

Ewing, R., Handy, S., Brownson, R.C., Clemente, O. and Winston, E. (2006) 'Identifying and measuring urban design qualities related to walkability', *Journal of Physical Activity and Health*, vol 3, S22-S240.

Granborn, M., Iwarsson, S., Kylberg, M., Pettersson, C. and Slaug, B. (2016) 'A public health perspective to environmental barriers and accessibility problems for senior citizens living in ordinary housing', *BMC Public Health*, vol 16, no 1, pp 1-11. Available at http://lup.lub. lu.se/record/875ddc11-bc87-413e-9e5a-b9a9a612426c

Holland, C., Clark, A., Katz, J. and Peace, S. (2007) *Social interaction in urban public places*, York: Joseph Rowntree Foundation.

I'DGO (no date) Street environment design guidance, Salford: Inclusive Design for Getting Outdoors. Available at www.idgo.ac.uk/design_ guidance/streets.htm#footpaths

Iwarsson, S. Jensen, G. and Stahl, A. (2000) 'Travel chain enabler: Development of a pilot instrument for assessment of urban public bus transportation accessibility', *Technology and Disability*, vol 12, pp 3-12.

Kirasic, K. (2000) 'Age differences in adults' spatial abilities, learning environmental layout, and wayfinding behaviour', *Spatial Cognition & Computation*, vol 2, pp 117-34.

Michael, Y. and McGregor, E. (2005) *Training manual: Senior Walking Environmental Assessment Tool – Revised (SWEAT-R)*, Portland, OR: Oregon Health & Science University.

Oswald, F. and Wahl, H-W. (2013) 'Creating and sustaining homelike places in residential environments', in G. Rowles and M. Bernard (eds) *Environmental gerontology*, New York: Springer, pp 53-77.

Peace, S. (2013) 'Social interactions in public spaces and places: A conceptual overview', in G. Rowles and M. Bernard (eds) *Environmental gerontology*, New York: Springer, pp 25-53.

Peace, S., Kellaher, L. and Holland, C. (2006) *Environment and identity in later life*, Maidenhead: Open University Press.

Planning Advisory Service (2009) *Knitting together planning and our ageing population*, Improvement and Development Agency.

Rowles, G. (1978) *Prisoners of space: Exploring the geographic experience of older people*, Boulder, CO: Westview.

Rowles, G. and Bernard, M. (2013) 'The meaning and significance of place in old age', in G. Rowles and M. Bernard (eds) *Environmental gerontology*, New York: Springer, pp 3-24.

Royal Town Planning Institute (2007) *Planning for an ageing society*, London: Royal Town Planning Institute.

Royal Town Planning Institute (2017) *Dementia and town planning: Creating better environments for people living with dementia*, January.

Rubinstein, R. and de Medeiros, K. (2004) 'Ecology and the aging self', in H. Wahl, R. Scheidt and P. Windley (eds) *Aging in context: Socio-physical environments*, New York: Springer, pp 59-84.

Scharf, T., Phillipson, C. and Smith, A. (2003) 'Older people's perceptions of the neighbourhood: Evidence from socially deprived urban areas', *Sociological Review Online*, vol 8, no 4. Available at www.socresonline.org.uk/8/4/scharf.html

Smith, A. (2009) *Ageing in urban neighbourhoods: Place attachment and social exclusion*, Bristol: Policy Press.

Ward Thompson, C., Curl, A., Aspinall, P., Alves, S. and Zuin, A. (2013) 'Do changes to the local street environment alter behaviour and quality of life of older adults? The "DIY Streets" intervention', *British Journal of Sports Medicine*, vol 48, no 13, pp 1059-65.

Welsh Government (2017) *Our housing agenda: Meeting the aspirations of older people in Wales. A report of the Expert Group on Housing an Ageing Population*. Available at http://gov.wales/topics/housing-and-regeneration/housing-supply/expert-group-on-housing-an-ageing-population/?lang=en

WHO (World Health Organization) (2015) *World report on ageing and health*, Geneva: WHO.

Wu, Y., Prina, M., Barnes, L., Matthews, F. and Brayne, C. and MRC CFAS (2015) 'Relocation at older age: Results from the Cognitive Function and Ageing Study', *Journal of Public Health*, pp 1-8. doi:10.1093/pubmed/fdv050

Zhong, J. and Moffat, S. (2016) 'Age-related differences in associative learning of landmarks and heading directions in a virtual navigation task', *Frontiers in Aging Neuroscience*, vol 8, doi:10.3389/fnagi.2016.00122

FOUR

Financial elder abuse

*Mary Gilhooly, Deborah Kinnear, Miranda Davies,
Kenneth Gilhooly and Priscilla Harries*

Introduction

A true story

The topic of financial elder abuse is rather closer to home than I might have wished. During this research project, my 94-year-old mother, and then subsequently my 95-year-old stepfather, fell for a financial scam. The scam consisted of a letter arriving in the post telling my mother that she had won US$800,000 in the Publishers Clearing House (PCH) sweepstakes. All that mother had to do was pay the taxes of US$800 and a cheque would be sent for the US$800,000. This is, of course, where mother should have become suspicious. However, PCH does run a sweepstake prize, and the letter certainly looked legitimate, containing the logo of PCH. All that mother had to do was go to Western Union and telegraph the tax money; this, she did, even though my stepfather by then was suspicious and warned against this action. Needless to say, the winnings never arrived.

My sister and I probably never would have found out about this, as clearly my mother felt humiliated for falling for this scam, but for the fact that they were then inundated with telephone calls and further letters saying that they had won money. Not knowing how to stop the calls and the mail, mother eventually revealed what had happened to my sister. My sister and I were both horrified and felt guilty. We felt guilty because we had never thought to warn about scams of this nature. One of the reasons for not discussing this with them was because they did not have a computer, and both of us were unaware of the number of very sophisticated scams that are sent through the post.

As if this was not bad enough, our stepfather then fell for the follow-up scam. He received a letter from a 'company' indicating that they understood that mother had been scammed and they were now receiving nuisance telephone calls and letters, and that for a fee of US$300 the company would intervene and stop the calls and letters. He paid the fee. Luckily my sister found out about this in time to stop the payment. However, he then received nasty letters threatening legal action if he did not make the payment.

Both my mother and stepfather are university-educated and both had full mental capacity. My sister and I certainly did not think of them as 'vulnerable' to such scams. As a researcher in this field, it still seems bizarre that this should have happened in my family while I was in the middle of a research project on detecting and preventing financial elder abuse. It did, however, make me very conscious of how and why such abuse does not come to the attention of the police or any professionals who could perhaps have intervened. Mother could hardly bring herself to admit to my sister and me that she had fallen for this scam, and certainly would not have been prepared to face further humiliation by going to the police. (Mary Gilhooly)

What is financial elder abuse?

This personal example could be labelled as a crime rather than financial abuse, and many in the field prefer to talk about 'exploitation' rather than abuse. Interestingly, there is no agreed definition of elder financial abuse or even agreed terminology in the area – the World Health Organization (WHO) report refers to 'elder maltreatment' (Sethi et al, 2011). In the UK, elder financial abuse is defined in the guidance document *No secrets* as '… including theft, fraud, exploitation, pressure in connection with wills, property or inheritance or financial transactions, or the misuse or misappropriation of property, possessions or benefits' (DH and Home Office, 2000, p 9, Section 2.7).[1] The National Center on Elder Abuse (NCEA) in the US defines financial exploitation as the 'illegal taking, misuse or concealment of funds, property, or assets of a vulnerable elder' (NCEA, 2014).

How common is financial elder abuse?

Are those who fall for scams in a small minority? The answer is hard to find. Most research has looked across the different types of elder abuse, with findings subsequently used to evidence the scale of the problem. In the US, Acierno et al (2010) conducted 5,777 telephone interviews with older people aged 60+ about their experience of abuse and neglect. A one-year prevalence figure of 5.2 per cent for financial abuse by a family member at the time of the interview was estimated. Another recent telephone survey (n=903) in the US examining racial differences in the prevalence of financial mistreatment found financial exploitation rates of 23 per cent for African Americans and 6.4 per cent for non-African Americans in the past six months (Beach et al, 2010).

To measure UK elder abuse prevalence rates using a larger and more representative sample than earlier attempts, Comic Relief and the UK Department of Health sponsored a prevalence study, which was conducted by O'Keeffe et al (2007). The study included people aged 66+ (n=2,111) across the UK living in the community; residential homes and NHS facilities were excluded. Financial abuse was the most prevalent form of elder abuse after neglect. The prevalence of financial abuse reported as occurring within the last year was 0.7 per cent, or around 56,000 older people in the UK.

There has been considerable variability in reported prevalence rates around the world. In a cross-sectional, population-based study of people over the age of 75 in rural villages in Gerona, Spain, Garre-Olmo et al (2009) found a prevalence rate of 4.7 per cent for financial abuse. Using a convenience sample, Dong et al (2007) found a prevalence rate of 13.6 per cent in an urban Chinese population. An Indian study by Chokkanathan and Lee (2006) of 400 community-dwelling older Indians found a prevalence rate of 5 per cent.

These various studies looked at a range of different types of financial abuse, not just the type of fraud in our 'True Story'. However, even if we postulated that around 3-4 per cent of older people are abused financially and that of those, a quarter represent postal or online fraud of the type my mother experienced, around the world that would indicate a large number of victims. As noted by Cassandra Cross in her study of online fraud, the cost of fraud victimisation extends beyond just the financial loss to emotional and psychological effects, and even through to general deterioration in physical health (Cross, 2012).

Are certain types of people more likely to be abused?

Unsurprisingly, little is known about those most likely to be financially abused. People who have been financially abused rarely put themselves forward for research, often even keeping the abuse secret from close friends and family, as my own personal case illustrates. Embarrassment, or a wish to keep the identity of the abuser a secret, are just two of the reasons why those who have been financially exploited are unlikely to reveal abuse. The main characteristics of abused people that have been of interest to researchers are age and gender.

Gender has been identified as a risk factor in relation to elder abuse, although the picture is unclear. In the ABUEL study (Abuse of the elderly in the European region), men were more likely than women to be victims of financial abuse (Soares et al, 2010). *The National Elder Abuse Incidence Study* (NCEA, 1998) reported that cases of financial elder abuse predominantly involved females. Some mixed UK results have, however, been reported, in that older men were at greater risk than younger men (O'Keefe et al, 2007), although women were at greater risk of maltreatment generally. That older men might be more at risk of financial abuse than older women may have to do with perceptions that men are more likely to control and have access to money.

Research on age, like that on gender, has produced conflicting results. Acierno et al (2010) reported that older people aged 60-69 were more likely to experience financial abuse than those aged over 70. O'Keefe et al (2007) conversely reported that males aged over 85 had a higher prevalence of financial abuse than those aged between 66-84. Increased likelihood of physical and mental problems with age is thought to increase vulnerability to abuse.

Framing the detection of elder abuse as 'bystander intervention'

It is often suggested that reported financial abuse is only the 'tip of the iceberg', indicating that financial abuse is often detected but no one intervenes. This appears to be the case even though abuse of older people is gaining attention from advocacy groups, policy-makers and professionals who deal with older people. The increase in absolute and relative numbers of older people in every country in the world, and their higher relative wealth and increased vulnerability to physical and mental health problems with age indicates that detecting and preventing financial abuse are going to be very important if we are to ensure the wellbeing of our ageing society. Unlike other countries, in England there is no mandatory reporting requirement for suspected elder financial abuse; and it is unlikely that legislation for mandatory reporting will be introduced in the near future. We must therefore come to a better understanding of the factors that make it hard to detect and prevent financial elder abuse. We believe that the bystander intervention model has considerable potential for underpinning research on elder abuse (Gilhooly et al, 2013, 2016).

The bystander intervention effect refers to a social psychological phenomenon in which the likelihood of helping in an emergency decreases as the number of passive bystanders increases. Research on this phenomenon was instigated by the rape and killing in 1964 of Ms Catherine Genovese in New York (Darley and Latané, 1968). Several people heard or saw this incident, but no one intervened until it was too late. Since then there have been many other real-life examples of the bystander effect. For example, many shoppers noticed a distressed James Bulger being led away from a shopping centre in England, but no one intervened to stop what turned into the murder of a three-year-old by two boys aged ten (Wikipedia, 2014). The bystander effect has been replicated many times over in numerous experiments (Latané and Nida, 1981). Latané and Darley (1970) proposed a five-stage psychological model for intervention. The bystander needs to: (1) notice the event; (2) construe the situation as an emergency; (3) develop a feeling of personal responsibility; (4) believe that he or she has the skills necessary to succeed; and (5) reach a conscious decision to help.

The same stages that are involved in cases of emergency bystander intervention must be gone through in non-emergencies as in elder financial abuse. In particular, the identification of elder financial abuse involves complex judgements to be made as part of the decision-making process.

Aims and methods

Project aim and theoretical underpinning

The aim of this project was to examine real-world decision-making in relation to the professional detection of financial elder abuse. We were interested in exploring the utility of the bystander intervention model to explain why elder financial abuse often goes unreported. Although developed to explain why people fail to act in emergencies, the bystander intervention model has considerable potential to help us understand decision-making in relation to the detection and prevention of elder financial abuse.

There are five stages to our modified professional bystander intervention model:

1. Noticing relevant cues to financial abuse
2. Construing the situation as financial abuse
3. Deciding the situation is a personal responsibility

4. Knowing how to deal with the situation
5. Considering the rewards and costs of intervening and not intervening.

Design

The aims of the four phases of the project were as follows:

- Phase I: Identify the 'cues' used in judging whether or not a case represents financial elder abuse
- Phase II: Test hypotheses about the factors that account for the greatest variance in decisions-making
- Phase III: Compare policy documents and guidelines with practice
- Phase IV: Disseminate findings and develop online training tools.

This chapter only considers findings from Phases I and II. Findings from Phase III can be found in Gilbert et al (2013). Details of Phase IV and the training tools we developed can be accessed free of charge via our Elder Financial Abuse Research and Training site (see www. elderfinancialabuse.co.uk; see also Harries et al, 2014a, b, 2016).

Phase I: Participants included 23 social care, 20 health and 20 banking and financial services professionals. Only those who had experience of dealing with older people and at least one experience of suspected elder financial abuse were included. In-depth interviews were carried out using the critical incident technique to generate an understanding of the cues used to determine that a case represents genuine financial abuse. Participants were asked to describe their most recent experiences (critical incidents) of a case of elder financial abuse. Only incidents in which participants had been directly involved (cases that were identified by them or reported to them) were included in the analysis.

Phase II: Participants included 82 health, 70 social care and 70 banking and financial sector professionals. Experiments used case scenarios (factorial surveys) to determine if some cues weighed more heavily in decision-making than others (Taylor, 2006). Case scenarios (see Figure 4.1) were created for social care and health professionals with seven factors that varied: age, gender, identifier of abuse, type of abuse/nature of financial problem, physical capacity, mental capacity and living arrangements. The case scenarios for banking and finance professionals also included 'who was in charge of the money' as a variable. Study participants made judgements about case scenarios in terms of

Figure 4.1: Example case scenario: Financial Elder Abuse Project

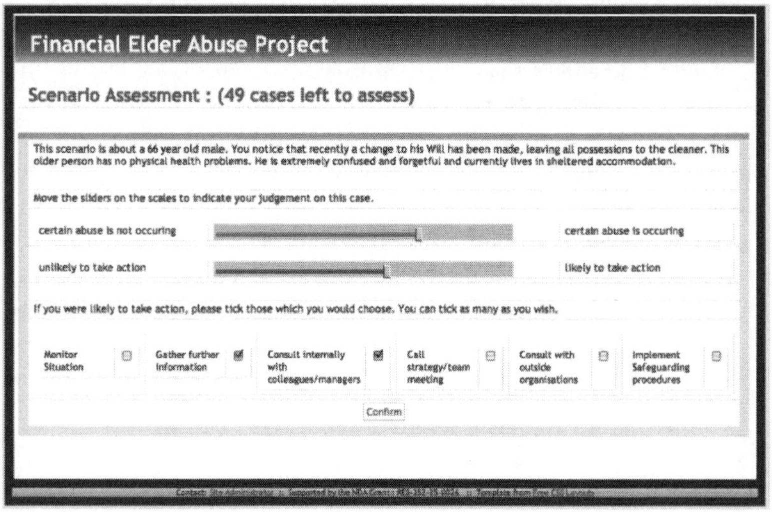

(1) certainty that financial abuse was taking place; (2) likelihood of taking action; and (3) action to be taken. We did not ask directly about perception of personal responsibility because piloting indicated that participants from these professional groups would almost always say that they would accept responsibility for acting where financial abuse was certain. In hindsight, however, leaving out a question of this nature was problematic given our interest in viewing the detection and prevention of elder financial abuse through the lens of the bystander intervention model. The health and social care professionals accessed the case scenarios via the web. They had 65 case scenarios to judge. Fifteen of the scenarios were repeats in order to check for consistency. Banking professionals also accessed the case scenarios via the web, but did so in their spare time due to restricted access within the workplace for security reasons. The banking professionals judged 46 case scenarios, with 11 repetitions.

Ethical approval and sample bias

Research ethics approval was obtained from the Research Ethics Committee of the School of Health Sciences and Social Care, Brunel University London, from the NHS Research Ethics Committee (Integrated Research Application System, IRAS) and from individual primary care trusts (PCTs). Site Specific Information (SSI) forms were completed for South West London, North West London, East & West

Berkshire and West Kent PCTs. The project was registered on the UK Clinical Research Network (UKCRN) portfolio and our Research Passport was obtained. From the date of submission of the IRAS form to Brunel University London for initial approval, to achieving final approval from the NHS Research Ethics Committee took over nine months. It was not, however, the time that these procedures took that was most problematic for the project. What may most have influenced the project was the requirement to insert in our information sheets a statement that we had to report negligence, if such negligence emerged in our interviews. We think it very likely that the requirement to report negligence would have influenced those willing to take part in Phase I of the study. By ensuring complete confidentiality, we had hoped to recruit professionals who were certain that abuse was taking place but did not intervene. An important aim of the study was to explore why people did *not* intervene. Although we have no way of knowing if only those who intervened volunteered to be interviewed, it seems very likely that the Phase I sample was biased. Readers need to take this potential bias into consideration when thinking about our findings.

Findings and discussion

In this chapter we consider five research questions, using a combination of both qualitative and quantitative findings.

How does elder financial abuse come to the attention of professionals?

In typical bystander intervention studies, participants witness an event that they judge to be an emergency or not. In the cases of real-world elder financial abuse reported by study participants there were two ways in which the 'event' came to the attention of a banking or health professional, namely, direct observation or reports by others. Those who reported cases included family members, friends, other professionals and the older person at the centre of the abuse.

Banking professionals directly observed more cases of abuse ($n=20$) than those reported to them by someone else ($n=15$). The higher number of directly observed cases is unsurprising given that these professionals work within the financial sector, deal with monetary issues and work closely with customers on a day-to-day basis. These professionals are also trained, as part of their role, to identify any unusual financial behaviours or transactions made by a customer.

Social care professionals, however, were more reliant on cases being reported to them (n=31) rather than directly observed (n=4). The higher number of reported (n=31) rather than directly observed cases (n=4) may be reflective of the formal processes by which adult protection cases are dealt with. It is also unsurprising that there were more reported cases or referrals than directly observed, as social care professionals work with a range of cases, not just those who are at risk of abuse.

In contrast, health professionals directly observed a similar number of cases (n=18) as those reported to them by someone else (n=24): health professionals are not only in a position to witness cases of potential abuse (for example, general medical practitioners or district nurses visiting patients at home), but they are also likely to be informed about cases of abuse. Patients are seen to hold them in a position of trust where sensitive information can be disclosed to them under the confines of patient confidentiality.

What cues lead to certainty that financial abuse is taking place?

The first stage of the bystander intervention requires that the event be noticed. Thus, we were interested in the nature of the 'cues' (case features) that raise suspicions of financial abuse. We were also interested in whether different cues are noticed by those in banking/finance, health and social care.

The in-depth interviews in Phase I revealed a large number of 'cues' that financial abuse might be taking place (Davies et al, 2011). As a consequence, we categorised the cues and explored variations between our three groups of study participants. What emerged was a similar picture for health and social care professionals, with three cue categories of importance in judgements: (1) types of abuse; (2) mental capacity; and (3) physical capacity. Interestingly, mental and physical capacity did not emerge as important cues for those in banking and finance. An important cue category for the banking and finance professionals was the 'person in charge of the money' (for example, third party signatory, lasting power of attorney, older person). The type of abuse was also important in judgements, although the subcategories of type of abuse were different. The differences can be seen in Table 4.1.

Table 4.1: Types of suspected financial abuse reported

Banking professionals		Health and social care professionals	
Types of abuse	Banking N	Types of abuse	Health N
Suspicious third party	11	Stealing from the home or person	16
Large cash withdrawal	10	Anomalies between living conditions and financial assets	12
Financial anomalies in accounts or bills	9	Unknown befriender or rogue traders	9
Scams	3	Exerting influence to change a will	2
Protecting inheritance	2	Financial anomalies in accounts or bills	2
		Misuse of power of attorney	1
Total	35	Total	42

Are some cues more influential than others in determining certainty that financial abuse was occurring?

Among our health and social care study participants, only two factors (cue categories) had a significant influence on social care and health sector professionals' certainty of abuse: mental capacity (~30 per cent of the variance) and the nature of the financial problem (~27 per cent of the variance) (Davies et al, 2013). Case scenarios involving misuse of power of attorney and rogue traders, compared to anomalies between finances and living conditions and anomalies in accounts or bills, were associated with higher certainty that abuse was occurring. The finding that two factors most influenced decision-making is in line with other research showing that only a few key features of cases influence judgements (Kahneman and Frederick, 2005).

Three factors were found to have a statistically significant influence on case scenario ratings of certainty of abuse among our banking and finance participants. These included the type of abuse (78 per cent of the variance), the older person's mental capacity (~14 per cent of the variance) and who was in charge of the individual's money (~3 per cent of the variance) (Davies et al, 2014).

The finding that type of abuse suspected had the greatest influence on banking professionals' judgements is perhaps a result of the focus of the banking professional role on the customer's financial management and the need to prevent fraud. Cases involving an out-of-the-ordinary cash withdrawal and an overdrawn account were judged as significantly lower certainty of abuse than other types of financial problems, and cases involving winning an overseas cash prize had significantly higher certainty of abuse than other categories. It is interesting that the type of abuse where certainty of abuse was rated as significantly lower than others were those were it could be argued that the extent of financial losses were lower. For instance, a cash withdrawal that was out of the ordinary for the customer's routine was likely to involve less financial loss than the potential loss where a relative has objected to the customer's house being sold.

Professionals' consideration of who is in charge of the older person's money as a cue may be expected given that it has previously been suggested that where an individual is not in charge of their own finances the opportunities for elder financial abuse increase (Edmonds and Noble, 2008). This observation is supported by the fact that there was no significant difference between certainty of abuse where the individual was under a lasting power of attorney in comparison to a third party signatory (that is, someone in charge other than the individual themselves). In both instances, certainty of abuse (and likelihood of action) was higher than where the individual was in independent control of their finances.

The presence of mental capacity as a key cue for the banking professionals was surprising given that this did not emerge as a cue in Phase I of the research where banking professionals described incidents of elder financial abuse. Using mental capacity as a cue of elder financial abuse may be associated with knowledge regarding who is in control of the individual's finances. The Queensland Assets and Ageing Research Programme reported that where older people are independently managing their money and have mental capacity to make financial decisions, there is less opportunity for financial abuse (Wilson et al, 2009). It may therefore be that consideration of mental capacity is associated with knowledge of who is in charge of the money.

Is uncertainty associated with lack of action?

In our case scenario study there was a high and statistically significant correlation between ratings of certainty of abuse and likelihood of taking action ($r=0.98$, $n=50$, $p<0.001$ for health and social care; $r=0.98$, $n=35$, $p<0.001$ for banking/finance samples). Although the bystander intervention model would lead to an expectation of a significant correlation between certainty that financial abuse was taking place and likelihood of action, what surprised us somewhat was that when comparing the mean ratings, the likelihood of taking action (health and social care mean = 63 per cent; banking/finance mean = 63 per cent) was greater than certainty that financial abuse was taking place (health and social care mean = 55 per cent; banking/ finance mean = 56 per cent) for all three groups. Thus the answer is yes, uncertainty is associated with less likelihood of action, but the ratings indicated that when in doubt, many professionals would play safe and take action to intervene.

However, the finding that participants from social care were more likely to take action, and to take stronger actions than participants from health and banking, could be because in the UK, those in social care are tasked with and trained for adult safeguarding. In terms of the bystander intervention model, we surmise that social care professionals are more likely than non-social care professionals to decide that the situation is a personal responsibility (Stage 3 of the model), and have the knowledge, and possibly some training, to deal with it (Stage 4 of the model).

What are the barriers to intervening in cases of suspected financial elder abuse?

Barriers to intervention were explored in the qualitative component of the project, namely, Phase I. The most frequent difficulty that all three professional groups mentioned in relation to detecting and preventing financial elder abuse was identifying the abuse:

> '… we're GPs, we're medical doctors, we're not sort of financial advisers and you know a person's finances are not really any of our business. However, you know, if someone's being abused, physically, mentally, psychologically, financially, there's someone who's taking advantage of somebody else, then you know we do have a duty of care, but it is a very, very difficult thing to pick up.' (GP partner)

However, even when it was relatively clear that abuse was taking place, participants in our study indicated that there were many barriers to acting. Our banking/finance participants were most likely to indicate that issues surrounding policy and legislation were barriers to acting:

> '… well the problem we have is Data Protection. Now we are very concerned, you know, if we breach that, you know, it's all very well and good if it turns out to be a genuine case but if we've misread the signs, then … whether we're in breach of Data Protection. So, you know, we're a bit unsure of what exact procedures we can take.' (Investment manager)

Banking professionals frequently highlighted the restrictions they faced particularly as a result of the Data Protection Act (UK Parliament, 1998) and the difficulty of reporting their suspicions for fear of consequences. Interestingly, there was generally an inability to explain what the Data Protection Act 1998 stipulated to prevent them from reporting a case of suspected abuse. According to the British Banking Association (2010), only the refusal of the customer's consent will prevent a case from being reported. If a bank suspects financial abuse but the customer either does not or is not prepared to admit they may be a victim, this is a difficult area for banks in terms of the customer mandate. There is only one reporting route, which is via the Suspicious Activity Reports (SAR) regime to the Serious Organised Crime Agency (SOCA) under the Proceeds of Crime Act 2002. Contacting any other organisation or person, whether it be the customer, law enforcement, social services or the victim's family, before a SAR has been made to SOCA constitutes an offence for which the bank may be criminally liable.

Social care, health and banking professionals reported that lack of experience in identifying and dealing with cases of financial abuse as well as uncertainty about how to deal with victims of abuse and potential abusers were sources of difficulties. Each group reported a need for guidance and training tools to be developed to enable them to improve their ability to accurately identify financial elder abuse and to make the appropriate decisions:

> '… if there was something set in stone, that says this is what you need to do, and this is what you can do within your own powers kind of thing.' (Team manager)

> '… it would be helpful to have some guidance I think … because that vulnerable population will be coming into contact with us more.' (Occupational therapist)

A further difficulty faced by professionals was working with other agencies. Cases of financial elder abuse rarely had a positive outcome often due to a lack of evidence to prosecute the perpetrator. Part of the problem involved working with various agencies that were unable to share information to support a case:

> '… we tried to make some enquiries via the bank very tentatively, and obviously even though she'd sort of said "right, this is my social worker and things put her on the

line, there's been some irregularity here, I don't understand what's happened", they obviously wouldn't really tell us anything...' (Team manager)

All professional groups reported the need for more collaborative interagency working when detecting and preventing elder financial abuse to address this difficulty.

Policy implications and theory development

It is concerning that our participants reported being more likely to decide that financial abuse was definitely taking place, and even more likely to act if the victim was mentally incapacitated. It is surely desirable that financial abuse be detected before mental incapacity has arisen.

Prioritising cases based on mental capacity could be due to pressure to direct services where the need is greatest. This issue was raised in Phase I of data collection when professionals explained the impact of resource and time limitations as a factor that could make taking action in cases of suspected elder financial abuse very difficult. Another possible implication of this focus on impaired mental capacity is that professionals are less likely to take action in cases where the victim has full mental capacity, and may not consent to intervention, either because of embarrassment or because the perpetrator of the financial abuse is known to the victim.

The finding that there were two particular types of abuse where certainty of abuse and likelihood of action was rated significantly higher – rogue traders and misuse of power of attorney – has implications for training. First, professionals should be particularly alert to these two sorts of financial problems and the potential they suggest for abuse. More importantly, training must also address the fact that financial abuse can be more subtle and professionals need to be made aware of, and have training in, how to address these more subtle forms of financial abuse, particularly financial abuse perpetrated by family members, friends and neighbours.

Misuse of power of attorney and what is known as rogue trading raise interesting issues about the definition of elder financial abuse. It is sometimes argued that these are both crimes and, hence, there is no need for the term 'elder financial abuse'. It may be that social care and health sector professionals weigh these types of financial abuse more heavily in decision-making precisely because they represent crimes rather than the more subtle forms of financial abuse that are perpetuated by relatives and other people known and trusted by the victim of the financial abuse.

Let us now consider implications for theory development in relation to the bystander intervention model.

At any one of the five stages of our professional bystander intervention model decisions could be taken that prevent abuse coming to the attention of those in a position to intervene. Exploring decision-making via the bystander intervention model has been instructive in a number of ways.

First, the bystander intervention model suggests that people will be less likely to take action in cases of suspected elder financial abuse where there is uncertainty that abuse is occurring. In Phase II we found that certainty of abuse and likelihood of taking action were highly correlated; where there was less certainty that abuse was taking place, likelihood of taking action was lower. However, we also found that likelihood of taking action was greater than certainty that abuse was taking place. Thus, it appears that many participants think it best to play safe and take action even if uncertain.

The third stage in our proposed professional bystander intervention model is assuming responsibility for acting when financial abuse seems certain. In this study we also found that participants from the social care sector were more likely to indicate that they would take action compared to those from healthcare, and that healthcare participants chose what we called 'less strong' actions. These sector differences are interesting and readily explicable given that in the UK adult safeguarding is primarily the responsibility of social services. Moreover, in Phase I of the project we found that GPs often detected financial abuse, but that doctor–patient confidentiality prevented them reporting the case to adult safeguarding teams or even reporting to the police. In Phase I of the project several cases were described in which patients were reported as asking their doctors not to reveal the abuse because the perpetrator was a family member on whom the older person was dependent.

The fourth stage of the bystander model is deciding that one has the skills to act. Again, Phase I was instructive in that participants revealed that sometimes they did not know what to do when confronted with a case of financial abuse. In countries with mandatory reporting of abuse suspicions, it is presumably obvious what people must do. The UK, however, does not hold any member of the public or any professional responsible for reporting suspected abuse.

Finally, the fifth stage of the professional bystander intervention model is taking some action, and there could be any number of barriers to taking action. Phase I explored barriers to actions qualitatively. Phase II did not directly address the issue of barriers to action, but provided interesting information about which factors do and do not play a key role in the likelihood that a social or health sector worker will intervene in some way when abuse is suspected.

Key findings

- Financial abuse of people with dementia or declining cognitive and physical functioning is of growing concern.
- It is equally important to protect professionals and carers from unfair allegations of financial abuse, as it is to safeguard the assets of vulnerable older people.
- There is little comparative evaluation of the efficiency of safeguarding procedures in different authorities, and no evidence base underpinning the effectiveness of decision-making in cases of suspected abuse. A major gap in policy exists in understanding the long-term effects of financial abuse on victims.
- It is apparent that the multi-agency procedures have only a limited focus on financial abuse, with the consequence that it features as secondary in importance to other forms of abuse.

Conclusions

The finding that 'mental capacity' was a key determinant of both certainty that abuse was taking place and likelihood of intervention is concerning. Prevention requires that such abuse is detected well *before* an older person loses mental capacity.

It may be that, like other countries, mandatory reporting is needed in the UK to help overcome the many barriers to reporting suspected financial elder abuse. Using the bystander intervention model to explore why it is that professionals often make decisions that delay or even prevent financial abuse from coming to the attention of those in a position to act could be a useful tool in training.

More research is, of course, needed to determine the utility of the bystander intervention model in detecting and preventing financial elder abuse. Only a small number of factors were varied in our study and there were only three dependent variables in Phase II; moreover, in many real-life cases there may be considerably less information on which to base a decision. Decision-making by other professional groups, such as the police, also needs to be investigated. However, we are of the view that the bystander intervention model has considerable potential for studying the decision-making of both professionals and the public in relation to not only elder abuse, but also even neglect in hospitals and care homes.

Acknowledgements

The research reported here was funded by the UK cross-Research Council New Dynamics of Ageing (NDA) programme (Economic and Social Research Council-administered) (grant number RES-352-25-0026). The views expressed in this chapter are those of the authors, and do not necessarily reflect the views of the funding body or our project partners and advisers. We would like to thank our co-investigators, Tony Gilbert, Catherine Hennessy, Bridget Penhale and David Stanley. The members of our Project Management Board – Gary Fitzgerald, Alison Toombs, Mary Cox, Gillian Dalley, David Sinclair, Gill Fairhurst, Ruth Cartwright, and Teresa LaFort – also deserve a big thank you. Our partner, HSBC, in particular, Mary Walsh and Neal Shadbolt, deserve a special thank you for providing a wonderful venue for Project Management Board meetings, including lunch, and for much needed help in obtaining study participants. We would also like to acknowledge the study participants who must, of course, remain anonymous. Dr Catherine Pearson provided invaluable insights into the importance of the finding that mental capacity is a major determinant of judgements.

Note

[1]   *No secrets* was applicable at the time of the study, but has been superseded by the Care Act 2014.

References

Acierno, R., Hernandez, M.A., Amstadter, A.B., Resnick, H.S., Steven, K., Muzzy, W. and Kilptrick, D.G. (2010) 'Prevalence and correlates of emotional, physical, sexual and financial abuse and potential neglect in the United State: The National Elder Mistreatment Study', *American Journal of Public Health*, vol 100, no 2, pp 292-7.

Beach, S.R., Schulz, R., Degenholtz, H.B., Castle, N.G., Rosen, J., Foz, A.R. and Morycz, R.K. (2010) 'Using audio computer-assisted self-interviewing and interactive voice response to measure elder mistreatment in older adults: Feasibility and effects on prevalence estimates', *Journal of Official Statistics*, vol 26, pp 507-33.

British Banking Association (2010) *Safeguarding vulnerable customers. Banking best practice: Advice for bank staff*. Previously accessed (but no longer available) at www.bba.org.uk/media/article/Fighting-fraud-keeping-safe

Chokkanathan, S. and Lee, A.E.Y. (2005) 'Elder mistreatment in urban India: A community-based study', *Journal of Elder Abuse & Neglect*, vol 17, no 2, pp 45-61.

Cross, C. (2012) *The Donald Mackay Churchill Fellowship to study methods for preventing and supporting victims of online fraud*, Report to the Winston Churchill Memorial Trust of Australia.

Darley, J.M. and Latané, B (1968) 'Bystander intervention in emergencies: Diffusion of responsibility', *Journal of Personality and Social Psychology*, vol 8, pp 377-83.

Davies, M.L., Gilhooly, M.L.M., Gilhooly, K.J., Harries, P.A. and Cairns, D. (2013) 'Factors influencing decision-making by social care and health sector professionals in cases of elder financial abuse', *European Journal of Ageing*, vol 10, no 4, pp 313-23. Available at http:// link.springer.com/article/10.1007%2Fs10433-013-0279-3#page-2

Davies, M.L., Harries, P.A., Gilhooly, K.J., Gilhooly, M.L.M. and Cairns, D. (2014) 'Detection and prevention of financial abuse against elders', *Journal of Financial Crime*, vol 20, no 4, pp 84-99.

Davies, M.L., Harries, P.A., Cairns, D., Stanley, D., Gilhooly, M.L.M., Gilhooly, K.J., et al (2011) 'Factors used in the detection of elder financial abuse: A judgment and decision making study of social workers and their managers', *International Social Work*, vol 54, no 3, pp 404-20.

DH (Department of Health) and Home Office (2000) *No secrets: Guidance on developing and implementing multi-agency policies and procedures to protect vulnerable adults from abuse*, London: DH.

Dong, X., Simon, M.A. and Gorbien, M. (2007) 'Elder abuse and neglect in an urban Chinese population', *Journal of Elder Abuse & Neglect*, vol 19, no 3-4, pp 79-96.

Edmonds, J. and Noble, P. (2008) *Responding to the financial abuse of older people: Understanding he challenges faced by the banking and financial services sector*, Bendigo: Loddon Campaspe Community Legal Centre.

Garre-Olmo, J., Planas-Uujol, X., Lopes-Pousa, S., Juvinya, D., Vila, A. and Vilalta-Franch, J. (2009) 'Prevalence and risk factors of suspected elder abuse subtypes in people aged 75 and older', *Journal of the American Geriatrics Society*, vol 57, no 5, pp 815-22.

Gilbert, A., Stanley, D., Penhale, B. and Gilhooly, M. (2013) 'Elder abuse in England: A policy analysis perspective related to social care and banking', *Journal of Adult Protection*, vol 15, no 3, pp 153-63, 24 June.

Gilhooly, M.M., Cairns, D., Davies, M., Harries, P., Gilhooly, K. and Notley, E. (2013) 'Framing the detection of elder financial abuse as professional bystander intervention: Decision cues, pathways to detection and barriers to action', *Journal of Adult Protection*, vol 15, no 2, pp 54-68.

Gilhooly, M.M., Dalley, G., Gilhooly, K.J., Sullivan, M.P., Harries, P., Levi, M., Kinnear, D.C. and Davies, M.S. (2016) 'Financial elder abuse through the lens of the bystander intervention model', *Public Policy and Aging Report*, vol 26, no 1, pp 5-11.

Harries, P.A., Gilhooly, M.M., Gilhooly, K.J. and Davies, M.S. (2016) 'Enhancing workforce capacity in the detection and prevention of elder financial abuse', *Public Policy and Aging Report*, vol 26, no 1, pp 30-3.

Harries, P.A., Davies, M.S., Gilhooly, K.J., Gilhooly, M.M. and Tomlinson, C. (2014a) 'Educating novice practitioners to detect elder financial abuse: A randomised controlled trial', *BMC Medical Education*, vol 14, no 21.

Harries, P.A., Davies, M.S., Yang, H., Gilhooly, K.J., Gilhooly, M.M. and Thompson, C. (2014b) 'Identifying and enhancing risk threshold in the detection of elder financial abuse: A signal detection analysis of novice health and social care professionals' decision making', *BMC Medical Education*, vol 14, no 1044.

Kahneman, D. and Frederick, S. (2005) 'A model of heuristic judgment', in K.J. Holyoak and R.G. Morrison (eds) *The Cambridge handbook of thinking and reasoning*, Cambridge: Cambridge University Press, pp 267-317.

Latané, B. and Darley, J.M. (1970) *The unresponsive bystander: Why doesn't he help?*, New York: Appleton-Century-Croft.

Latané, B. and Nida, S. (1981) 'Ten years of research on group size and helping', *Psychological Bulletin*, vol 89, pp 308-24.

NCEA (National Center on Elder Abuse) (1998) *The National Elder Abuse Incidence Study, Final report*, Alhambra, CA: NCEA in collaboration with Westat, Inc. Available at www.acl.gov/sites/default/files/programs/2016-09/ABuseReport_Full.pdf

NCEA (2014) 'Frequently Asked Questions'. Available at https://ncea.acl.gov/faq/index.html

O'Keeffe, M., Hills, A., Doyle, M., McCreadie, C., Scholes, S. and Constantine, R. (2007) *UK study of abuse and neglect of older people: Prevalence survey report*, London: National Centre for Social Research.

Sethi, D., Wood, S., Mitis, F., Bellis, M., Penhale, B., Marmalejo, I.I. et al (eds) (2011) *European report on preventing elder maltreatment*, Geneva: World Health Organization. Available at www.euro.who.int/__data/assets/pdf_file/0010/144676/e95110.pdf

Soares, J.J.F., Barros, H., Torres-Gonzales, F., Ioannidi-Kapolou, E., Lamura, G., Lindert, J. et al (2010) *Abuse and health among elderly in Europe*, Kaunas: Lithuanian University of Health Sciences Press.

Taylor, B.J. (2006) 'Factorial surveys: Using scenarios to study professional judgement', *British Journal of Social Work*, vol 36, no 7, pp 1187-207.

UK Parliament (1998) *Data Protection Act*, London: HMSO.

Wikipedia (2014) 'Murder of James Bulger'. Available at http://en.wikipedia.org/wiki/Jamie_Bulger_murder_case

Wilson, J., Tilse, C., Setterlund, D. and Rosenman, L. (2009) 'Older people and their assets: A range of roles and issues for social workers', *Australian Social Work*, vol 62, no 2, pp 155-67.

FIVE

Maintaining dignity and independence

Liz Lloyd, Michael Calnan, Ailsa Cameron, Jane Seymour, Randall Smith and Kate White

Introduction

The perspectives of older people on dignity in care have been largely overlooked in British policies, and the tendency has been to look at ways in which care providers should 'deliver dignity' by reference to agreed standards. For example, the Dignity Challenge developed in 2006 identified 10 dignity tests against which services could be evaluated (Cass et al, 2009). In this project, the research team took the view that a better understanding of dignity in later life was needed, which was informed by the experiences of older people, including, but not limited to, those with experiences as service users.

Four questions shaped the research:

1. What preparations do older adults who are facing death at a near but uncertain time make for the process of dying and death?
2. What accounts are given about dignity in daily life by older adults during this phase in their life?
3. What resources are available to these older adults to draw on?
4. What factors are perceived to support or undermine a sense of dignity?

Dignity has both personal and social meanings, and the two are closely interrelated. The theoretical model developed by Nordenfelt (2004) was a valuable starting point for this project, as it takes both into account. It proposes four 'varieties' of dignity. First, the *dignity of merit* refers to the high rank of individuals because of the social role they occupy (the historical meaning of dignity) as well as to dignity earned through socially valued achievements. The *dignity of moral stature* concerns individual conduct and is linked to self-respect, which is shaped by prevalent cultural values, giving it a social as well as personal meaning. Importantly, this type of dignity also draws attention to the conduct of staff in care services and the impact of this on *their* dignity and moral stature. The third variety – the *dignity of identity* – is as Nordenfelt expressed it, 'the dignity that we attach to ourselves as integrated and autonomous persons' (2009, p 33). It is evidently challenged in old age by failing health and the loss of capacity for self-care. The dignity of identity also has social as well as personal meaning, exemplified in the institutionalisation of older people and the associated loss of individual identity. The fourth of Nordenfelt's varieties is the *dignity of being human*. He argues that unlike the other three varieties, this is fixed and immutable, irrespective of age or ability. It provides the basis of laws on human rights and procedures for upholding these.

Dignity and health in later life

Dignity in later life is inextricably linked to the earlier life course (James and Hockey, 2007). The concept of the life course captures individual experiences over time and in context. It highlights the contingent nature of individual health in later life, and the combined effects on old age of interpersonal relationships, socioeconomic status and other social and cultural factors experienced throughout life. Theories of the life course identify a division between the third and fourth ages of the life course. Although this division is not clear-cut, the third age is associated with personal growth, development and active citizenship and the fourth with dependency, frailty, loss and decline (Twigg, 2006; Gilleard and Higgs, 2010). From this point of view, the problems and difficulties associated with old age are concentrated in the fourth age, the period of life adjacent to death, when dignity in both personal and social forms is at risk. The perception of dignity in the context of death and dying is contentious, with supporters and opponents of assisted dying invoking the concept to support their cause (Lloyd, 2004).

According to Nordenfelt's model (2009), individual autonomy and bodily integrity are essential to the dignity of identity and thus, the loss of these in the fourth age has *inevitable* consequences for dignity. This point of view is not universally accepted (Wainwright and Gallagher, 2008), although Nordenfelt (2009) argues that in any circumstances, the dignity of being human prevails, and primary responsibility for upholding it would rest on caregivers. Differences between older people in terms of how they experience the loss of bodily integrity and autonomy and how these differences reflect inequalities in resources and access to support, technological aids and therapeutic interventions also play a crucial part in maintaining dignity. The indignities associated with health problems (falls and continence problems are two examples) can be mitigated by appropriate support. The means by which this can be achieved were the focus of our analysis. A further factor to take into account is the way in which support services are provided. In the UK, the policy context favours the idea of self-care and health literacy among people with long-term health problems. This model seeks to maximise patient control over health with the support of health professionals. Self-care and patient control are strongly associated with the maximisation of dignity, but there are questions about how health itself is understood in the self-care model. Is the focus merely on functional health, or does it also embrace psychological and spiritual wellbeing?

Debates concerning the provision of support raise questions about the policy imperative of limiting the cost of care for older people, which also has important implications for dignity. Pleschberger (2007) and Woolhead et al (2004) reflect on the impact on frail older people of almost daily reminders that their care represents an economic burden on society. Woolhead et al (2004) also argue that the social and economic contexts of health services are not conducive to supporting their human rights or dignity of identity, and that where staff succeed, it is often despite, not because of, the organisational and policy context. Dignity *within* care relationships is inextricably linked with the broader political and economic contexts *of* care relationships.

Aims and methods

A longitudinal qualitative methodology was adopted so that fluctuations and changes in participants' circumstances and their perspectives on these could be examined in real time. This methodology also made it possible to explore sensitive issues at an appropriate time, thus reducing pressure on both participants and researchers. For example, questions about the end of life could be raised when the participants had come to know and trust the researchers. There were significant ethical issues to be considered in this project related to capacity to consent, the wellbeing of potentially vulnerable participants and the subject matter of the interviews, which had the potential to be upsetting. We also took into account the length of participants' involvement and the importance of ongoing consent. Following the Mental Capacity Act 2005 guidance we adopted the rule that capacity would be assumed unless there was evidence to the contrary. We followed a protocol of asking participants at each interview if they could remember who we were and what the research was about. Taking into account participants' wellbeing, we invited them to nominate a supporter for the duration of the study. Ten of them did so, and most participants living with partners wished to have them present at interviews, whether or not they were nominated as supporters. We conducted full interviews with six supporters, including two following the deaths of participants.

We aimed to recruit 40 participants aged 75 and over with ongoing needs for support and care that enabled them to remain living in the community. In order to achieve some variation within the participant group, we aimed for three groupings:

• People who had had an unscheduled stay in hospital during the previous 12 months that resulted in ongoing support needs.
• People with ongoing high support needs, requiring help with, for example, bathing, dressing, food preparation or regular nursing care.
• People with ongoing lower level need for support in order to remain living at home. This included help with shopping, cleaning and transport.

Using an opting-in approach, we began recruitment through three GP practices (two in Bristol and one in Nottingham). Potential participants were sent a letter of invitation from their GP with a stamped addressed envelope and a reply slip. Recruitment in this sphere of inquiry is often a challenge, and conditions imposed by the local NHS Research Ethics Committee complicated the process. They required us to limit our invitations to participate to exactly the number of people we wished to have in the study, so as to avoid the possibility that potential participants would be disappointed if more responded than we needed. This requirement slowed down recruitment, and after nine months we had only 29 participants. Thanks to the help of an Advisory Group member we boosted numbers to 34 through recruiting from day centres, also using an opting-in approach. Table 5.1 provides an outline picture of the group at the point when they joined the study. Participants have been given pseudonyms.

Interviews were conducted between June 2008 and January 2011 in participants' own homes. In round 1 the focus was on participants' everyday life, their experiences of being helped and their thoughts about ageing and dignity. In round 2, the focus was participants' earlier life course and how this had influenced their current beliefs, values and approach to life. In round 3 we examined the changes that had occurred in participants' health, mobility, living arrangements and relationships since the first interview, including their experiences of treatment and help. In round 4, if the subject of the end of life had not previously arisen, it was addressed at this point. In this round we also provided feedback to each participant on the data we had gathered from them and clarified this. In addition to the pre-planned themes, each round was influenced by the findings from previous ones. For example, in rounds 1 and 2 the subject of medication emerged as a strong interest of participants and was covered more fully in round 3.

In addition to the general themes there were also specific points of focus tailored to each individual. We reflected on events between interviews and followed up on what participants had talked about in the previous interview, particularly if they had referred to planned events. Eighteen participants were interviewed four times and nine five times in order to follow up important changes occurring at the time of the fourth interview. Those who were interviewed once, twice or three times included those who had died during the project. At round 4 we also asked participants to comment on their participation in the research and their motivation for joining. All said they had enjoyed taking part, and most explained their motivation as a wish to 'give something back' to society.

At the end of the study we held a social event in each of the two cities, at which participants were given a report and presentation. This provided further validation for the findings as well as a way of showing appreciation to the participants for their contributions. Ending the data gathering appropriately was a serious responsibility on the research team. Over the years the trusting relationships that were integral to the research design also had an impact on the individual participants who had shared personal, often very emotional, information.

Findings

Interview data were transcribed verbatim as the research progressed, and analysis was ongoing throughout the study. Both researchers read the transcripts and emerging findings were presented to the wider research team at six-monthly meetings. At the end of the study a full analysis was conducted using the analytic hierarchy developed by Spencer, Ritchie and O'Connor (2009). After initial sorting of the data, 10 descriptive categories were developed: health and illness; functional health and mobility; treatment and help; significant relationships; home and environment; everyday life and activities; thoughts about ageing; thoughts about changes occurring during the study; reflections on earlier life course; and thoughts about the future.

Table 5.1: Participant characteristics at first interview

Participant	Sex	Age	Marital status	Previous occupation	Health condition (self-described)
Henry	M	90	Married	Firefighter	Skin cancer
George	M	87	Married		Bowel cancer; died after first interview
Edward	M	85	Married	Upholsterer	Falls, fractured ribs, blood clot, irregular heartbeat, gout
Adrian	M	81	Married	HGV driver	Non-Hodgkin lymphoma
Jonathan	M	85	Married	Own business franchise	Heart triple bypass, knee injury, allergy to medication
Lena	F	80	Widowed	Comptometer, wages clerk	Emphysema, arthritis, lost use of arm, leg ulcer, sleep problems
Andrew	M	80	Divorced	Company director	Cancer, arthritis, hip replacement (awaiting second)
James	M	82	Single	Coachbuilder, factory worker	Parkinson's, diverticulitis, IBS, colostomy, allergy to medication
Alice	F	80	Divorced	Secretarial, PA, sales coordinator	Mastectomy (breast cancer), low energy
David	M	84	Married	Teacher	Diabetes, leg cramps, chest pains, triple bypass surgery
Brenda	F	83	Widowed	Factory worker	Diabetes, osteoporosis, angina, triple bypass, hip replaced; registered blind
Graham	M	78	Married	Lawyer	Stroke
Jane	F	75	Married	International conference administrator	Sodium deficiency, irregular heartbeat, asthma, broken ankle
Michael	M	84	Married	Careers adviser	Ankylosing spondylitis, fall, pneumonia, eye problems
Brian	M	89	Single	Army office, writer	Painful knee, accidental injuries
Rose	F	84	Widowed	School clerical, shop assistant	Stroke, diabetes, problems with feet
Margaret	F	82	Married	Manager dry-cleaning chain	Stroke
Peter	M	78	Married	Mechanical engineer for council	Cancer of the colon, mini-stroke, polymyositis
Stephen	M	83	Widowed	Army, administrator, geological surveyor, park ranger	Stroke, cataracts, hernia

(continued)

Table 5.1: Participant characteristics at first interview (continued)

Participant	Sex	Age	Marital status	Previous occupation	Health condition (self-described)
Samuel	M	82	Married	Own business	Skin cancer, detached retina
Frederick	M	81	Civil Partnership	Company rep	Heart problems, diabetes, arthritis
Doreen	F	80	Married	Factory machinist	Lymphoma, cancer of womb and bowel, cataracts, vertigo, diabetes
Robert	M	83	Married	Painter and decorator, factory worker	Arthritis, knee replacement, broken wrist, hoarseness (under investigation)
Daniel	M	83	Married	Post office telecom line manager	Arthritis, funny turns – fainting
Norman	M	88	Widowed	Miner	Emphysema, high blood pressure, deafness, two knee replacements
Harry	M	90	Married	Business manager (drapery)	Heart failure, angina, colostomy, deafness, cataracts, carpal tunnel syndrome, gall bladder removed
Howard	M	83	Widowed	Photographer, insurance agent	Aortic aneurism, macular degeneration, hernia, painful feet
May	F	87	Widowed	Lace market; laundry, office and factory worker	Arthritis, low sodium, painful legs
Phillip	M	88	Married	Civil servant	Abdominal pain, cataracts removed
Ruth	F	88	Widowed	Catering, post office TV licences	Parkinson's, cramps, thyroid problem, knee replacement
Dorothy	F	75	Married	Hospital drugs dispenser	Osteoporosis, psoriasis, DVT, two aortic aneurisms, lichen planus
Valerie	F	70	Divorced	Factory worker, care worker	Severe anxiety, depression, asthma
Elizabeth	F	70	Widowed	Shop worker	Tumour behind eye, arthritis, high BP, high cholesterol.
Irene	F	88	Widowed	Factory, shop, office worker	Fall, poor eyesight, osteoporosis, painful shoulders

Following this, cross-cutting conceptual themes were developed, as discussed below.

Change and loss

The twin themes of change and loss arose frequently in participants' accounts from the outset and were highly indicative of their views about dignity. As indicated in Table 5.1, participants had all experienced significant changes in their health prior to the study, and these continued throughout the period we were interviewing them. For example, 12 participants had serious falls necessitating hospital treatment, and others were hospitalised because of serious symptoms. Six participants received new diagnoses, including cancer, heart failure and kidney failure, while others had ongoing serious symptoms for which they had no diagnosis. Deteriorating health conditions led to difficult decisions for some about treatment and medication. James (aged 82), for example, refused to take statins because he said he would prefer to die of a heart attack than live longer with Parkinson's disease.

All participants referred to the way in which they were 'slowing down' and losing their mobility, strength and agility, and the implications of this for their ability to live independently and to maintain their activities were evidently felt very keenly. They gave detailed accounts of how their daily routines and activities had changed as a consequence of declining health and mobility. Seven out of the 16 participants who were driving at the beginning of the study gave up for health-related reasons and felt the impact of this on their social life. Activities such as golf, dancing, travel and going to concerts, cinema and theatre were curtailed or stopped altogether. Sight problems and arthritis had also affected participants' home-based activities, such as reading, sewing and knitting.

Changes in living arrangements were an important theme. Four participants moved to a care home or to sheltered housing. With one exception, where a participant felt he had no control over the process, this was a positive experience. Other changes that preoccupied participants included decisions about whether to have houses adapted or to convert a downstairs room to a bedroom. Several participants talked about making a move but at the end of the study were still living in the same place as at the beginning. For a few, the decision was hard to make, especially when they had lived in the same house for many years.

Changes in relationships and family life also featured strongly in participants' accounts. All experienced bereavements during the study including family members and friends. Eight of these bereavements were of close family relationships, including one being widowed. Two participants had spouses move to care homes and several others experienced major changes when their spouse became too ill to care for them. For some, separate sleeping arrangements because of disturbed nights provided a solution to an immediate problem but had significant wider implications in terms of participants' personal life and long-term relationships. There were examples of positive changes. These included treatments like cataract removal and joint replacement, which had enabled some participants to regain their ability to walk more easily or to watch TV again, for example. Changes in living arrangements had also relieved pressure and engendered a sense of security for some. Overall, however, participants' accounts of change and their feelings about ageing were negative.

Precariousness

The accounts of changes discussed above concerning health, relationships, activities and living arrangements generated the conceptual theme of precariousness. This reflected the sense of instability and loss of control evident in participants' accounts. It was striking, for example, how participants described their illnesses as having "come out of the blue", as a shock. In addition, they realised that their experiences raised the likelihood of more – and more serious – changes in future, as expressed by Doreen (aged 80):

> 'Well ... I'd be quite happy if we could stay as we are, but ... I mean as things go, I mean I realise uh ... what's happened in the last five years has sort of uh ... there's quite a bit changed for us – *had* to change. And in the next five, I don't know what will happen. Or the next one or two really.'

Participants' views about the future in relation to the relative closeness of death were expressed in very vague and general terms, on the whole. Five of them had made arrangements with relatives for lasting power of attorney. Views on wills and funerals were easier to express than views on dying. Some expressed the view that it was pointless to think about the future because one never knew what was around the corner. "I'll take pot luck" was how Edward (aged 85) expressed it. Living day to day was a way of coming to terms with the momentous changes that were experienced in the recent past and the present and anticipated in the future. The nearness of death was commented on in a wide range of ways, with some saying that they dare not or would not allow themselves to think about it while others, particularly the minority with religious beliefs, were more philosophical. The frequent bereavements that participants experienced increased their sense of precariousness about the nearness of death. Participants' views on the end of life were not always consistent. Hence, Andrew (aged 80) commented at one time that he would have no complaints "if my maker should call me tomorrow", while on another he described how he planned to take his own life when he felt the time was right. Some expressed strong views about not being resuscitated and referred to conversations with family members, but had not formalised these wishes. Only five participants had made formal plans, such as advance decisions or lasting power of attorney.

Participants' accounts were peppered with expressions such as 'still', 'as long as', 'until' and 'at the moment', reflecting the instability of their lives. This required significant efforts to adapt. As Robert (aged 83) said: "As things opened up I've gone along with them." Not all were able to maintain the efforts, however. Describing his loss of confidence as a result of his problems with walking, Norman (aged 88) commented, "I've lost a bit of that fight now, to be honest. Otherwise I should be going out." The perception that changes were often beyond participants' control was evident in the way that they talked about ageing and about the future. For example, Doreen (aged 80) commented that old age is "just sort of sprung on us, isn't it." This sense of loss of control was also reflected in how she saw the future: "I think the time's going to come ... when we've got to think about being looked after. And of course you hear all these horrifying things about [it]." The loss of independence was thus seen in terms of increased vulnerability to potential ill treatment as a result of needing to be cared for.

Perseverance

Many used the term 'perseverance' to describe the daily efforts they made to maintain their health and to avoid the need for care services and becoming a burden on others. Perseverance referred to an attitude of mind that required a degree of acceptance of change coupled with the determination to make the most of their abilities and to 'keep going'. As Frederick (aged 81) described it: "I try to be as philosophical as I can. It's difficult sometimes, but there we are", while Jane (aged 75) said, "I wish I could walk better, but never, mind, I can still go out."

Preventing ill health was an important aspect of 'keeping going' day to day. Most of the participants referred to their special diets, vitamins and other supplements, 'flu jabs and other preventive activities. Those who were able to walk made an effort to get out of the house every day or exercised in the house. Word puzzles, Sudoku or other mental exercises were popular as ways of staying alert. Monitoring their health because of their long-term conditions was also an important focus, and self-care was normal for these participants. Check-ups and tests with GPs and hospital consultants on blood, urine, stools, blood pressure, eyes, ears and hearts were common. Self-care also included stoma care, the management of continence problems and learning to use mobility aids and adaptations, such as motor scooters. Participants had also learned new ways of doing familiar things to accommodate their impairments. For example, James (aged 82), who had Parkinson's disease, taught himself to stir his tea from the shoulder rather than the wrist to avoid spilling it, while Lena (aged 80) invented a new way to change her bed linen when she lost the use of her right arm. Self-care demanded emotional as well as physical and mental effort. Rose (aged 84), for example, described how her experience of going out in a wheelchair for the first time made her feel that she had "had it".

The management of medication was an important aspect of self-care. Of the 28 participants alive at the end of the study, 15 had refused, changed or stopped the medication they had been prescribed and another 5 had discussed with their doctors the possibility of reducing or stopping it. Many described the socially embarrassing side effects of medication, such as sweating, rashes and dizziness. Water tablets were disliked by many because they generated the need to urinate urgently, and this was a major deterrent to going out. Self-care extended to developing knowledge about the medications through the internet or through direct contact with pharmaceutical companies. Daniel (aged 83) found out that it was his medication for a hiatus hernia that had made him prone to falling and caused irreparable damage to his kidneys. Most participants regarded medication as something to be avoided if possible because, in addition to concern about side effects, there was a moral aspect to managing without it. As Margaret (aged 82) said: "I've never been a pill-taker."

These health-related activities add up to a significant amount of physical, mental and emotional effort, summed up in the term 'perseverance' that several of them used. Their perseverance also reflects how participants strove to retain a degree of control over their lives. On the other hand, it was also true that many found these demands exhausting and that they would have welcomed more support from services. Where support such as community transport was provided it had a very positive impact on participants' experiences of services.

Independence and dependency on others

Independence was described by all participants as extremely important, and for most was strongly related to their perception of dignity. However, a range of meanings could be identified in their use of the term. Independence was frequently linked to functional health, being able to look after one's self and not being a burden on others. It was also seen as the ability to exert control and to do what you choose to do. The ability to stay in one's own home was also an indicator of independence. Perceptions of independence shifted with changing circumstances as people became accustomed to receiving help, particularly if they felt the helpers were happy to provide it. There was a strong moral dimension to participants' views on dependency associated with concern about what others would think of them. May (aged 87) was reluctant to ask for help, because "I always feel that I look all right on the outside", while Norman (aged 88) said, "I feel a fraud."

Independence and dependency were sometimes in tension. Peter (aged 78) described himself as being "independent to the point of being daft about it" yet thought that he should have had more help when he was discharged from hospital following a stroke. This tension was managed in a number of ways, for example, participants restricting their requests for help to particular jobs, such as gardening and cleaning. Some preferred to pay for help while others preferred to obtain help from friends or family, but either way, participants spoke of how this helped them maintain their independence. Phillip (aged 88) described how he helped his wife to the bathroom every morning in order to "give her a little bit of independence." Thus, the subjective *feeling* of independence was crucial to their dignity and self-respect.

Participants' accounts also showed how personal relationships were central to their efforts to adapt to changing circumstances and maintain their dignity and self-respect. They provided bonds of affection and a sense of security at a time when life was becoming more precarious while the practical help many provided sustained participants' familiar ways of life. This point was reinforced in the context of those participants who were widowed, estranged from or unable to turn to their family and those who had been bereaved of close friends. Being alone increased their sense of vulnerability and loss as they became dependent on 'strangers' for help. Family support overlapped with formal support, as discussed above, but the overlaps were more extensive. Families provided help with decisions about where to live and how to obtain the best help from services.

It is important to note, too, that there were also several examples in the study of participants being the helpers as well as being helped. They offered financial help and housing to children and grandchildren, supported relatives who were bereaved, provided advice and guidance within a church community and looked after school-aged grandchildren after school. Some were active in creating and maintaining friendship groups, which kept alive a social life as well as being a source of support.

Respect and self-respect

In relation to their use of services, most participants said that they were satisfied on the whole with the treatment they received, but there were also accounts of disrespectful and unacceptable treatment by health and care practitioners. What many said they felt was missing from services was the recognition of the significance for them as individuals, of their health problems, as indicated by this extract from Lena's description (aged 80) of a visit to her GP:

> 'The doctor said to me "What does Dr X say is wrong with you?" and I said "He doesn't know". She said, "Well you've got Parkinson's. When you see him in a month's time mention it to him."'

There were some instances of rudeness, as when James (aged 82) was laughed at by a nurse when he raised his concern about the possibility of sexual impotence as a result of his treatment. More commonplace were examples of being overlooked and neglected when asking for a bedpan or a drink of water in hospital. Participants talked candidly about how keenly these instances of disrespectfulness were felt at the time, and how they felt they were 'invisible' to the care staff. There were also many examples of occasions when professionals were late, harassed and too busy to listen or to look at participants. A common concern was that it was all too easy to become overwhelmed by the bureaucracy of health and care systems and to become "just a number".

On the contrary, participants also described how pleasantly surprised they were to find that their dread of services had been misplaced, and that the kindness, cheerfulness and thoughtfulness of front-line staff enabled them to see their circumstances in a more hopeful and positive light. Services that were well coordinated, informative, efficiently organised and provided with courtesy were highly regarded. A point made by several of the participants was that they appreciated their needs being anticipated so they were offered help without having to ask. Being treated with respect was valued by participants not least because it promoted their sense of self-respect.

Policy and practice implications

The accounts provided by participants in this study show the massive scale of the challenges faced by older people as their health declines, and highlights the efforts they make to maintain their health and wellbeing. Health services and, to a lesser extent, social care services, had become a core aspect of the lives of participants in this study and the impact of their encounters with services had a lasting impact, which can be understood as affecting their dignity in several ways. Their need for help was seen as out of character and presenting them with moral and ethical questions about the conditions in which it was right to ask for help. Participants would often stress how they "had no choice" about calling the doctor or other help or that they would only ask "for a proper reason", showing their real concern about how they would be judged by others, including people working in health and other services. Reassurance that their rights to services are recognised is therefore fundamental to upholding older people's dignity.

The findings discussed above show how challenges to dignity are compounded or mitigated by encounters with practitioners. Negative experiences of services are not confined to people in old age, but the impact on them needs to be understood in the context of the precariousness of later life, as discussed above. Participants often explained poor treatment by reference to the pressure that practitioners were under and to the wider culture of organisations. Services that were spoken about positively were those where there was an understanding of how the individual was feeling about what they were going through. This helps explain the high value placed on the provision of transport to get to a hospital appointment or a home visit from a GP. Being supported in this way indicated that services were attuned to their general state of health and wellbeing. The older people in this study had accepted the model of self-care but at times expressed the view that a great deal had been expected and demanded of them. This was a consistent theme in relation to hospital discharge, for example.

The wide variations in how participants understood and 'felt' independence are important to recognise. The older people in this study had not given up on self-determination, and the decisions they made concerning their treatment and living arrangements were made carefully, using knowledge, skills and values they had built up over a lifetime. Nevertheless, they understood that increasing dependency on others was inevitable, although difficult to contemplate or plan for. This underlines the value of skilled interventions that recognise the impact of declining health on each individual person's sense of self, their identity and self-respect.

Key findings

- Focusing on the day to day, participants view their struggles with illness and increasing disability as a fact of life that requires a great deal of perseverance to deal with.
- Not surprisingly, the loss of independence or self-reliance is hard for people to accept and is seen by most as inevitably leading to a loss of dignity.
- Not wanting to be a burden but having to accept a growing reliance on others is the complex task that older people face, and their identity and dignity are bound up in this task.
- Participants frequently spoke in terms that reflected the shifting and precarious nature of life. Typical expressions were: "At the moment I'm still able to cook my own food" and "As long as we're able to manage, we'll stay living where we are." These expressions convey the instability of their current circumstances and the prospect of further change ahead. Needing help from strangers with personal, bodily care was often dreaded: "The very thought of having somebody washing me, you know", said May. Most find that personal care is not as bad in reality as expected, but this depends on how the help is given.

Conclusions

The findings from this study reinforce the importance of understanding dignity as a complex concept with interrelated personal and social meanings. The changes and losses that participants experienced challenged their dignity in many ways. The sense of being 'a fish out of water' indicates the enormity of those changes and challenges as life becomes increasingly precarious. In the face of this precariousness, older people persevere and strive to maintain a sense of identity and self-respect. Perseverance is an ongoing necessity, because in the context of declining health, the process of adjustment is never complete.

Participants in this study drew on the values, skills and knowledge they had built up throughout their life course, and often showed great ingenuity in the practical ways they adapted to impaired mobility or dexterity. For most, the task was eased by the presence of family and friends who could be relied on in future when needs became greater while those who were more isolated found it harder to persevere. Maintaining dignity when supportive care is needed in later life involves more than ensuring good standards in services, although these are essential. Personal dignity depends on recognition of individual difference. Maintaining dignity means supporting older people in their efforts to maintain their identity and self-respect through this turbulent and challenging period of the life course.

References

Cass, E., Robbins, D. and Richardson, A. (2009) *Dignity in care*, SCIE Guide 15, London: Social Care Institute for Excellence (SCIE).

Gilleard, C. and Higgs, P. (2010) 'Aging without agency: Theorizing the fourth age', *Aging & Mental Health*, vol 14, no 2, pp 121-8.

James, A. and Hockey, J. (2007) *Embodying health identities*, Basingstoke: Palgrave Macmillan.

Lloyd, L. (2004) 'Mortality and morality: Ageing and the ethics of care', *Ageing and Society*, vol 24, pp 235-56.

Nordenfelt, L. (2004) 'The varieties of dignity', *Health Care Analysis*, vol 12, pp 69-81.

Nordenfelt, L. (2009) 'The concept of dignity', in L. Nordenfelt (ed) *Dignity in care for older people*, Oxford: Wiley-Blackwell, pp 26-51.

Pleschberger, S. (2007) 'Dignity and the challenge of dying in nursing homes: The residents' view', *Age and Ageing*, vol 36, pp 197-202.

Spencer, L., Ritchie, J. and O'Connor, W. (2009) 'Analysis: Practices, principles and processes', in J. Ritchie and J. Lewis (eds) *Qualitative research practice: A guide for social science students and researchers*, London: Sage, pp 199-218.

Twigg, J. (2006) *The body in health and social care*, London: Palgrave.

Wainwright, P. and Gallagher, A. (2008) 'On different types of dignity in nursing care: A critique of Nordenfelt', *Nursing Philosophy*, vol 9, no 1, pp 46-54.

Woolhead, G., Calnan, M., Dieppe, P. and Tadd, W. (2004) 'Dignity in older age: What do older people in the United Kingdom think?', *Age and Ageing*, vol 33, no 2, pp 165-70.

SIX

Families and caring in South Asian communities

Christina R. Victor, Maria Zubair and Wendy Martin

Introduction

Like other Western societies, the UK is undergoing important social and demographic changes, most notably the continued 'ageing' of the population and the increasing ethnic diversity of the older population. In the UK ethnicity is defined on the basis of self-identification from a standard list of categories included in routine administrative data collection, social surveys and the decennial census. This approach recognises that ethnicity is a multidimensional concept that embraces a constellation of characteristics including country of birth, skin colour, language(s) spoken, nationality, culture and religion, and which represents an individual/group identity that is grounded in shared origins or social background; shared culture and traditions that are distinctive and maintained between generations; and a common language and/or religious tradition. Fundamental to the concept of ethnicity is that it represents an individual's self-assessment of their status and, consequently, may change over time and is not externally attributed or imposed by others. In terms of diversity, the 2011 Census data report that 16 per cent of the population of England and Wales self-define themselves as non-White compared with 5 per cent in 1991, with approximately 4 per cent self-defining as Black/African-Caribbean and 5 per cent as South Asian (2.5 per cent Indian, 2 per cent Pakistani and 0.8 per cent Bangladeshi).

These two demographic trends noted above intersect with the ageing of the communities of migrants who came to the UK from the Caribbean and India in the 1950s, from Pakistan in the 1970s, with the Bangladeshi group arriving in the late 1970s and early 1980s. For these groups migration was for a range of reasons including economic opportunities, family reunification or because of expulsion from their country of residence in the case of the Ugandan Asians. Eighteen per cent of the White population of England and Wales are aged over 65 compared with 14 per cent of the African Caribbean group, 8 per cent of the Indian community and 4 per cent each for the Pakistani and Bangladeshi populations (Lievesley, 2010). A key feature of these ageing members of our minority populations is that they are almost exclusively comprised of first-generation migrants (Herbert, 2008; Qureshi, 1988). Thus 10 per cent of the combined Asian group (Indian, Pakistani and Bangladeshi) aged 65+ moved to the UK in later life, as did 4 per cent of the Black Caribbean/African populations.

The experience of ageing for minority elders is not homogeneous. There are important variations in the experience of ageing, between and within groups as well as with gender and social class. The specific spatial context within which minority ethnic elders lead their daily lives influences their experiences of ageing. Black and minority ethnic populations in the UK are not evenly distributed across the country but concentrated in specific geographical areas. Approximately half of all minority ethnic groups live in the Greater London area, increasing to three-quarters when London is combined with the conurbations of the West Midlands (Birmingham), East Midlands (Leicester), West Yorkshire (Bradford and Leeds) and Greater Manchester compared with 25 per cent of the White population. One-quarter of the total Bangladeshi population is resident in two London boroughs, Tower Hamlets and Newham, both in the East End of London, and 95 per cent of Bangladeshi migrants to the UK came from the rural Sylhet district (Gardner, 2006).

The Bangladeshi and Pakistani communities, the focus of our research, are especially vulnerable, being characterised by profound material and health inequalities and social exclusion when compared with both the general population and other minority groups (Bécares, 2013; Botsford, 2011; Victor et al, 2012a). Geographers, sociologists and anthropologists who have focused on these two populations have rarely engaged with issues of age and ageing (Anwar, 1985; Brice, 2008; Herbert, 2008; Shaw, 1998, 2000), with Gardner's (2006) study of older Bengalis living in East London a notable exception. Work from an explicitly gerontological perspective demonstrates a strong pre-occupation with issues of health service access and/or the relationships between informal and formal care services and/or the support needs and experiences of informal carers (Dobbs and Burholt, 2010; Giuntoli and Cattan, 2012). Research with an explicit focus on broader issues of older age and later life is rarer (Norman, 1985; Blakemore and Boneham, 1994; Afshar et al, 2008). Consequently, we know little about the daily lives of older Pakistani/Bangladeshi populations, who are predominantly first-generation migrants, and how these are contextualised by their local, national and transnational connections (Victor et al, 2012b; Victor, 2014, 2015; Burholt et al, 2016, 2017).

Aims and methods

Gerontologists must engage with the realities of old age and later life among our minority communities regardless of how challenging – methodologically, conceptually or empirically – this research agenda is (Phillipson, 2015; Torres, 2015; Zubair and Norris, 2015; Zubair and Victor, 2015). By examining how ageing is experienced and navigated by minority elders we can start to consider if and how the cultural, religious and family lifestyles of specific minority groups influence the experience of later life and ageing. In our project 'Families and caring in South Asian communities', we focused on understanding the experiences and perceptions of old age and later life among Bangladeshi and Pakistani elders, looking at their (1) social identities and levels of participation in transnational, national and local communities; (2) perceptions and experiences of family lives, social networks, 'place' and locality; and (3) ideas, meanings and experiences of 'care' and 'support'. In this chapter we discuss our key methodological challenges that have wider resonance for research with minority elders, and summarise our key substantive themes and consider how different these ideas are (or are not) from the general population in order to start to distil the unique or novel dimensions of the experience of ageing among these populations.

The growing field of environmental gerontology demonstrates recognition of the importance of both space (the physical environment at both micro and macro level) and place (the meanings and experiences of specific environments) for ageing and later life (see Peace et al, 2006). The concentration of our populations of interest, that is, Bangladeshi and Pakistani populations, in specific geographical areas of the UK noted earlier is reflected in previous research work focusing on large urban areas such as London (Phillipson et al, 2003; Ahmed and Jones, 2008), Birmingham (Burholt, 2004a, b), Bristol (Brice, 2008), Leicester (Anwar, 1985; Herbert, 2008) and Glasgow/Edinburgh (Bowes and Dar, 2000). We opted to conduct our study in a medium-sized town in southern England where minority ethnic communities are smaller, with less critical mass and 'visibility', and that have been subject to much less research (Shaw, 2008).

This decision was not 'research neutral': the size of the communities had implications for the achievement of our target sample and posed challenges in terms of preserving the anonymity of both respondents and the communities where the research was located. Census data from 2011 reports that 1 per cent of the total population of our study area (approximately 1,000 individuals) were from Bangladesh and 4.5 per cent (approximately 7,000) were from Pakistan. The geographical dispersal of our Bangladeshi community as compared with our more concentrated Pakistani group complicated the fieldwork logistics. The unfamiliarity of these populations with research meant that the fieldwork took longer to complete as our research team had to develop trust and rapport with the local communities (Zubair et al, 2010, 2012a, b).

Our guiding aim in answering our research questions was to generate a sample of participants that would represent the breadth of experiences across our communities of interest. Consequently we used a broad range of strategies to recruit participants including the existing social networks of our two bilingual researchers, established links with local community organisations and the immersion, visibility and familiarity of researchers within these communities. We explicitly opted not to limit recruitment to members of organisations, recipients of services or via community 'gatekeepers'. Our researchers spent extensive time 'in the field' establishing the credentials of our project and gaining recognition among the populations by frequenting the local area, shops and mosques and community meeting places before attempting to recruit participants (Zubair et al, 2010). Once individuals had been successfully recruited to the project we then used snowballing and chain recruitment to achieve our target sample size.

Crucial to the successful recruitment of participants in any research project is the identity and role of the researcher. This is especially so for 'hard-to-reach groups' such as minority ethnic communities where ethnic/language matching between researcher and researched is seen as essential. Ethnic matching presumes a reduction in the 'social distance' between researchers and researched, and gives primacy to ethnic/linguistic variables, making the simplistic presumption that the researcher, simply by virtue of their ethnicity, is competent to navigate the research encounter (Sin, 2007). Using the example of our Pakistani community, we demonstrate that linguistic matching of researchers is a necessary, but not sufficient, requirement to ensure either a good response or 'rapid' recruitment. The youth and female gender of our researcher, her privileged urban-educated background and unconventional living arrangements were as important in engaging and recruiting participants as her Pakistani heritage and language (Zubair et al, 2012a, b). Hence, gender, age and class are also important elements of the research encounter and are not subsumed by the commonality of ethnicity or language (Wray and Bartholomew, 2010).

Our aim was to recruit 60 Pakistani and 60 Bangladeshi participants, with an equal distribution between men and women and across three broad age groups, 50-59, 60-69 and 70+. This sample size was designed to achieve saturation within each of the age/gender/ethnicity sub-groups and to ensure that both men and women's voices were heard and that we captured the perspectives of those in old age as well as those on the cusp of later life. We achieved our target for our Pakistani group but, despite extending our fieldwork area and timetable by six months, we under-recruited for our Bangladeshi group. This reflects the small absolute size of this population, their highly dispersed settlement pattern and the very small numbers of people aged 70+ (see Table 6.1).

Recruitment to the study was determined by three inclusion criteria: age, gender and ethnicity. We encountered a fluidity of reported ages that conflicted with our pre-determined rigid age-based sampling framework. Some participants had two 'ages' – their 'official' passport age and an unofficial age that could vary by several years in either direction. For women this differential is largely, although not exclusively, linked with the operational immigration entry criteria (for example, minimum age of marriage) when they migrated to the UK. Latifah, a 53-year-old Pakistani female who migrated to UK as a spouse, described her actual chronological age as being five years less than her 'official' age. She explained, "When people used to come from Pakistan earlier, they used to have their age increased. Marriages happened in younger ages ... they had their age written as more than actual. That's why I got married at 16 years, so my age is written as more." Mahmood, a Pakistani male with an 'official' age of 73 explaining a five-year difference in his 'real' and 'official' age stated, "The reason for that is – I will tell you. I will tell you now –

Table 6.1: Key characteristics of the study participants

	Bangladeshi		Pakistani	
	Male	Female	Male	Female
Age				
50-59	14	18	12	13
60-69	6	6	6	14
70+	4	2	12	3
Mean age (years)	58	54	64	58
Mean length of residence in the UK (years)	22	19	33	24

actually, the reason was that my mother wasn't that literate ... and she had my age written according to calculations based on the Islamic calendar. According to that, my age came out as less. Otherwise, my age at the moment is 78....'' We used the official age of participants in our analysis as this was consistent across groups, but acknowledge that for some participants this does not mesh with their 'true' age. This serves to both question our unstated assumptions that everyone has 'one' accurate chronological age and, more specific to this study, illustrates the way that official processes and procedures frame and contextualise the lives of members of migrant communities, including their experiences of age.

To answer our research questions, we collected data using four linked components: (1) a standard demographic profile of the participants recording age, gender, marital and employment status, household composition (distinguishing single, two- and three-generational households), religion, education and length of residence in the UK and in the current community; (2) a memo summarising the interview context; (3) a social network 'map' detailing the interviewees' most significant social relationships; and (4) an in-depth semi-structured interview using a guide framed around our three key research questions, based on existing literature and revised in the light of our pilot study involving the first 20 interviews (see Table 6.2 for the key topics covered in the interview guide). This provided a consistent framework for our data collection but was sufficiently flexible to adapt to the circumstances of our participants.

Interviews were undertaken in the preferred language of the participant and recorded (with the permission of the participant). These lasted for approximately an hour (with a range of 25 to 100 minutes). Extensive field notes were taken for the 28 non-recorded interviews, the majority of which (18) were in the pilot phase of our study. Five interviews were conducted in English but respondents often used English words when discussing specific concepts or issues. These are underlined in the transcripts to distinguish them from translated words and terms. We used a 'forward' translation strategy with interviews transcribed verbatim into English by a team of bilingual translators. The two researchers checked the completeness and quality of the translations to ensure that they represented, as well as possible, the views and opinions of participants (Birbili, 2000). It is important to acknowledge that our data are translated (Temple and Young, 2004), and that we were attempting to generate equivalenced rather than 'literal' translations (Ross, 2010). This means that some words and terms may have been lost or changed meaning in translation since

Table 6.2: Interview guide: key themes

Biographical	Focus on brief life history, key life events and social relationships
Migration history	Reasons for moving to Britain and internal migration history
General overview of current circumstances	Key activities and the things identified as important to individuals
Everyday life	Description of daily life and activities
Family life	Description of family membership, contact with family and giving/receiving of care and support within family
Social networks and locality	Description of friendship networks and places where they meet friends/acquaintances
Care and support and health	Understandings and expectations of care and support. Evaluation of health status and specification of key health issues and service use
Age and ageing	Meanings, perceptions and experiences of age and ageing
Social ties, sense of belonging and wellbeing	Comparison of (and preferences in relation to) life/old age in Britain and Bangladesh/Pakistan

translation is itself an interpretative process. This had both conceptual and analytical implications, as our reliance on translated transcripts inevitably means some loss of nuance and meaning (Regmi et al, 2010) and imposed some 'distance' between the data, the transcripts and the research team.

Our analytical strategy was broadly inductive. We could not conform to the strictures of grounded theory as data collection and analysis was not co-terminus because of the constraints imposed by the requirements for translation before we could begin our analysis. However, a general inductive approach is appropriate when the analysis is guided by specific objectives and where we needed to ensure that the links between our data and research questions are transparent and robust but that also enables the key themes (defined by significance, frequency or novelty) to emerge by minimising preconceptions when approaching the data. Coding of the data was led by one of our researchers (MZ) who was deeply immersed in the data collection and supervision of translations. An initial set of 26 primary codes were derived and cross-checked independently by the principal investigators (WM and CV) who confirmed their veracity after resolving any discrepancies in the use of specific codes/concepts through discussion.

Findings

Our analysis identified five key themes – understanding and experiencing ageing; the context of ageing; resources for ageing; transitions; and culture and identity (see Figure 6.1) – and we present examples from each theme here to illustrate how they relate to the experience of growing old as first-generation migrants in the UK. In reporting our findings, all participants are referred to by pseudonyms.

Understanding and experiencing ageing

Our participants had moved from countries with comparative low life expectancies at birth of around 50 to one where it is 30 years longer. Participants acknowledged this differential with comments such as, "You have to think about it. I am getting old and going on. After 50 years, it's a <u>bonus</u> ... in Pakistan, life is short. Age wise – you age quicker in Pakistan" (Taaj, Pakistani male aged 54). Chronological age did not carry the same connotations for our participants as a marker of ageing as is common in Western notions of ageing and later life: "Ageing means you are gradually getting towards end of your life" (Danish, Bangladeshi male aged 54). When participants spoke explicitly about the characteristics and key signifiers of age and ageing, the narrative was dominated by discourses of physical ill health and dependency: "Ageing means being ill and dependent

Figure 6.1: Key study themes

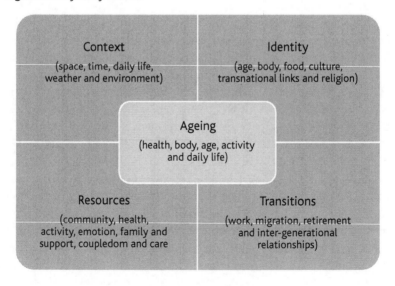

on others.... Becoming a diabetic has given me age"; "Age means weakness, not having enough strength to look after yourself" (Ishrat, Pakistani female aged 62); "To me ageing means hardship, loss of identity and dependence on others. For me it is the end of life" (Laila, Bangladeshi female aged 52). Individuals gave examples of their own realisation of being 'old': "When I meet someone and s/he respects me by salam [Islamic greeting], I understand that I have become an aged person" (Adil, Bangladeshi male aged 46). However, the context within which participants were growing old was located within a culture of respect for older people – "You know we have a tradition that we should respect our murubbi [elder], but here they do not show much respect to the elderly" (Kashifa, Bangladeshi female aged 57) – and age-appropriate behaviour by the elders: "I buy clothes that are appropriate to wear for my age ... and also I am aware that I should behave as people expect from a murubbi [elder] in our culture" (Iffat, Pakistani female aged 60). Sabira, a 45-year-old Bangladeshi woman, typified the view that ageing was not something that individuals could mediate: "Obviously I will get old, some people will die first, and some will die later. There is no reason to worry about that, I cannot do anything about it."

The context of ageing

We identified a range of contextual factors: weather, sociospatial environment, importance of space/place and time in the experience of ageing. Here we focus on the example of religion as forming a contextual framework for experiencing ageing and daily life. Participants were predominantly Muslim, and a strong religious faith provided an important context for ageing as it had for earlier phases of the life course. Participants, both male and female, expressed a very strong religious belief that each individual's life expectancy was determined by the will of God. Ageing is therefore less of a worry for them as individuals don't need to (or should not) contest the decisions made for them by God:

> 'I don't worry because what I believe is, the time is fixed [that is, the time to die] from Him. When it comes, He won't wait for nothing. So, as far as I have to live, I'll live. This is what even in my holy book says, the God has fixed the age. You will die at a certain age. He don't reduce, he don't increase, so I think these things we should leave it to God.' (Barkat, Pakistani male aged 75)

The rhythm of daily life was shaped by religious observance:

> 'I get up in the morning at six o'clock to offer prayers. Then I go [back] to sleep; then I sleep until eleven o'clock. Then I get up; I have breakfast. We have our breakfast at eleven o'clock [laughs]. Then I clean the house; I cook the food. So then it is time for zuhar [afternoon prayer]. I offer the asar prayers [prayers performed some time before the sun is about to start setting]; offer the maghrib prayers [prayers performed at the time of sunset] – so that's all; the whole day goes past like this. After offering the isha prayers [prayers performed after it turns completely dark], I go to sleep.' (Darakhshan, Pakistani female aged 51)

Indeed, Sadiqa, a 66-year-old Pakistani female, moved house to live alone and separate from her family so that she could focus on her religion in her later years. She observed, "That's why I have separated myself, because sometimes there is no time to do household chores. Now I pray to Allah [God] with complete focus. Now I like that I keep on praying like this."

Resources for ageing

Three key sets of factors provide the resources that older people bring to the experience of later life: health, material resources and social resources including statutory services, family, friends and the wider community. Family are central to the experience of later life (see Victor et al, 2012b), and our participants drew a clear contrast between themselves and the general population who were characterised as 'less caring' in terms of their older relatives: "You have to make yourself understand that English people here, the children leave when they are over 17, 18 years; they do not look after their parents or their grandparents. We have been looking after our families like our forefathers, take caring, and looking after" (Fakhir, Bangladeshi male aged 58). The Bangladeshi and Pakistani communities and friends were seen as a positive resource for general support, these ties were not robust for those with fewer other resources which made reciprocity in the relationship problematic, "because it's [friendship] a relation that's been made – it's not a blood relation; it's a relation that can break anytime; anytime, it can break; so, what can I expect from them?" (Ghazi, Pakistani male aged 62). Most participants expressed the expectation that their children would care for them in old age:

'... now ... it is their duty ... that if my father is old, or my mother is old ... I hope according to the upbringing we have given them, they won't let us down, they look after us.... So expectations are good.' (Khalid, Pakistani male aged 66)

'... we are a Bangladeshi family, I looked after my parents until their death, we did not need a nurse to help our parents. Our hope is that our children will do that, inshallah. Why shouldn't they do it! If I did it for my parents then they would do it for their parents.' (Jaan, Bangladeshi male aged 46)

However, this was tinged with awareness that the community was changing, as Batool, a 57-year-old Pakistani female acknowledged: "but, gradually, as the time is passing – they won't enquire after anyone. Why – because they will get so busy in their jobs, and worries about their kids, and they will forget about everyone else." Rani, a 64-year-old Bangladeshi, was unusual in both planning for her (potential) future dependency and instructing her children to opt for a care home rather than cope themselves: "if I become bed dependent or, in the meantime, if anything happens to me, I have advised my children to send us in care home. I know all of my money will be spent but we will be in good health in care home." The more usual discourse was that of Luqmaan, a 54-year-old Pakistani male, for whom a care home was a last resort and a statement that resonates with the sentiments of the more general population: "I hope my family will look after me otherwise I will go to care home."

Transitions

Our participants experienced a range of transitions across the life course including migration, widowhood and retirement. Here we focus on migration as most of our participants had moved to the UK as young adults. Typically the migration history was characterised by a 'chain' pattern with adult males arriving first and then the wives and children following, and migration was not always a clear and distinct 'break' with the country of origin, as these quotations illustrate: "first, my father came here. Then he brought my brother. Then ... the third time I came here. Then my mother came" (Mahfooz, Pakistani male aged 57). Aalim, a Pakistani male aged 54, described an international pattern of migration moving between Europe and the UK:

'I came to England in [19]67. Then I went to Pakistan again in [19]74 and then came back to England. I returned to England in [19]74. Then I went to Austria in [19]79 and lived there. I lived in Germany for three-and-a-half years after that, and returned to England again in [19]83. I went to Pakistan in [19]88 and came back to England in [19]99.'

Retirement from the labour market is a transition demonstrated by the general population. In this study retirement from work was predominantly commented on by men rather than women. Unusually, Inder, a 72-year-old Bangladeshi male, commented, "my wife, she is always here, she's retired so she is the main carer", while Rani, a 64-year-old Bangladeshi female, described herself as retired: "Previously I had little time to read books, now I feel very interesting in reading books. I have retired now." Retirement was seen as a time to focus on religious observance or for the opportunity to travel back home or visit children: "I achieved what I set out to achieve, and now is the right time. So that I can travel the world. See other parts of the world, and be happy, while I can. And that's it" (Tariq, Pakistani male aged 69). However, for some they were unable to return to Pakistan at retirement as they had hoped, and for many time sat heavy:

'But as I am retired I would like to stay there for the rest of my life and enjoy there. What is here? You wake up, drink tea, eat toast and turn the TV on and you sit all day. Even when you meet friends here how long can you spend time with them here, half an hour, one hour? Each person is busy here so how long can you spend with them? Because I do not do anything here so it is difficult to pass the time here and easier to pass the time in Pakistan.' (Ghaffaar, Pakistani male aged 72)

These comments serve to illustrate the diversity of the experience of retirement and how this is linked in with the broader context of resources.

Culture and identity

Our participants held a range of linked identities of which being a Muslim was central alongside a British identity, with other important roles such as spouse, parent and grandparent resonating with the general population, along with specific relationships such as parents-in law and roles (daughter-in-law). As these quotations illustrate, "of all … we are Muslim … I am proud of being a Muslim" (Nabeela, Pakistani female aged 51) and "This is our country because I am a [sic] British now, after 45 years of life here" (Dawood, Pakistani male aged 54). Class and gender identities were also evident, as the comments of Farah, a 52-year-old Pakistani woman, highlights:

> 'Because I look at them [older white women], elderly, old people, ladies, they go to the market, for shopping – lipstick, eye shadow, blusher; they don't think they have grown old [whereas] our Pakistanis think, "No, no, we have now grown old." If someone says to me, "I have grown old", I tell them, "No, you have not grown old at all".'

Policy and practice implications

Policy and practice are based on the presumption that everyone has an 'accurate' chronological age, which was not the case for all of our participants, and that there is a broadly shared notion of when 'old age' starts. Our participants articulated ideas about the onset of old age that were at least a decade younger than for the general population. Strong religious beliefs with life expectancy pre-ordained by God does not mesh with policy/practice discourses on active/healthy ageing while religious observance forms a pattern of daily life that does not readily conform with the temporal patterns of service providers (Ahmet and Victor, 2015). Our data also highlight the importance of diversity in terms of both gender and social class and the evolving nature of these communities as the UK-born children of these migrants move towards old age. Perhaps the key implication of our project for both policy and practice is in terms of recognising the diversity of experience within these communities and their evolving nature in terms of notions of ageing, the resources that they bring and norms and expectations of families and family-based care.

Key findings
- The onset of 'old age' is not linked to a specific age such as 65 or 70 but by key 'life events' such as the marriage of their children or the birth of (grand) children that involve changes in family roles and responsibilities.
- Family networks are very strong and locally focused. There are ties back to Bangladesh and Pakistan that are weakening over time. New global links are being established as their children move to Europe and other countries.

These highly complex and interlocking sets of family/social networks have implications for both expectation and provision of care and support.

- Strong links with the local community are the norm, and these provide vital resources in coping with growing old in a foreign land, give a focus for social engagement and provide support in times of celebration (weddings) or stress (bereavement).
- Expectations of their children providing care for old age are strong, and 'state' care services are viewed as only to be used as a last resort. However, some participants are uncertain if their expectations will be realised in the future and others are ambivalent about having such expectations of their children.

Conclusions

In the next two decades the UK will see the increasing ethnic and cultural diversity of the older population resultant from the increase in both the absolute and relative number of elders from minority ethnic backgrounds. We have focused on older people from Bangladeshi and Pakistani communities as they represent one of the most deprived and least researched ageing minority groups within Britain the UK. We have sought to extend the analytical gaze beyond the narrow but important focus on health and informal care that has characterised previous research, to encompass the daily lives of older people from these communities. The gender balance in our sample allows for the voices of both women and men to be represented equally while the age range offers the opportunity for those of different generations to present their experiences. This is important since the experience of ageing for minority elders is heterogeneous with gender, age and generation (among other things) contextualising the experiences of our participants.

Our study raised a number of methodological challenges. We argue that, while ethnic matching of researchers to participants is important, we need to acknowledge other dimensions of researcher identity such as age and gender when developing recruitment and engagement strategies with minority ethnic populations and other hard-to-reach groups (Zubair et al, 2012a, b). However, for the near future at least, linguistic matching of participants and researchers will be required when conducting research with minority ethnic older people with the issues of using translated interviews as primary data and resultant issues around translation and meaning of words. The need for researchers to articulate clear rules about the translation process is irrefutable, but the logistics when doing this across a range of languages remains challenging. The 'distance' that this process imposes between the research team and the data is a rarely discussed but not inconsiderable issue that requires further articulation and debate.

Our participants challenged taken-for-granted assumptions of both researchers and policy-makers. For example, chronological age was not a significant component of their identity and furthermore, the meaning of a specific age was often interpreted with reference to their country of origin rather than a British/Western European context. Hence we saw participants in their 50s readily ascribing themselves as being 'old' at ages that the general population might ascribe as being mid-life. Key areas for future research are to more fully explore the diversity in the experience of ageing and later life in terms of gender and class and to consider factors such as family norms and expectations, especially around the provision of informal care, longitudinally, to determine if these are changing for those born and brought up in the UK.

Ethical approval

This was given by the University of Reading Ethics Committee and all participants gave written informed consent.

Acknowledgements

This study was funded by Economic and Social Research Council (ESRC) grant reference RES-352-25-0009A as part of the New Dynamics of Ageing programme directed by Professor Alan Walker of the University of Sheffield. We wish to formally acknowledge Dr Subrata Saha for her work on the project between 2007-09, and are especially grateful to all those who participated in the study.

References

Afshar, H., Franks, M., Maynard, M. and Wray, S. (2008) *Women in later life: Exploring race and ethnicity*, Maidenhead: Open University Press/McGraw Hill.

Ahmed, N. and Jones, I. (2008) '"Habitus and bureaucratic routines": Cultural and structural factors in the experience of informal care: A qualitative study of Bangladeshi women living in London', *Current Sociology*, vol 56, pp 57-78.

Ahmet, A. and Victor, C.R. (2015) 'Understanding definitions and experiences of care and caring among Hindu and Muslim older people. The role of religion', in T. Hjelm (ed) *Is God back?*, London: Bloomsbury, pp 191-204.

Anwar, M. (1985) *Pakistanis in Britain: A sociological study*, London: New Century.

Bécares, L. (2013) 'Which ethnic groups have the poorest health? Ethnic health inequalities 1991 to 2011', Centre on Dynamics of Ethnicity (CoDE) Briefing, Manchester: Manchester University.

Birbili, M. (2000) 'Translating from one language to another', *Social Research Update*, vol 31, pp 1-7.

Blakemore, K. and Boneham, M. (1994) *Age, race and ethnicity: A comparative approach*, Maidenhead: Open University Press.

Botsford, J. (2011) 'Research and dementia, caring and ethnicity: A review of the literature', *Journal of Research in Nursing*, vol 16, pp 437-49.

Bowes, A. and Dar, N. (2000) 'Researching social care for minority ethnic older people: Implications of some Scottish research', *British Journal of Social Work*, vol 30, pp 305-21.

Brice, J. (2008) 'Migrants and the second generation: Health inequalities in Bristol's Bangladeshi community', *Durham Journal of Anthropology*, vol 15, no 1, pp 59-105.

Burholt, V. (2004a) 'The settlement patterns and residential histories of older Gujaratis, Punjabis and Sylhetis in Birmingham, England', *Ageing and Society*, vol 24, pp 383-409.

Burholt, V. (2004b) 'Transnationalism, economic transfers and families' ties: Intercontinental contacts of older Gujaratis, Punjabis and Sylhetis in Birmingham with families abroad', *Ethnic and Racial Studies*, vol 27, no 5, pp 800-29.

Burholt, V., Dobbs, C. and Victor, C. (2016) 'Transnational relationships and cultural identity of older migrants', *GeroPsych: The Journal of Gerontopsychology and Geriatric Psychiatry*, vol 29, pp 57-69.

Burholt, V., Dobbs, C. and Victor, C. (2017) 'Social support networks of older migrants in England and Wales: The role of collectivist culture', *Ageing and Society*. doi:10.1017/s0144686x17000034

Dobbs, C. and Burholt, V. (2010) 'Caregiving and carereceiving relationships of older South Asians', *GeroPsych: The Journal of Gerontopsychology and Geriatric Psychiatry*, vol 23, no 4, pp 215-25.

Gardner, K. (2006) *Age, narrative and migration: The life course and life histories of Bengali elders in London*, Oxford: Berg.

Giuntoli, G. and Cattan, M. (2012) 'The experiences and expectations of care and support among older migrants in the UK', *European Journal of Social Work*, vol 15, no 1, pp 131-47.

Herbert, J. (2008) *Negotiating boundaries in the city: Migration, ethnicity and gender in Britain*, Aldershot: Ashgate.

Lievesley, N. (2010) *The future ageing of the ethnic minority population of England and Wales*, London, Runnymede Trust and Centre for Policy on Ageing.

Norman, A. (1985) *Triple jeopardy: Growing old in a second homeland*, London: Centre for Policy on Ageing.

Peace, S., Kellaher, L. and Holland, C. (2006) *Environment and identity in later life*, Buckingham: Open University Press.

Phillipson, C.R. (2015) 'Placing ethnicity at the centre of studies of later life: Theoretical perspectives and empirical challenges', *Ageing and Society*, vol 35, no 5, pp 917-34.

Phillipson, C.R., Ahmed, N. and Latimer, J. (2003) *Women in transition: A study of the experiences of Bangladeshi women living in Tower Hamlets*, Bristol: Policy Press.

Qureshi, T. (1988) *Living in Britain: Growing old in Britain: A study of Bangladeshi elders in London*, London: Centre for Policy on Ageing.

Regmi, K., Naidoo, J. and Pilkington, P. (2010) 'Understanding the processes of translation and transliteration in qualitative research', *International Journal of Qualitative Method*, vol 9, no 1, pp 16-26.

Ross, J. (2010) 'Was that infinity or affinity? Applying insights from translation studies to qualitative research transcription', *Forum: Qualitative Social Research*, vol 11, no 2, Art 2.

Shaw, A. (1988) *A Pakistani community in Britain*, Oxford: Basil Blackwell.

Shaw, A. (2000) *Kinship and continuity: Pakistani families in Britain*, London: Routledge.

Sin, C.H. (2007) 'Ethnic matching in qualitative research: Reversing the gaze on "white others" and "white" as "other"', *Qualitative Research*, vol 7, pp 477-99.

Temple, B. and Young, A. (2004) 'Qualitative research and translation dilemmas', *Qualitative Research*, vol 4, no 2, pp 161-78.

Torres, S. (2015) 'Expanding the gerontological imagination on ethnicity: Conceptual and theoretical perspectives', *Ageing and Society*, vol 35, no 5, pp 935-60.

Victor, C.R. (2014) 'Understanding physical activity in the daily lives of Bangladeshi and Pakistani elders in Great Britain', *ISRN Geriatrics*, vol 8.

Victor, C.R. (2015) 'A preliminary analysis of the prevalence of loneliness among older Indian migrants to England and Wales', *International Journal of Contemporary Sociology*, vol 52, no 1, pp 77-92.

Victor, C.R., Burholt, V. and Martin, W. (2012a) 'Loneliness and ethnic minority elders in Great Britain: An exploratory study', *Journal of Cross Cultural Gerontology*, vol 27, no 1, pp 65-78.

Victor, C.R., Martin, W. and Zubair, M. (2012b) 'Families and caring amongst older people in South Asian communities in the UK: A pilot study', *European Journal of Social Work*, vol 15, no 1, pp 81-96.

Wray S. and Bartholomew, M. (2010) 'Some reflections on outsider and insider identities in ethnic and migrant qualitative research', *Migration Letters*, vol 7, pp 7-16.

Zubair, M. and Norris, M. (2015) 'Perspectives on ageing, later life and ethnicity: Ageing research in ethnic minority contexts', *Ageing and Society*, vol 35, pp 897-916. doi:10.1017/S0144686X14001536

Zubair, M. and Victor, C. (2015) 'Exploring gender, age, time and space in research with older Pakistani Muslims in the United Kingdom: Formalised research "ethics" and performances of the public/private divide in "the field"', *Ageing and Society*, vol 35, no 5, pp 961-85.

Zubair, M., Martin, W. and Victor, C.R. (2010) 'Researching ethnicity: Critical reflections on conducting qualitative research with people growing older in Pakistani Muslim communities in the UK', *Generations Review*, January.

Zubair, M., Martin, W. and Victor, C.R. (2012a) 'Embodying gender, age, ethnicity and power in "the field": Reflections on dress and the presentation of the self in research with older Pakistani Muslims', *Sociological Research Online*, vol 21.

Zubair, M., Martin, W. and Victor, C.R. (2012b) 'Doing Pakistani ethnicity, the female way: Issues of identity, trust and recruitment when researching older Pakistani Muslims in the UK', in M. Leontowitsch (ed) *Researching later life and ageing: Expanding qualitative research agendas and methods*, Basingstoke: Palgrave, pp 63-83.

Part Two:
Biological perspectives

SEVEN

Understanding immunesenescence

Anna C. Whittaker (previously Phillips), Jane Upton,
Niharika Arora Duggal, Chadni Deb, Charanjit Randhawa,
Jan Oyebode and Janet Lord

Introduction

With the ageing of the population, hip fractures are a growing issue in the UK (Dennison et al, 2006). At least half of older adults who have suffered a hip fracture never regain their previous function (Stevens and Olson, 2000), with mortality at one year after the fracture recorded as high as 33 per cent (Roche et al, 2005). The factors influencing recovery from hip fracture are poorly understood. These include depression, a common co-morbidity in these patients (Nightingale et al, 2001).

The prevalence rate for depression in people who have had a hip fracture across eight US and UK studies ranged from 9 to 47 per cent (Holmes and House, 2000). Importantly, depression in people who have suffered a hip fracture has been associated with increased risk of infections and poor survival (Nightingale et al, 2001), impaired recovery and a reduced ability to regain pre-fracture levels of physical functioning (Mossey et al, 1990).

It is well documented that ageing is accompanied by poor functioning of the body's immune system (Dorshkind et al, 2009; Panda et al, 2009). This is called immunesenescence, or immune ageing, and contributes to the increased risk of infection in old age (Gavazzi and Krause, 2002). Particular aspects of immune ageing can be observed in specific important immune system cells. For example, neutrophils are key cells in the immune system that are responsible for providing protection against bacteria such as those that cause hospital-acquired infections and pneumonia. Ageing is accompanied by a decline in neutrophil ability to ingest such bacteria (Butcher et al, 2001), and their ability to kill the bacteria once ingested (Tortorella et al, 2000). Similar reductions in efficacy have been shown in other immune cells, such as monocytes, with advancing age (Shaw et al, 2011).

An additional important component of the immune system are natural killer (NK) cells, which are capable of destroying cancer cells and cells infected with viruses (Farag et al, 2003). Older adults have an age-related decrease in NK cell function (Hazeldine et al, 2012), which may explain why they are more susceptible to cancer and virus infections such as influenza. Further, ageing is also accompanied by changes in immune cells that are very focused and kill specific infections because they have encountered them before – this is termed 'immune memory', or because the older adult has had a vaccination to protect them. These cells, called lymphocytes, do not function as well in older adults and this reduces the ability to benefit from vaccines in old age. In addition, some of these cells have a specific role in dampening down immune responses to prevent autoimmune disorders – these are called regulatory cells (Blair et al, 2010). Interestingly, a recent study in our group has reported an age-related decrease in the numbers and function of this type of cell that might contribute towards an increased risk of autoimmune diseases such as rheumatoid arthritis with age (Duggal et al, 2013b).

Interestingly, there is accumulating evidence suggesting that the effects of psychological stress and ageing are additive, with chronic stress worsening the effects of ageing on immunity in older adults (Kiecolt-Glaser and Glaser, 1999). For example, older adults who had suffered stressful life events, such as bereavement and marital dissatisfaction, have lower levels of antibody production in response to the annual 'flu vaccination than those who had not experienced these stressors (Phillips et al, 2006). In addition, neutrophils are susceptible to the effects of stress, with their ability to kill bacteria reduced in older people who have suffered the trauma of a hip fracture (Butcher et al, 2005) or bereavement (Khanfer et al, 2011).

One of the ways in which stress affects bodily systems, including the immune system, is via the production of stress hormones. Stress is sensed in the brain by the hypothalamus that signals the adrenal gland to produce stress hormones that circulate in the blood and reach immune cells and influence their function (Tsigos and Chrousos, 2002). Cortisol is the main stress hormone and is a potent immune system suppressor and can also contribute to the development of depression (Fischer et al, 2017). Dehydroepiandrosterone sulphate (DHEAS) is another steroid hormone produced by the adrenal gland, and has the opposite actions to cortisol, being anti-depressive (Hough et al, 2017) and immune-enhancing, including the ability to increase the bacterial killing mechanisms of neutrophils (Hazeldine et al, 2010; Radford et al, 2010). Although cortisol levels generally may not increase with ageing, they are higher in relation to DHEAS that decreases with age in men and women (adrenopause), thus ageing is accompanied by an elevated cortisol:DHEAS ratio; this may be a key factor contributing towards age-associated immune dysfunction (Buford and Willoughby, 2008). As stress increases cortisol production, this age-related dysfunction is made worse by stress. Our group reported a raised cortisol:DHEAS ratio in older hip fracture patients versus young comparable trauma patients, and these higher cortisol levels were also accompanied by reduced neutrophil bacterial killing ability and increased incidence of bacterial infections like pneumonia (Butcher et al, 2005).

Cortisol levels are often higher in individuals with depression (Lesch et al, 1988; Deuschle et al, 1997). Higher cortisol levels in older adults have also been associated with frailty, including poor standing and walking performance (Peeters et al, 2007). Low levels of DHEAS have also been related to poorer physical function (Berkman et al, 1993). Importantly, the cortisol:DHEAS ratio is higher in older hip fracture patients than in healthy older adults (Dubin et al, 1999) and younger comparable fracture patients (Butcher et al, 2005). This hormone imbalance may thus be a major determinant of frailty in older people following hip fracture, as well as their susceptibility to infections, particularly in those with concomitant depression.

A pilot study, as part of this larger project, focused on patients' perceptions of their illness. There is evidence to support the connection between illness perceptions and outcomes in a range of conditions including chronic fatigue syndrome (Moss-Morris et al, 1996), Addison's disease (Heijmans and De Ridder, 1998) and multiple sclerosis (Jopson and Moss-Morris, 2003). Illness perceptions have been found to be related to wellbeing and mood (Murphy et al, 1999), and to participation in rehabilitation programmes (Cooper et al, 1999). Further, there is evidence that minority cultural groups hold illness perceptions that differ in various respects from the majority in the UK (Kim et al, 2012). For research into minority ethnic groups to produce useful findings, studies need to acknowledge variations in religion and culture by working with defined groups. Consequently, these issues were also considered in the present project.

Aims and methods

The 'Synergistic effects of physical and psychological stress upon immunosenescence' New Dynamics of Ageing (NDA) study sought to test whether psychological distress, specifically depressive symptoms emerging after a hip fracture, would act additively on top of the physical stress of hip fracture to amplify the effect of ageing on immunity (immunesenescence) and physical frailty. It also examined the role of the cortisol : DHEAS ratio and cytokines (immune messengers) as potential mechanisms that might explain any of the effects on immunity and frailty.

An integrated pilot study within this overall project aimed to explore the implications of attitudes to hip fracture of a significant minority ethnic patient group in the UK, and the consequent implications for tailoring approaches to rehabilitation. Therefore in this pilot study the intention was to recruit only hip fracture patients from the Punjab region of India (excluding Punjabis from Pakistan, a different religious group).

Participants with hip fracture were 101 White British older adults, of whom 81 were female. A parallel pilot study of Punjabi-speaking older adults was recruited elsewhere for comparison, as discussed below. The participants had an average age of 83.9 and had been admitted to hospital as in-patients with a fractured neck of femur (hip fracture). Participating hospitals were all located in the West Midlands, UK. Participants were all aged 60+ and did not have any existing medical conditions or medications that could affect the immune system, dementia, taking anti-depressants or having a previous diagnosis of depression before the age of 50. In this way we aimed to recruit individuals who had likely developed depression post-fracture, rather than those who already had a history of depression. Fifty healthy older adults were also recruited from the community as a control group via the Birmingham 1,000 Elders cohort of healthy older adults involved in research at the University of Birmingham. These controls also had to meet the criteria above, but not have a hip fracture. We also involved a sub-sample of these healthy controls to advise us on the usability of the questionnaire packs and tests that were administered during the study.

For the integrated pilot study, we attempted to recruit an additional 30 Punjabi hip fracture patients concurrently with White patients from five hospitals in the West Midlands. Only one Indian Punjabi patient was recruited, who later withdrew. Our Steering Group Committee, including an age- and ethnicity-relevant advisory member, had considered barriers to participation in advance, and translated validated questionnaires as well as employing a Punjabi-speaking technician to assist with recruitment, although this did not make a difference to the poor recruitment of this sub-sample.

The main research study compared these three groups of older adults: hip fracture patients with or without depressive symptoms and healthy older adults at six weeks post-fracture. This is the first time that previously non-depressed patients have been assessed for emerging depression post-hip fracture. All hip fracture patients were recruited while in hospital, then completed questionnaires, structured interviews and provided a blood sample six weeks and six months after hip fracture. Control participants completed a depression and anxiety symptoms scale and basic demographic information when attending the university for blood sampling around the same time as the patients' six-week sample. Blood samples were taken between 08:00 and 11:00 to minimise any effect of daily variations in steroid levels. None of the participants had an acute infection at the time of blood sampling. Interviews were performed either in hospital or the participant's home.

The assays for neutrophil and monocyte function, namely, phagocytosis (bacteria ingesting ability) and superoxide production (bacteria killing ability) were performed on blood the same day as blood sampling. We also looked at the numbers of regulatory immune cells. Serum from the blood samples from hip fracture patients and healthy control subjects were analysed for stress hormones, namely, cortisol and DHEAS.

The interviewer recorded standard sociodemographics (age, sex, occupation), health behaviour information, and all other illnesses present, and medications (prescription and over-the-counter). The psychological status of the participant was assessed by means of validated psychological questionnaires. Depression was evaluated using the Geriatric Depression Scale (GDS) (Yesavage et al, 1982). Depression was defined as a GDS score greater than or equal to 6 (Sheikh and Yesavage, 1986). The Hospital Anxiety and Depression Scale (HADS) was also used to confirm the presence of depression and anxiety (Zigmond and Snaith, 1983). The Oxford Hip Score (OHS) (Dawson et al, 1996) is a 12-item questionnaire validated to assess activities of daily living (ADL) and ability in patients undergoing hip replacement surgery. Physical frailty was assessed in part by the OHS but, in addition, upper body strength was measured as handgrip strength using a hydraulic hand dynamometer, and lower body strength using the Timed Up and Go (TUG) test (Podsiadlo and Richardson, 1991), which is getting up and walking speed over three metres and back, and the Berg Balance Scale (BBS) (Berg et al, 1992). The BBS comprises activities to assess balance standing and during the performance of tasks. Body mass index (BMI) was computed as kg/m^2 from measured height and weight. Health behaviours, including smoking, alcohol intake, diet, exercise and sleep duration, were recorded using a simple questionnaire adapted from the Whitehall study (Marmot et al, 1991).

For the pilot study, given the difficulties of recruitment of Punjabi-speaking participants, an alternative strategy was developed by the Steering Group. Two University of Birmingham medical students, with work placements in the Punjab region of India, agreed to collect pilot data in India. The limitations of collecting comparative data in India rather than the UK were recognised and are discussed below. However, the study research team agreed that data from the Punjab may guide the development of future studies addressing illness perceptions of South Asians in the UK. Patients were recruited from two hospitals in the city of Jalandhar, Punjab: Orthonova Joint and Trauma Hospital and Civil Hospital. Inclusion criteria were as for the UK sample except that to facilitate recruitment, those with concurrent depression, diabetes, cancer or chronic obstructive pulmonary disease were included, and the lower age limit was 60 for men as well as women.

Pilot study participants in India completed translated versions of the Brief Illness Perception Questionnaire (BIPQ) (Broadbent et al, 2006), OHS, HADS, and patient basic sociodemographic information. Where validated translated versions were not available, such as for the BIPQ, questionnaires were translated into Punjabi, and independently back-translated. Discrepancies were then discussed, and agreement reached concerning the most appropriate wording.

Findings

All of our findings were published in peer-reviewed journals (Duggal et al, 2013a, 2014a, b, 2015; Phillips et al, 2013, 2015; Lord et al, 2016). In summary, 101 hip fracture patients and 43 controls were recruited for the six-week study. By six months, 66 hip fracture patients remained in the study. Withdrawals were due to death, being too unwell to be tested, being non-contactable or no longer meeting the inclusion criteria (for example, taking anti-depressant medication). The flow of participants through the study is shown in Figure 7.1.

For the pilot study in India, 22 patients who met the inclusion criteria were recruited.

Participant characteristics

Patients were classified into two groups on the basis of their depression scores: 37 per cent of the hip fracture patients had depressive symptoms

Figure 7.1: Flow of participants through the study

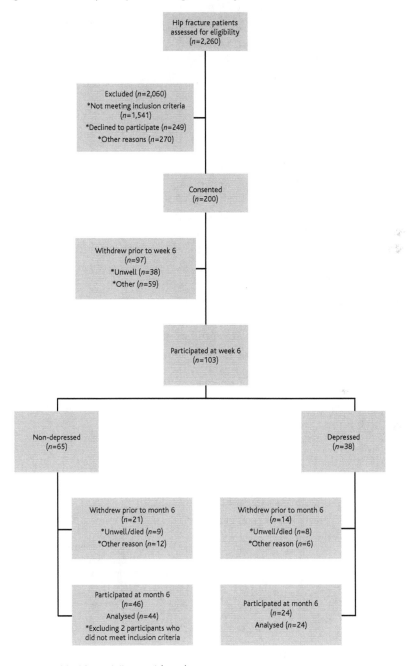

Source: Modified from Phillips et al (2013)

six weeks after their fracture. These groups differed on age and BMI, such that the non-depressed group was slightly younger and had a higher BMI. However, there were no significant differences between the two hip fracture groups on other variables. At month 6, data were available for 66 hip fracture patients, 29 per cent of whom were depressed. Participants classified as depressed had significantly higher GDS scores by an average of 5.6 at week 6. At month 6, this difference remained significant.

Length of hospital stay and infections

A range of hospital-related and community-acquired infection data were collected from patients' hospital and GP notes within the six months post-hip fracture. The depressed group spent a significantly longer entire length of stay in hospitals or rehabilitation centres, although the length of in-patient stay at the hospital their surgery took place at did not significantly differ (Phillips et al, 2015). Hip fracture patients were significantly more likely to be discharged to a rehabilitation unit, and there was a slightly increased number of readmissions to hospital (Phillips et al, 2015). However, depressed patients did not have a greater number of infections while in hospital. Although they had a slightly higher number of infections in the six months following their hip fracture, this was not statistically significant (Phillips et al, 2015). The types of infections experienced by depressed and non-depressed patients were not significantly different between groups.

Table 7.1: Characteristics of participants

Variable	Hip fracture patients (N=65)	Hip fracture patients with depressive symptoms (N=38)	Healthy controls (N=43)
Week 6	Number/average		
Age (years)	83.8	84.0	74.9
Sex (female)	58	25	26
Body mass index (BMI) (kg/m²)	23.5	22.7	27.2
Alcohol consumption (one or more units per week)	13	24	13
Sleep (<8 hours per night)	19	28	23

Physical performance in hip fracture patients

Physical frailty was assessed using four measures as described above. Patients with symptoms of depression were less able to engage in activities of daily living (ADL) than non-depressed patients at week 6 and month 6, although ADL significantly improved over time. Participants with depression took significantly longer to complete the Timed Up and Go (TUG) walking speed test at week 6 and month 6 compared to the non-depressed group (Phillips et al, 2013). Both groups were far slower than age-related norms at both time-points, although walking speed improved over time in both groups. Depressed patients also scored significantly worse on the Berg Balance Scale (BBS) at week 6 compared to the non-depressed patients, but there was no significant difference by month 6 (Phillips et al, 2015).

Neutrophil functioning in hip fracture patients

When we compared neutrophil numbers between our hip fractured participants with and without depression and the healthy control group, significantly lower numbers were observed in healthy older adults compared with both groups of older adults with hip fracture, although all were within the normal range. Neutrophil phagocytosis (eating ability) did not differ significantly between the two groups of hip fracture patients and healthy controls. Neutrophil superoxide production (killing ability) in response to stimulation differed between our three groups, but the significant impairment was restricted to the hip fractured participants who developed depressive symptoms. Hip fracture patients with higher GDS scores had poorer neutrophil superoxide production (Duggal et al, 2013a).

Monocyte functioning in hip fracture patients

Similar to neutrophils, monocytes play a key role in removal of pathogens and providing protection against infections. We compared the monocyte count between our three groups, but no significant differences were detected nor for monocyte phagocytic (eating) ability. Monocyte superoxide production (killing ability) was different between the three groups, but the significant impairment was restricted to the hip fracture patients who developed depression (Duggal et al, 2014a), similar to our neutrophil data. Further, higher depression scores related to lower monocyte superoxide production (Duggal et al, 2014a), again in the same way as depression scores related to neutrophil function.

Natural killer cell numbers and cytotoxicity in hip fracture patients

On examining NK cells in the participants, similar to the results above, we did not find any significant differences in percentages or absolute numbers of NK cells between our three groups. However, a significant impairment in NK cell killing capacity was restricted to the hip fractured participants with new onset depression compared to healthy controls and those without depressive symptoms (Duggal et al, 2015). Again, depressive symptoms predicted a reduction in NK cell killing ability, such that hip fracture patients with greater depressive symptoms had poorer NK cell activity.

Hormone imbalance in hip fracture patients with depressive symptoms

Analysis of stress hormone levels from the blood samples revealed significant differences: higher cortisol levels, reduced DHEAS levels and an elevated serum cortisol : DHEAS ratio was observed in hip fracture patients with depressive symptoms compared to those with hip fracture alone and controls (Phillips et al, 2013). Elevated serum cortisol : DHEAS ratios have been previously reported as an indicator of individuals at risk of depression (Young et al, 2002). Here, the higher the depression scores, the higher the cortisol : DHEAS ratio. However, the hormone ratio was not related to neutrophil, monocyte or NK cell function, suggesting that it is not the main underlying link between depressive symptoms and impaired immune function.

Interestingly, the ratio between these hormones did relate to physical function. The cortisol : DHEAS ratio was related to walking speed as measured by the TUG at month 6, such that the higher the cortisol : DHEAS ratio, the longer it took the participant to walk three metres (Phillips et al, 2013). This suggests that although this hormone ratio was not the link between depression and the immune changes we observed in participants with hip fracture, it may have a role to play in the markers of frailty we measured, at least in walking speed.

Circulating cytokine levels in hip fracture patients with depressive symptoms

Next, on measuring serum cytokine (immune messenger) levels in participants, we observed that hip fracture patients with depressive symptoms also had higher levels of pro-inflammatory cytokines, which are associated with higher levels of inflammation in the body, including

IL6 and TNFα. We also observed higher levels of anti-inflammatory cytokines, such as IL10, in the participants with depression compared with non-depressed participants and controls, but overall depression scores did not positively relate to these levels (Duggal et al, 2013a). It is therefore unlikely that these immune messengers were the underlying link between depressive symptoms and immune function changes in our subjects.

Reduced T cell numbers in hip fracture patients with depressive symptoms

In an attempt to examine the effect of physical and psychological distress on adaptive immune cells (immune memory), we found several differences in cell numbers. T cell (so-called as they mature in the thymus gland) numbers were significantly lower in our group of hip fracture patients with depressive symptoms compared with those without depression or healthy controls (Duggal et al, 2014b). T cells are composed of two main subsets, CD4 T cells (helper T cells that help other cells recognise pathogens) and CD8 T cells (cytotoxic T cells that kill infected cells directly). However, on examining the percentage of CD4^{+ve} T cells and CD8^{+ve} T cells, no significant differences were observed between our three groups, or the ratio of these types of cells, which is sometimes higher in older or particularly stressed groups.

Numerical and functional deficit in regulatory B cells in hip fracture patients with depressive symptoms

B cells are a type of cell involved in recognising pathogens in the body and producing antibodies against them. There are also specific types that help to regulate the function of the immune system to prevent over-activity that might result in autoimmune disease. In this study, there were no differences in the total numbers of B cells between the three groups. However, a significant decline was seen in the percentage and absolute numbers of regulatory B cells in hip fracture patients with depressive symptoms compared with healthy controls and hip fracture patients without depressive symptoms (Lord et al, 2016). Further, participants with higher depressive symptoms (GDS score) had lower frequency of regulatory B cells (Lord et al, 2016). All of these immune, hormonal and physical function differences between the depressed and non-depressed participants at week 6 are summarised in Table 7.2.

Table 7.2: Main group differences

	Direction of group difference		
GDS score*	Depressed	>	Not depressed
Neutrophil phagocytosis	Depressed	=	Not depressed
Neutrophil superoxide generation*	Depressed	<	Not depressed
Monocyte phagocytosis	Depressed	=	Not depressed
Monocyte superoxide generation*	Depressed	<	Not depressed
NK cell %/numbers	Depressed	=	Not depressed
NK cell killing*	Depressed	<	Not depressed
Cortisol*	Depressed	>	Not depressed
DHEA*	Depressed	<	Not depressed
Cortisol:DHEAS ratio*	Depressed	>	Not depressed
Pro-inflammatory cytokines*	Depressed	>	Not depressed
T cell %/numbers*	Depressed	<	Not depressed
CD4/CD8 T cell numbers/ratio	Depressed	=	Not depressed
Regulatory B cell %*	Depressed	<	Not depressed
Regulatory B cell cytokine production*	Depressed	<	Not depressed
OHS*	Depressed	<	Not depressed
Hand grip mean (kg)	Depressed	=	Not depressed
TUG (seconds)*	Depressed	>	Not depressed
BBS score*	Depressed	<	Not depressed
Length of hospital/rehabilitation centre stay*	Depressed	>	Not depressed

Note: * Denotes significant differences between the groups at week 6.

Long-term effect of depressive symptoms on hip fracture patients

Finally, the long-term effect of depressive symptoms on hip fracture patients was evaluated six months post-surgery. We observed that during the six-month follow-up, neutrophil superoxide production had improved in both hip fracture groups, but monocyte and NK cell functioning in hip fracture patients with depressive symptoms still remained suppressed six months post-surgery. Further, the serum cortisol:DHEAS ratio remained high in the depressed group of hip fracture patients six months post-hip surgery. This was not influenced by any change in reported depressive symptom scores at six weeks and six months; in fact, there was very little change over time between the groups – six individuals who were not originally classified as depressed were depressed at month 6, and 11 who were initially depressed had recovered by month 6. However, the biggest groups by far were those who had been depressed and remained so, and those who were not depressed and remained so.

Pilot study results

Next, our Punjabi sample was compared to our UK-based group of hip fracture patients on basic characteristics. The Punjabi sample was somewhat younger than the Caucasian sample, and there were more males. However, levels of anxiety and depression and ADL scores were comparable across the samples. From the BIPQ, the Indian Punjabi group reported that they were significantly more affected by their hip fracture, perceived that the treatment had helped their hip fracture far less, and reported significantly more emotional distress resulting from their hip fracture compared to the UK sample. These differences are shown in Table 7.3, and were not driven by age and sex differences between the samples. Further, the Indian Punjabi group also reported higher levels of understanding about their hip fracture, but this became non-significant when taking age and sex differences into account in statistical analyses.

All of the participants in both groups had fallen, but the reasons for the fall were perceived differently between the ethnic groups. The main cause provided by the UK Caucasian participants was that the hip fracture was due to the way that they had fallen (22 per cent). This

Table 7.3: Demographic and questionnaire pilot data in both samples

	Mean (Standard Deviation) or number (%)	
	UK	India
Age	84 (7.96)	71 (9.76)
Sex (male)	20 (20%)	11 (50%)
ADL	27.5 (9.24)	22.5 (9.57)
HADS depression score ≥ 8	26 (27%)	8 (36%)
HADS anxiety score ≥ 8	29 (30%)	5 (23%)
How much does your hip fracture affect your life?	6.0 (2.63)	7.45 (3.16)
How long do you think your hip fracture will continue?	4.9 (2.63)	4.1 (3.29)
How much control do you feel you have over the recovery from your hip fracture?	5.5 (2.9)	6.4 (3.4)
How much do you think your treatment helped your hip fracture?	7.4 (2.7)	1.6 (2.11)
How much do you experience symptoms from your hip fracture?	4.3 (2.65)	3.7 (3.62)
How concerned are you about your hip fracture?	4.6 (3.07)	5.8 (4.24)
How well do you feel you understand your hip fracture?	5.4 (3.5)	7.4 (3.5)
How much does your hip fracture affect you emotionally?	3.9 (3.16)	6.8 (4.08)

Note: Scores ranges from 10 = high or best to 0 = low or worst.

cause was not perceived by any of the Indian Punjabi participants, who attributed the main cause to be 'fate' (41 per cent). However, difficulties in answering this open-ended question about the reason for the hip fracture in the Punjabi sample meant that this question was followed up with an additional probe: 'Some people think that their fracture was due to fate or bad diet, do you think any of these factors caused your illness?' This is likely to have introduced some bias into the distribution of answers across the samples. Other perceived causes of hip fracture are shown in Table 7.4.

Table 7.4: Participants' perceptions of causes of hip fracture

	Number (%)	
Perceived cause of hip fracture	UK	India
The way they fell and landed	22 (22)	0 (0)
Bone-related cause (osteoarthritis or low calcium levels)	9 (9)	1 (4.5)
Blamed themselves (eg, for being careless)	7 (7)	0 (0)
Dizziness	4 (4)	1 (4.5)
Age	4 (4)	2 (9)
Fate	0 (0)	9 (41)
No cause known/given	55 (55)	9 (41)

Policy and practice implications

The clear implication arising from this research is that depression in older adults post-hip fracture is not only common, but can have a range of catastrophic consequences including poorer immunity across a whole range of immune measures, worse physical frailty and recovery and longer stays in NHS facilities. Our findings support the need for preventing and treating depression and depressive symptoms to improve outcomes in older people with hip fracture, and that this should become common practice.

One particular difficulty that this immediately raises is that patients with hip fracture are not routinely screened for depression symptoms, thus we would recommend this be integrated into normal clinical practice. The use of a short scale such as the GDS would not add significant workload but would identify those patients at risk of poorer outcomes. Interestingly, as well as group differences, our findings also showed that all immune outcomes were worse among those with the highest depression scores, meaning that for some individuals, the effects of untreated depressive symptoms post-fracture are very severe.

Poorer immune outcomes means that these patients are more at risk of infection (Butcher et al, 2005), which often results in mortality or at least a return to hospital. Poor physical function outcomes means that these patients lose independence and are more likely to need to be admitted to rehabilitation facilities, or may not ever be fit enough to return home. Consequently, it is of great importance to identify such patients in terms or improving their health and wellbeing as well as reducing NHS costs in the longer term. Use of such a measurement would also indicate those patients struggling most emotionally after the physical trauma of their fracture, and thus identify those most in need of supportive care for up to six months post-fracture.

There are also a number of obvious routes for intervention in these patients. Although participants' GPs were informed of their involvement in the study and high depressive symptoms scores, this resulted in only two participants being prescribed anti-depressive medication. This may reflect that patients' hip fracture is the main cause for concern and focus of treatment at this time, or also that common anti-depressant medications are contra-indicated in frail older adults due to interactions with osteoporosis and the risk of further serious injury. However, the difficulties inherent in not assessing and treating such symptoms are outlined above, thus it is likely that some type of psychological or pharmaceutical depression treatment would be helpful for these patients, not only in terms of psychological wellbeing, but also in terms of physical health and day-to-day functioning.

The link with the cortisol : DHEAS ratio in the present study also suggests another route for intervention. As a higher ratio was related to poor physical frailty and slower walking speed recovery, it is possible that an intervention to adjust this ratio would have beneficial effects on recovery. DHEA tablets given as a nutritional supplement have been shown previously to be effective at increasing wellbeing and mood in older adults (Arlt et al, 1999, 2000), improving some measures of physical function (Buvat, 2003), as well as being safe and well tolerated at doses of 50mg (Arlt et al, 1998). Further, DHEA supplementation is also known to modify immune function (Arlt and Hewison, 2004) – for instance, an immune-enhancing effect of DHEAS has been reported on neutrophil superoxide generation (Radford et al, 2010) and NK cell cytotoxicity (Casson et al, 1993; Solerte et al, 1999). Although some studies have shown limited effectiveness in healthy populations, we believe the real effects of DHEA supplementation are likely to be seen among those with adrenal insufficiency or at acute risk of a high cortisol : DHEAS ratio, such as in our elderly depressed hip fracture patients. DHEA is also a cheap nutritional supplement, thus would not cost as much as testing as introducing a new anti-depressant that is safe among older adults, or time-intensive psychological therapies. It is also possible that such treatment could be combined with some type of psychological support such as social support or talking therapy for older adults with depressive symptoms, which might result in even more positive health and wellbeing outcomes. Further research on the likely effectiveness as well as cost-effectiveness of such interventions is our next plan.

The implications of our pilot research are limited by the inability to identify and recruit sufficient UK-based Punjabi patients. This reflects both low numbers of this group having hip fracture as well as difficulty with recruitment, even with a Punjabi-speaking research assistant. Given this, our data are based on Punjabi patients in India where time since hip fracture and age of patients differed to our UK sample, making it difficult to generalise this group to a Punjabi patient group in the UK. However, it was interesting to note that Punjabi patients felt more affected and less effectively treated than UK Caucasian patients, and it would be interesting to conduct further research to see whether this might also be the case within the UK NHS or whether it is specific to India.

Further, Punjabi patients were more likely to attribute their hip fracture to fate, whereas UK Caucasian patients attributed it to the way they had fallen. However, caution should be taken here, as the questionnaires were conducted as interviews in the Punjab, and when answers were not forthcoming, the research assistants gave prompts based on previous patients' answers, which are likely to have biased self-reports. However, if further research were to replicate this finding without prompting from the researchers, it would raise interesting questions regarding patients' understanding of illness and reasons for illness within the healthcare system in India, suggesting that more communication and education about the source of illness and reasons for treatment might be necessary. This would be important as illness perceptions can affect patient engagement with the healthcare system and rehabilitation, with consequent effects on patient health and wellbeing outcomes.

Key findings

- One-third of older hip fracture patients develop new onset depression within six weeks after hip fracture.

- Hip fracture patients who develop depression have significantly poorer physical function, for example, walking speed, at both six weeks and six months after surgery, and poorer balance at week six.
- There was an increase in the stress hormone cortisol, which is an immune suppressor, and a decrease in the immune-enhancing hormone dehydroepiandrosterone sulphate (DHEAS), leading to an increase in the cortisol : DHEAS ratio in depressed hip fracture patients compared with non-depressed patients or healthy controls.
- Patients with higher depression scores have a higher cortisol : DHEAS ratio.
- Slower walking speed is related to a higher cortisol : DHEAS ratio in the depressed group, suggesting that this hormonal imbalance might contribute to the reduced physical function in these patients.
- An Indian Punjabi group of hip fracture patients reported that they were more affected by their hip fracture, perceived that the treatment had helped their hip fracture far less and felt significantly more emotional distress resulting from their hip fracture than the UK White patients.

Conclusions

In conclusion, this NDA project reported for the first time that development of depressive symptoms in older people who have suffered hip fracture can result in the suppressive effect of psychological distress of depressive symptoms on neutrophil, monocytes and NK cell functioning in older hip fracture patients. Additionally, certain aspects of immunity in the participants with hip fracture and new onset depression remained suppressed even six months post-surgery. Further, the development of depressive symptoms post-hip fracture induces hypothalamic–pituitary–adrenal (HPA) axis activation, resulting in elevated cortisol levels in people with hip fracture patients and depressive symptoms. Additionally, a reduction in serum DHEAS levels were also observed in these participants, resulting in an overall elevated serum cortisol : DHEAS ratio in hip fracture patients with new onset depression that remained elevated even six months post-surgery. We have also reported a reduced frequency of circulating B regulatory cells in hip fracture patients with depressive symptoms.

These findings suggest that the development of depressive symptoms after a hip fracture in older adults is the main driver of immune suppression, as we failed to find an immune decline as a result of hip fracture alone. Further, depression emerging post-hip fracture in older adults impaired physical function, including walking speed, balance and ADL. This showed for the first time that depressive symptoms in the absence of longer-term pre-fracture depression diagnosis relate to recovery and physical frailty. Effects on walking speed were mediated by alterations in the cortisol : DHEAS ratio that was heightened among the depressed group. Finally, the adults with hip fracture who developed depression were also more likely to spend longer in NHS facilities overall, incurring significant cost to the health service as well as an inconvenience to patients not well enough to return home.

This novel finding implies that in order to speed the recovery of physical function, immunity and infection protection and independence following hip fracture, patients should be assessed and treated for depressive symptoms. This is of relevance to surgeons and health professionals alike involved in rehabilitation post-fracture surgery who currently do not screen this patient group for depressive symptoms. Identification and treatment of depression in these patients would improve patient outcomes and quality of life as well as having an impact on health service costs incurred through treatment of those with slower recovery and decreased independence post-fracture.

We propose that correcting the cortisol : DHEAS imbalance by oral supplementation with DHEA may be one means of improving depressed mood and contributing to better physical function after hip fracture. However, such an intervention would need to be cautiously informed by the intervention literature in order to determine an effect dosage and regime for an effect in these patients. It is possible that some form of psychological support on top of DHEA treatment might result in the best outcomes for patients who have developed depressive symptoms. Consequently, the next stage in our research will be to pilot a randomised controlled trial of DHEA supplementation with and without psychological support in older adults with hip fracture and depression and ascertain effects on wellbeing, physical frailty and immunity.

Acknowledgments

We are grateful to the following hospital consultants for their assistance: Professor Sir Keith Porter and Mr Martin Goodman (Queen Elizabeth Hospital, Birmingham), Mr Edward Davis (Russells Hall Hospital, Dudley) and Mr Sanjay Mistry (Heartlands Hospital, Birmingham). We are also grateful to the National Institute for Health Research (NIHR)/Wellcome Trust Clinical Research Facility, Queen Elizabeth Hospital Birmingham, for their research nurse and testing facilities support.[1]

Note

[1]   This work was supported by funding from the Research Councils UK New Dynamics of Ageing initiative (Grant Number RES-356-25-0011).

References

Arlt, W. and Hewison, M. (2004) 'Hormones and immune function: Implications of aging', *Aging Cell*, vol 3, pp 209-16.

Arlt, W., Callies, F. and Allolio, B. (2000) 'DHEA replacement in women with adrenal insufficiency – Pharmacokinetics, bioconversion and clinical effects on well-being, sexuality and cognition', *Endocrine Research*, vol 26, pp 505-11.

Arlt, W., Justl, H.G., Callies, F., Reincke, M., Hubler, D., Oettel, M., et ak (1998) 'Oral dehydroepiandrosterone for adrenal androgen replacement: Pharmacokinetics and peripheral conversion to androgens and estrogens in young healthy females after dexamethasone suppression', *Journal of Clinical Endocrinology and Metabolism*, vol 83, pp 1928-34.

Arlt, W., Callies, F., van Wlijmen, J.C., Koehler, I., Reincke, M., Bidlingmaier, M., et al (1999) 'Dehydroepiandrosterone replacement in women with adrenal insufficiency', *New England Journal of Medicine*, vol 341, pp 1013-20.

Berg, K.O., Maki, B.E., Williams, J.I., Holliday, P.J. and Wood-Dauphinee, S.L. (1992) 'Clinical and laboratory measures of postural balance in an elderly population', *Archives of Physical Medicine and Rehabilitation*, vol 73, pp 1073-80.

Berkman, L.F., Seeman, T.E., Albert, M., Blazer, D., Kahn, R., Mohs, R., et al (1993) 'High, usual and impaired functioning in community-dwelling older men and women: Findings from the MacArthur Foundation Research Network on Successful Aging', *Journal of Clinical Epidemiology*, vol 46, pp 1129-40.

Blair, P.A., Norena, L.Y., Flores-Borja, F., Rawlings, D.J., Isenberg, D.A., Ehrenstein, M.R. and Mauri, C. (2010) 'CD19(+)CD24(hi) CD38(hi) B cells exhibit regulatory capacity in healthy individuals but are functionally impaired in systemic Lupus Erythematosus patients', *Immunity*, vol 32, pp 129-40.

Broadbent, E., Petrie, K.J., Main, J. and Weinman, J. (2006) 'The brief illness perception questionnaire', *Journal of Psychosomatic Research*, vol 60, pp 631-7.

Buford, T.W. and Willoughby, D.S. (2008) 'Impact of DHEA(S) and cortisol on immune function in aging: A brief review', *Applied Physiology, Nutrition, and Metabolism*, vol 33, pp 429-33.

Butcher, S.K., Killampalli, V., Lascelles, D., Wang, K., Alpar, E.K. and Lord, J.M. (2005) 'Raised cortisol:DHEAS ratios in the elderly after injury: potential impact upon neutrophil function and immunity', *Aging Cell*, vol 4, pp 319-24.

Butcher, S.K., Chahal, H., Nayak, L., Sinclair, A., Henriquez, N.V., Sapey, E., et al (2001) 'Senescence in innate immune responses: Reduced neutrophil phagocytic capacity and CD16 expression in elderly humans', *Journal of Leukocyte Biology*, vol 70, pp 881-6.

Buvat, J. (2003) 'Androgen therapy with dehydroepiandrosterone', *World Journal of Urology*, vol 21, pp 346-55.

Casson, P.R., Andersen, R.N., Herrod, H.G., Stentz, F.B., Straughn, A.B., Abraham, G.E. and Buster, J.E. (1993) 'Oral dehydroepiandrosterone in physiologic doses modulates immune function in postmenopausal women', *American Journal of Obstetrics and Gynecology*, vol 169, pp 1536-9.

Cooper, A., Lloyd, G., Weinman, J. and Jackson, G. (1999) 'Why patients do not attend cardiac rehabilitation: Role of intentions and illness beliefs', *Heart*, vol 82, pp 234-6.

Dawson, J., Fitzpatrick, R., Carr, A. and Murray, D. (1996) 'Questionnaire on the perceptions of patients about total hip replacement', *The Journal of Bone and Joint Surgery. British Volume*, vol 78, pp 185-90.

Dennison, E., Mohamed, M.A. and Cooper, C. (2006) 'Epidemiology of osteoporosis', *Rheumatic Disease Clinics of North America*, vol 32, pp 617-29.

Deuschle, M., Schweiger, U., Weber, B., Gotthardt, U., Korner, A., Schmider, J. et al (1997) 'Diurnal activity and pulsatility of the hypothalamus-pituitary-adrenal system in male depressed patients and healthy controls', *Journal of Clinical Endocrinology and Metabolism*, vol 82, pp 234-8.

Dorshkind, K., Montecino-Rodriguez, E. and Signer, R.A. (2009) 'The ageing immune system: Is it ever too old to become young again?', *Nature Reviews Immunology*, vol 9, pp 57-62.

Dubin, N.H., Monahan, L.K., Yu-Yahiro, J.A., Michael, R.H., Zimmerman, S.I., Hawkes, W. et al (1999) 'Serum concentrations of steroids, parathyroid hormone, and calcitonin in postmenopausal women during the year following hip fracture: Effect of location of fracture and age', *The Journals of Gerontology. Series A, Biological Sciences and Medical Sciences*, vol 54, M467-73.

Duggal, N.A., Upton, J., Phillips, A.C. and Lord, J.M. (2013a) 'Depression is associated with reduced neutrophil function in hip fracture patients', *Brain, Behavior & Immunity*, vol 33, pp 173-82.

Duggal, N.A., Upton, J., Phillips, A.C., Hampson, P. and Lord, J.M. (2014b) 'Depressive symptoms post hip fracture in older adults are associated with phenotypic and functional alterations in T cells', *Immunity and Ageing*, vol 11.

Duggal, N.A., Upton, J., Phillips, A.C., Hampson, P. and Lord, J.M. (2015) 'NK cell immunesenescence is increased by psychological but not physical stress in older adults associated with raised cortisol and reduced perforin expression', *Age*, vol 37.

Duggal, N.A., Upton, J., Phillips, A.C., Sapey, E. and Lord, J.M. (2013b) 'An age-related numerical and functional deficit in CD19 CD24 CD38 B cells is associated with an increase in systemic autoimmunity', *Aging Cell*, vol 12, no 5, pp 873-81.

Duggal, N.A., Beswetherick, A., Upton, J., Hampson, P., Phillips, A.C. and Lord, J.M. (2014a) 'Depressive symptoms in hip fracture patients are associated with reduced monocyte superoxide production', *Experimental Gerontology*, vol 54, pp 27-34.

Farag, S.S., Vandeusen, J.B., Fehniger, T.A. and Caligiuri, M.A. (2003) 'Biology and clinical impact of human natural killer cells', *International Journal of Hematology*, vol 78, pp 7-17.

Fischer, S., Strawbridge, R., Vives, A.H. and Cleare, A.J. (2017) 'Cortisol as a predictor of psychological therapy response in depressive disorders: Systematic review and meta-analysis', *British Journal of Psychiatry*, vol 210, pp 105-9.

Gavazzi, G. and Krause, K.H. (2002) 'Ageing and infection', *Lancet Infectious Diseases*, vol 2, pp 659-66.

Hazeldine, J., Arlt, W. and Lord, J.M. (2010) 'Dehydroepiandrosterone as a regulator of immune cell function', *The Journal of Steroid Biochemistry and Molecular Biology*, vol 120, pp 127-36.

Hazeldine, J., Hampson, P. and Lord, J.M. (2012) 'Reduced release and binding of perforin at the immunological synapse underlies the age-related decline in natural killer cell cytotoxicity', *Aging Cell*, vol 11, pp 751-9.

Heijmans, M. and De Ridder, D. (1998) 'Structure and determinants of illness representations in chronic disease: A comparison of Addison's Disease and chronic fatigue syndrome', *Journal of Health Psychology*, vol 3, pp 523-37.

Holmes, J.D. and House, A.O. (2000) 'Psychiatric illness in hip fracture', *Age and Ageing*, vol 29, pp 537-46.

Hough, C.M., Lindqvist, D., Epel, E.S., Denis, M.S., Reus, V.I., Bersani, F.S., et al (2017) 'Higher serum DHEA concentrations before and after SSRI treatment are associated with remission of major depression', *Psychoneuroendocrinology*, vol 77, pp 122-30.

Jopson, N.M. and Moss-Morris, R. (2003) 'The role of illness severity and illness representations in adjusting to multiple sclerosis', *Journal of Psychosomatic Research*, vol 54, pp 503-11; discussion pp 513-14.

Khanfer, R., Lord, J.M. and Phillips, A.C. (2011) 'Neutrophil function and cortisol:DHEAS ratio in bereaved older adults', *Brain, Behavior, and Immunity*, vol 25, no 6, 1182-6.

Kiecolt-Glaser, J.K. and Glaser, R. (1999) 'Chronic stress and mortality among older adults', *JAMA*, vol 282, pp 2259-60.

Kim, Y., Evangelista, L.S., Phillips, L.R., Pavlish, C. and Kopple, J.D. (2012) 'Racial/ethnic differences in illness, perceptions in minority patients undergoing maintenance hemodialysis', *Nephrology Nursing Journal*, vol 39, pp 39-48; quiz p 49.

Lesch, K.P., Laux, G., Schulte, H.M., Pfuller, H. and Beckmann, H. (1988) 'Corticotropin and cortisol response to human CRH as a probe for HPA system integrity in major depressive disorder', *Psychiatry Research*, vol 24, pp 25-34.

Lord, J.M., Phillips, A.C., Duggal. N.A. and Upton, J. (2016) 'Development of depressive symptoms post hip fracture is associated with altered immunosuppressive phenotype in regulatory T and B lymphocytes', *Biogerontology*, vol 17, no 1, pp 229-39.

Marmot, M.G., Davey-Smith, G., Stansfield, S., Patel, C., North, F., Head, J., et al (1991) 'Health inequalities among British civil servants: The Whitehall II study', *Lancet*, vol 337, pp 1387-93.

Moss-Morris, R., Petrie, K.J., Large, R.G. and Kydd, R.R. (1996) 'Neuropsychological deficits in chronic fatigue syndrome: Artifact or reality?', *Journal of Neurology, Neurosurgery, and Psychiatry*, vol 60, pp 474-7.

Mossey, J.M., Knott, K. and Craik, R. (1990) 'The effects of persistent depressive symptoms on hip fracture recovery', *Journal of Gerontology*, vol 45, M163-8.

Murphy, H., Dickens, C., Creed, F. and Bernstein, R. (1999) 'Depression, illness perception and coping in rheumatoid arthritis', *Journal of Psychosomatic Research*, vol 46, pp 155-64.

Nightingale, S., Holmes, J., Mason, J. and House, A. (2001) 'Psychiatric illness and mortality after hip fracture', *Lancet*, vol 357, pp 1264-5.

Panda, A., Arjona, A., Sapey, E., Bai, F., Fikrig, E., Montgomery, R.R., Lord, J.M. and Shaw, A.C. (2009) 'Human innate immunosenescence: Causes and consequences for immunity in old age', *Trends in Immunology*, vol 30, pp 325-33.

Peeters, G.M., van Schoor, N.M., Visser, M., Knol, D.L., Eekhoff, E.M., de Ronde, W. and Lips, P. (2007) 'Relationship between cortisol and physical performance in older persons', *Clinical Endocrinology (Oxford)*, vol 67, pp 398-406.

Phillips, A.C., Upton, J., Carroll, D., Arora Duggal, N. and Lord, J.M. (2015) 'New onset depression following hip fracture is associated with increased length of stay in hospital and rehabilitation centres', *SAGE Open*, April-June, pp 1-4.

Phillips, A.C., Upton, J., Duggal, N.A., Carroll, D. and Lord, J.M. (2013) 'Depression following hip fracture is associated with increased physical frailty in older adults: The role of the cortisol: dehydroepiandrosterone sulphate ratio', *BMC Geriatrics*, vol 13, p 60.

Phillips, A.C., Carroll, D., Bums, V.E., Ring, C., MacLeod, J. and Drayson, M. (2006) 'Bereavement and marriage are associated with antibody response to influenza vaccination in the elderly', *Brain Behavior and Immunity*, vol 20, pp 279-89.

Podsiadlo, D. and Richardson, S. (1991) 'The timed "Up & Go": A test of basic functional mobility for frail elderly persons', *Journal of the American Geriatrics Society*, vol 39, pp 142-8.

Radford, D.J., Wang, K., McNelis, J.C., Taylor, A.E., Hechenberger, G., Hofmann, J., et al (2010) 'Dehdyroepiandrosterone sulfate directly activates protein kinase C-beta to increase human neutrophil superoxide generation', *Molecular Endocrinology*, vol 24, pp 813-21.

Roche, J J., Wenn, R.T., Sahota, O. and Moran, C.G. (2005) 'Effect of comorbidities and postoperative complications on mortality after hip fracture in elderly people: Prospective observational cohort study', *BMJ*, vol 331, p 1374.

Shaw, A.C., Panda, A., Joshi, S.R., Qian, F., Allore, H.G. and Montgomery, R.R. (2011) 'Dysregulation of human Toll-like receptor function in aging', *Ageing Research Reviews*, vol 10, pp 346-53.

Solerte, S.B., Fioravanti, M., Vignati, G., Giustina, A., Cravello, L. and Ferrari, E. (1999) 'Dehydroepiandrosterone sulfate enhances natural killer cell cytotoxicity in humans via locally generated immunoreactive insulin-like growth factor I', *Journal of Clinical Endocrinology and Metabolism*, vol 84, pp 3260-7.

Stevens, J.A. and Olson, S. (2000) 'Reducing falls and resulting hip fractures among older women', *MMWR Recommendations and Reports*, vol 49, pp 3-12.

Tortorella, C., Piazzolla, G., Spaccavento, F., Vella, F., Pace, L. and Antonaci, S. (2000) 'Regulatory role of extracellular matrix proteins in neutrophil respiratory burst during aging', *Mechanisms of Ageing and Development*, vol 119, pp 69-82.

Tsigos, C. and Chrousos, G.P. (2002) 'Hypothalamic-pituitary-adrenal axis, neuroendocrine factors and stress', *Journal of Psychosomatic Research*, vol 53, pp 865-71.

Yesavage, J.A., Brink, T.L., Rose, T.L., Lum, O., Huang, V., Adey, M. and Leirer, V.O. (1982) 'Development and validation of a geriatric depression screening scale: A preliminary report', *Journal of Psychiatric Research*, vol 17, pp 37-49.

Young, A.H., Gallagher, P. and Porter, R.J. (2002) 'Elevation of the cortisol-dehydroepiandrosterone ratio in drug-free depressed patients', *American Journal of Psychiatry*, vol 159, pp 1237-9.

Zigmond, A.S. and Snaith, R.P. (1983) 'The hospital anxiety and depression scale', *Acta Psychiatrica Scandinavica*, vol 67, pp 361-70.

EIGHT

Towards understanding the biological drivers of cell ageing

Lynne S. Cox and Penelope A. Mason

Introduction

Ageing of the human body results in gradual loss of tissue and organ function, with consequent frailty and illness leading to poor quality of later life for many older people. Such ageing is thought to result from an accumulation of senescent cells that are unable to divide, leading to failure to replenish or repair the body – such non-dividing cells are said to be 'senescent'. In this New Dynamics of Ageing (NDA)-funded project, we aimed to investigate what causes cell senescence at the very fundamental level of the genes involved and the proteins they encode.

The human body is composed of trillions of cells, some of which are as old as the individual and some of which are renewed on an almost daily basis (Spalding et al, 2005). Cells of the same type are organised into tissues, and then organs are made up of different types of tissues comprising a range of cells with highly specialised functions. Organs such as the heart cooperate with other tissue and organs within the body to form organ systems such as the cardiovascular system.

The health of the individual is intimately linked to the health of each organ system, organ and tissue, which depends ultimately on the correct functioning of the cells comprising each component. While the experience of ageing varies hugely between individuals, according to an inextricable combination of genetics, environment and lifestyle, it is an incontrovertible fact that people's physical and often mental functionality diminishes with increasing chronological age; whether one likes it or not, ageing is the single biggest risk factor for morbidity and death, and many older people are living with a range of co-morbidities (multiple different diseases) that seriously affect their quality of life and risk of death (Pilotto et al, 2012). For example, the primary causes of admissions to care homes are stroke, dementia and incontinence (van Rensbergen and Nawrot, 2010; Maxwell et al, 2013). Major killers in later life are cardiovascular disease (ischaemic heart disease and stroke) and cancer (WHO, 2014), usually involving a long period of ill health prior to death. Other common late-life morbidities include chronic obstructive pulmonary disorder, non-healing ulcers, osteoporosis, muscle wasting, arthritis, progressive blindness and greatly increased susceptibility to infectious disease (to name only a subset) (Bowker et al, 2012).

Ageing *does* equate to detriment, to a greater or lesser extent, for the vast majority of the older population. Objectively, this can be measured: the last five years of life cost more to health services than the whole of the rest of the life course together (see, for example, Kelley et al, 2015). Although enormous, this financial costing does not take into account quality of life costs to the individual and to the family. Ageing well or badly is not a choice; it is a biological lottery in which genes play a large role. Age-related diseases happen even to the most abstemious and conscientious, and to suggest self-causation and ascribe blame is insulting and demeaning to the huge number of older people who suffer age-related disease. Biological ageing and its associated morbidities are not simply social constructs: animals as diverse as mice, horses and non-human primates (Colman et al, 2009; Yuan et al, 2011; Peffers et al, 2013) all suffer many of the same age-related changes and diseases as older humans – even microscopic nematode worms age in ways that biochemically are very similar to our own ageing (reviewed in Kenyon, 2010; Lees et al, 2016).

Mechanisms of biological ageing

Cell theory and cell senescence

It is current clinical practice to treat each disease of ageing as a separate entity: age-related macular degeneration is dealt with by an ophthalmologist, cancer by an oncologist, heart disease by a cardiologist, and so on. At the clinical level, this makes perfect sense, but does it make sense at the biological level? Is there a common factor that drives the onset of age-related diseases, and if so, can that common factor be modulated to delay or even prevent such diseases from developing? This is where we return to the cellular composition of the human body. It has been known since the landmark studies of Hayflick in 1961 that normal human cells have only a finite ability to divide when grown in culture (Hayflick and Moorhead, 1961). Once cells have undergone a specific number of cell divisions, they permanently lose the ability to divide further and are termed *senescent*.

Telomere attrition as a cause of replicative senescence

Some of the biological mechanisms underlying this finite cell division capacity have been uncovered by biological research. Every time a cell divides, it needs to copy its genetic material (the DNA) so that an exact copy is passed on to both resulting daughter cells. In healthy human cells, the tip of each of our 46 chromosomes is protected by a cap of proteins that promotes the DNA ends to tuck in on themselves and protects them from damage – this structure is called the telomere, and is made up of repetitive DNA sequences wrapped into a loop and coated with a protective 'shelterin' protein complex (Longhese et al, 2012). Because of the nature of DNA replication, a short region of DNA at the telomere is lost at each round of copying (Kipling, 1995). Eventually, such losses accumulate to the point at which telomeres become critically short and are detected by the cell as DNA damage (von Zglinicki et al, 2005). Cells respond to damage signals by up-regulating a host of proteins involved ultimately in preventing the damaged cell from ever dividing again – this is a critical cellular response, since passing on damaged DNA can lead to cells becoming cancerous. Telomere attrition is now known to be a major cause of cellular senescence (Wang et al, 2009; Fumagalli et al, 2012). Since senescence thus occurs as a consequence of multiple cell divisions, senescent cells are detected most in tissues with high cell turnover – the skin (Herbig et al, 2006; Jeyapalan et al, 2007; Waaijer et al, 2012), lining of the digestive tract (Saffrey, 2014) and lining of blood vessels (Chang and Harley, 1995). It is notable that these tissues are subject to shearing forces with concomitant loss of cells, and hence regular cell division is needed to replenish cells that have been shed. Indeed, failure of vascular bypass and stent operations after a period of time is related to accumulation of senescent cells at the junctions of the grafts, possibly exacerbated by the inclusion of slow-release drugs (Imanishi et al, 2006).

Low socioeconomic status and early life stresses are associated with greater disease burden and shorter lifespan (see, for example, ONS, 2014), and it has recently been shown that African-American boys from unstable family backgrounds have much shorter telomeres even by the age of nine than their peers from more stable families (Mitchell et al, 2014), which may contribute to lower life expectancy. The importance of telomere length in organismal ageing has been demonstrated experimentally in mice, where telomerase was reactivated in middle age; such mice showed marked regeneration of tissues that had undergone age-related decline, including gut, testes and brain

(Jaskelioff et al, 2011, reviewed in Cox and Mason, 2010). Because of the strong link between telomerase reactivation and cancer (and the finding that telomerase expression makes pre-existing cancers more aggressive; see Ding et al, 2012), we would not advocate the use of telomerase activators as a strategy to avoid senescent cell accumulation, but it is a notable proof of principle that telomere attrition-dependent cell senescence is a major contributor to age-related decline of tissue and organ function throughout the body.

Stress-induced premature senescence and oncogene-induced senescence

Cell turnover with telomere shortening is not the sole cause of cell senescence; the process has also been well documented to result from other types of damage, both endogenous and exogenous (reviewed by Chen et al, 2007).

One such senescence trigger is actually oxygen. Although we need oxygen to live, it can also pose dangers to our cells – within the mitochondria, particularly, where oxygen is used in the production of cellular energy, dangerous reactive oxygen species (ROS) can be generated. As demonstrated by a combined approach using experimental induction of senescence of cultured human cells, together with computational systems biology modelling, the earliest step towards senescence can be triggered by cells sensing high levels of ROS, which can damage DNA. The cellular signalling pathways invoked then lead to a positive feedback loop whereby the cells produce further ROS and reinforce the programme to enter senescence (Passos et al, 2010).

In addition to internal ROS, DNA damage caused by external agents such as excess sunlight, X-rays or toxic chemicals can lead to 'stress-induced premature senescence' (abbreviated to SIPS). Such senescent cells are metabolically and morphologically similar to those that have accumulated through telomere attrition, presumably because the initial trigger is in both instances the same – detection of DNA damage by the cells (Correia-Melo et al, 2014) – although there are also 'molecular scars' resulting from the initial trigger (Dierick et al, 2002). The DNA damage response (DDR) is thus an important component in senescence.

Some of the factors that lead to induction of senescence are important as sentinels against the development of cancer, and indeed senescence has been described as a tumour-suppressive mechanism (Campisi, 2001). It relies on key proteins that protect us from cancer from other causes, and loss of such factors (particularly a major tumour suppressor known as p53; see Rodier et al, 2007) will allow cells that should have entered senescence to continue dividing. Of note, then, is that senescence can also be triggered by inappropriate activation of cellular oncogenes (cancer-causing genes); our cells can detect unusual activity resulting from oncogene activation, such as high rates of DNA copying (Aird and Zhang, 2015), and respond by sending cells into the essentially irreversible state that is senescence. Note that 'irreversibility' is not strictly true of senescence, as further deleterious genetic mutations can lead to the re-entry of previously senescent cells into the cell division cycle, a process termed 'crisis' when it occurs in cultured cells, which results in oncogenic (cancerous) transformation. However, we have recently demonstrated a more physiological return to cell proliferation in non-cancerous senescent cells using drugs that target specific biochemical pathways (Walters et al, 2016, Latorre et al, 2017).

Senescence is therefore a response to a variety of cellular stresses, including imbalances in rates of protein production through changes in the levels of ribosomal proteins (Nishimura et al, 2015), as well as a response to unfolded proteins in mitochondria or the endoplasmic reticulum (Pluquet et al, 2015). In evolutionary terms, however, senescence may serve a somewhat different role, at the very beginning of human life. Formation of the surface of the placenta (the syncytiotrophoblast) occurs through cell fusion, resulting in a vast single cell that is responsible for providing boundary function; it also synthesises proteins needed to maintain the pregnancy and remodel the uterine lining to support the invasion of foetal blood vessels (reviewed in Cox and Redman, 2016). This fusion-induced senescence (Chuprin et al, 2013) may be an evolutionary side effect of the response to viruses that cause cell fusion, such as measles – indeed, one of the key proteins needed for placental formation is thought to derive from a viral gene that became incorporated into the mammalian genome millions of years ago (Mallet et al, 2004). It is notable that senescence has been shown to occur in early development (Muñoz-Espin et al, 2013; Storer et al, 2013; Davaapil et al, 2017) and in limb regeneration in salamanders (Yun et al, 2015). It is possible that senescence in response to cellular stresses evolved from essential developmental processes.

Impact of senescent cells on the body

Senescent cells are not simply passive within a tissue in which they accumulate. Significant changes in their metabolism can be measured biochemically by expression of senescence-associated-β-galactosidase (SA-β-gal), which, in simple terms, allows us to visualise senescent cells, as they can be stained blue by a specific dye that responds to SA-β-gal activity (Dimri et al, 1995). This change correlates with major intracellular stresses that suggest cells are unable to cope with accumulated damaged components including proteins and lipids that are biochemically altered: a younger cell would simply break down damaged components and recycle the useful building blocks, but this process of autophagy is disrupted in senescence (García-Prat et al, 2016). Moreover, gene expression patterns change markedly, and senescent cells have been shown to secrete a range of proteins that have detrimental effects on the surrounding cells and tissue structures, including inflammatory signalling molecules such as IL-6 and TNF-α. This is termed the senescence-associate secretory phenotype, or SASP (Coppe et al, 2008, 2010). It is possible that SASP signalling evolved to attract the immune system so that senescent cells can be effectively cleared from tissue (Muñoz-Espin et al, 2013; Storer et al, 2013; Davaapil et al, 2017), but as the immune system also ages (Vitlic et al, 2014), invocation of an inflammatory response instead results in local tissue destruction and chronic inflammation. It may be of particular significance that elevated TNF-α and IL-6 correlate with adverse cardiac outcomes in elderly people (Vasan et al, 2003). These results suggest that senescent cells (for example, circulating in the blood or in blood vessel endothelium) might directly contribute to heart attacks, one of the major causes of age-related disability and death.

In addition to invoking a chronic inflammatory state, senescent cells also generate enzymes that break down structures supporting tissues. For example, metalloproteases, including collagenase, that are secreted as part of the SASP by senescent cells, degrade the basement membrane that normally demarcates tissue boundaries and ensures the integrity of blood vessels. SASP-dependent chronic inflammation combined with tissue breakdown provides an ideal microenvironment for the spread of any cancerous cells, leading to dangerous metastases (Rodier and Campisi, 2011). Cancer incidence increases exponentially with age, and this may, in part, be due to changes in tissues that promote cancer spread. Hence the presence of senescent cells in tissues is detrimental, both locally and systemically. Experimental removal of senescent cells in prematurely ageing mice leads to significant improvements in many measures of tissue integrity and health (Baker et al, 2011); such work has now been extended to show the same rejuvenation properties of senescence cell removal in normal mice following treatment at middle age (Baker et al, 2016), further confirming the detrimental nature of senescent cells. The health benefits of senolytic drugs that selectively kill senescent cells in specific tissues such as fibrotic lungs and osteoarthritic joints are apparent in mouse studies, and such drugs are likely to be used in the human clinic within the very near future (reviewed by Kirkland et al, 2017).

Using progeroid syndromes to study ageing

The role of senescent cells in age-related disease is becoming widely accepted, but studying the biochemical pathways that sense senescence triggers and relay or mediate the cellular response is experimentally challenging, not least because of the multifactorial nature of ageing. However, although the products of many genes are likely to act in concert to influence the rate and outcomes of cellular ageing, it is remarkable that single genetic mutations can have disproportionately large effects on the entire ageing process from the level of molecules up to the whole body. Once such case is that of human progeroid Werner syndrome (WS) (reviewed in Goto, 2001; Cox and Faragher, 2007). WS patients experience a large range of age-associated changes, but highly prematurely. Their hair greys and thins from their teens onwards and their voices are often hoarse. They fail to undergo the pubertal growth spurt and are short in stature, with a very low body mass and little subcutaneous fat, although with fat redistribution to the abdomen. Skin wrinkling is common, and many patients suffer from non-healing ulcers, to the extent of requiring amputation in a relatively high percentage of cases. Metabolically, patients show poor blood sugar regulation and develop diabetes very early. Moreover, they prematurely develop atherosclerosis and cardiovascular disease because of lipodystrophy. The two leading causes of death in WS patients are cancer and cardiovascular disease (presumably from the aberrant regulation of fat with too much 'bad' fat circulating in the blood stream). So WS patients essentially mimic the normal ageing process, and patients with the syndrome develop many diseases normally associated with increasing chronological age (Goto and Miller, 2001). It is fair to say that WS is the best genetic model we currently have of 'normal' human ageing.

What makes the syndrome useful to study biochemically is that all these age-related changes result from mutation of a single gene, WRN (Yu et al, 1996). This gene encodes a large protein with two distinct enzymatic functions: it can remove broken DNA ends using its exonuclease function and it can untangle intertwined DNA using its helicase activity (Gray et al, 1997; Huang et al, 1998). When either of these activities is dysfunctional, the cell's DNA becomes unstable. Additionally WRN protein has binding sites for both DNA and other proteins within the cell, allowing it to interact directly with important cellular regulatory factors. We have previously shown that WRN is required for normal copying of the DNA prior to every cell division (Rodriguez-Lopez et al, 2002) and that it is present at a subset of all sites where DNA is being made, associating with a critical replication/ repair protein called PCNA (Rodriguez-Lopez et al, 2003). WRN is also implicated in telomere maintenance, by binding to the shelterin proteins (Opresko et al, 2002) and possibly also by virtue of its exonuclease and/or helicase activities (Opresko et al, 2004). Production of cellular RNA is also aberrant when WRN is non-functional (Balajee et al, 1999). Thus WRN has multiple biochemical effects within the cell and is said to be pleiotropic in action.

Importantly, when considering using WS as an investigative tool to study cell ageing, cells from WS patients prematurely enter cell senescence when cultured *in vitro* (Faragher et al, 1993). Gene expression analyses have validated WS as an extremely useful model for studying human ageing, as changes in gene expression normally detected in very old cells are observed in young WS patient-derived cells (Kyng et al, 2003), even under conditions of stress (Kyng et al, 2005). Genome-wide association studies have also implicated WRN in normal ageing: Finnish centenarians have been reported to carry a specific variant of the WRN gene that may contribute to their longevity (Castro et al, 2000), and similarly single nucleotide polymorphism analysis suggests that certain WRN variants are more generally associated with longevity (Lunetta et al, 2007). It is therefore likely that cells expressing WRN are protected from early ageing, and that those in which WRN is dysfunctional or absent will age quickly.

Aims of the research

We now believe that there is sufficient hard evidence from both observation and intervention to support the assertion that senescent cell accumulation is not only correlative with ageing, but also causative of detrimental changes. Thus this project set out to study the biochemical pathways leading to cell senescence in order to permit future development of targeted strategies to ameliorate age-related morbidity. To do this, we explored two main experimental objectives:

1. Generation of molecular tools designed to knock down WRN: We developed an experimental system using molecular biology

tools to generate novel DNA constructs that we introduced into cells, to enable us to down-regulate WRN protein levels at will in human cells in culture.

2. Analysis of changes in protein composition of cells as they undergo replicative senescence in culture: First, we had to age cells in culture and verify senescence. We examined cells down the microscope to assess shape and size, in combination with known biomarkers of ageing, to be confident that we had obtained senescent cells. We then conducted studies using mass spectrometry to assess the protein composition of cells at different stages as they progressed towards senescence.

Methodology

We adopted parallel experimental approaches to achieve our aims and objectives. First, we needed to develop a genetic tool to induce cellular senescence, and we chose to do this by switching off the anti-ageing gene WRN in human cells, to recapitulate WS in isogenic cell lines, that is, without the problem of underlying genetic diversity found between WS patients and avoiding accumulated DNA damage that occurs over time in patient cells lacking WRN function.

We employed short hairpin RNAi to target WRN through the pathway of RNA interference (Paddison et al, 2002), to reduce WRN expression. DNA constructs were generated by standard molecular biology techniques, amplified, purified and verified by DNA sequence analysis. They were then transfected into proliferating human cells in culture. We validated the level of WRN reduction, using immunoblotting and immunofluorescence microscopy with anti-WRN antibodies compared with controls (to ensure that an equal amount of cells and proteins were being tested in all cases). These molecular tools were designed to knockdown WRN as soon as they were introduced into human cells. We then went on to test whether the cells with decreased WRN levels showed phenotypes typical of WS patient cells, in particular, sensitivity to the anti-cancer drug camptothecin. DNA constructs were therefore transfected into growing human cells in culture, the cells were treated with 10 μM camptothecin and the degree of DNA damage assessed by looking for DNA fragmentation in a 'comet' assay, whereby treated cells are immobilised in agarose and exposed to an electrical field that draws any broken DNA out of the nuclei. This part of the project was conducted as a collaboration with the laboratories of Professor Richard Faragher in Brighton, UK and Professor Judy Campisi of the Buck Institute for Research on Aging, Novato, USA, who provided other shRNAi constructs and additional WRN knockdown tools termed ribozymes, for comparison of the impact of hairpin RNAi versus ribozyme-mediated WRN knockdown.

We also set out to develop a more complex system with the aim of being able to control the timing and degree of WRN knockdown, rather than causing knockdown at the point at which the molecular tools first enter the human cells. This was important as long-term loss of WRN leads cells to undergo senescence (and cease dividing) prematurely, whereas we wanted to be able to generate large number of cells prior to switching off WRN, in order to obtain sufficient biological material to test for differences between senescent and proliferating cells of the same genetic lineage.

Using standard molecular biology techniques, we obtained a synthetic DNA cassette encoding a hairpin RNA structure with sequence homology to the human WRN gene, fused to the coding sequence for jellyfish green fluorescent protein (GFP). We then attempted to clone this into a plasmid vector (a small circular DNA molecule that can be propagated in human cells) using standard genetic engineering techniques of restriction enzyme digestion, DNA fragment purification and ligation (molecular joining of the DNA backbone using a enzyme called DNA ligase). The acceptor vector contained a DNA sequence to which a specific regulatory protein called a transcription factor could bind. The construct proved challenging to produce using traditional molecular cloning methods, so we developed a method to generate the correct construct using polymerase chain reaction (PCR) to make multiple copies of the cassette, which were then used as 'mega primers' in a subsequent PCR to generate the final plasmid. The plasmid was amplified by growing up in *E. coli* bacteria, and the DNA purified. To check that the generated plasmid was correct, we conducted diagnostic restriction enzyme digests and DNA sequencing reactions.

To permit regulated expression of the anti-WRN cassette, we transfected the plasmid into human cells grown under sterile conditions in plastic tissue culture flasks in Dulbecco's Modified Eagle's Medium with high glucose and glutamine plus 10% FCS in 5% CO_2/air atmosphere in a humidified incubator at 37°C. We co-transfected in a plasmid encoding the transcription factor to which our engineered cassette is responsive. This transcription factor is expressed constitutively (that is, all the time), and is able to bind the regulatory region of the engineered cassette. However, it is inactive until the addition of a small drug-like molecule derived from an insect hormone, whereupon it changes shape and drives gene expression from the DNA under its control. The added 'drug' readily enters cells, is non-toxic and does not affect endogenous cellular proteins. Moreover, the expression from the engineered cassette should be proportional to the amount of drug added, and the expression should be reversible simply by removal of the drug from the cell culture medium.

Because this is a complex regulatory loop requiring all aspects of the engineered DNA cassette, transcription factor and drug to function correctly, it was necessary to conduct preliminary proof of concept tests looking for drug-induced expression of a measurable factor (looking for expression of something not normally present is easier than testing for something to be turned off). For this, we chose to use the fire-fly luciferase gene under the control of the regulatory region in the first plasmid, and looked for light emission on addition of the drug to cells.

To address the second aim, we aged cells by growing them in culture to allow both assessment of markers of senescence and collection of material for protein analysis. Primary human fibroblasts were grown (as above) in tissue culture. Cells were seeded to a density that covered approximately a quarter of the flask surface, and harvested before they became confluent, with cell density assessed visually and/or by counting cell number using a Cellometer T4™ (Nexcelom). Population doublings were calculated according to the formula:

$$PD = $$
$$(\log_{10} (\text{number of cells harvested/number of cells seeded}))/\log_{10}(2)$$

Cumulative population doublings (CPD) were hence determined and plotted as a function of time in culture. CPD was correlated with cell morphology as determined by phase contrast, fluorescence and immunofluorescence microscopy and immunohistochemistry. Because of telomere shortening at every cell division (see the section on cell theory), sub-culturing cells in the laboratory over many months (or years) can result in an entire population of cells that have undergone senescence. It was necessary to be able to distinguish 'young' from 'old' cells biochemically as well as by their chronological age or number of population doublings, so we adopted a standard dye assay (SA-β-gal; see Dimri et al, 1995) as well as testing other potential markers of cell ageing.

Cells were harvested at several stages during the natural ageing process in order to extract all of the proteins, the proteins were broken down into small peptide units (by trypsin digestion) and then the molecular mass of the peptide fragments determined using mass spectrometry (LCMSMS orbitrap; see Walther and Mann, 2010). Mascot bioinformatics software (Matrix Science, 2014) was used to analyse the data in order to identify both the peptide fragments based on their mass (PeptideProphet) and the parent protein, according to the frequency, mass and predicted sequence of matching peptide fragments (ProteinProphet). It was also possible to determine relative levels of proteins between samples. Identified proteins that showed significant changes during the ageing process (either increased/decreased or absent/present) were manually curated into functional categories.

Findings

To obtain senescent cells in the laboratory takes many months or even years of painstaking cell culture under strict sterile conditions, with regular feeding and sub-culturing – an average experiment will take at least six months to complete, with a further few months to analyse outcomes. Bearing in mind that at least three biological replicates are commonly performed to ensure validity, data generation using senescent cells can take two to three years to answer individual experimental questions. To try to develop a physiological system in which we can enhance the rate of cell senescence in culture (and hence speed up the rate of biochemical pathway discovery), we chose to exploit the naturally occurring human premature ageing WS. Since loss of function of the single WRN protein can lead to many of the changes of ageing, we reasoned that experimentally removing WRN from cultured human cells would similarly lead to premature senescence.

In order to alter WRN levels in cells, we had to interfere with the process of gene expression. Genes are stretches of DNA that code for functional products. The three-letter genetic code (made up triplets from the four building blocks, A, T, G or C) needs to be decoded into amino acids in order to make functional proteins. This occurs by a two-step process. First, the DNA is transcribed into a transient copy called messenger RNA (chemically similar to DNA and still using the triplet code). The RNA is then decoded in a process fittingly called translation, to make a functional protein. To interfere with WRN gene expression, we therefore designed a tool to prevent translation of the WRN mRNA, by exploiting a cellular mechanism of control through very small RNA molecules (Paddison et al, 2002). We designed in essence a small anti-WRN gene to block WRN protein production, in order to deplete WRN levels in cells.

Using both short hairpin and ribozyme tools, we successfully depleted WRN protein in human cells in culture and moreover showed that even limited levels of WRN depletion could lead to the development of WS-like features such as hypersensitivity to the anti-cancer drug camptothecin. This work was published (Bird et al, 2012), with the suggestion that the impact of camptothecin or similar drugs to treat cancer might be enhanced by agents that reduce WRN levels.

Furthermore, we successfully generated an engineered plasmid containing a regulatable WRN knockdown construct, although the genetic engineering and cloning steps required to produce this expression system were complex and time-consuming. Transfection of the engineered plasmid into human cells in culture (a rapidly growing cancer cell line called HeLa, and importantly also normal human fibroblasts) together with the transcription factor-encoding plasmid was also successfully achieved. The dual level of control allowed us to start selection for cell lines that had incorporated both anti-WRN and transcription factor-encoding vectors, before switching on the anti-WRN cassette. In addition, by fusing the GFP gene to the anti-WRN cassette, we were able to monitor expression of the anti-WRN product using GFP fluorescence as a proxy readout. The positive control (expressing luciferase) showed regulatable expression on drug addition, validating the system. Once the drug was added to cells containing the WRN-knockdown construct, the anti-WRN-GFP fusion gene was expressed as RNA, normal human enzymes present within the transfected cells cleaved the anti-WRN RNA that was processed to form a functional inhibitory RNA and the adjacent GFP-encoding RNA was then translated into functional protein by the normal cellular translation machinery, making the cells that had expressed the construct glow green under fluorescence microscopy. WRN levels were shown to be decreased on drug addition, as assayed by immunoblotting with anti-WRN antibodies, hence drug-dependent knockdown of WRN was achieved.

Analysis of protein differences between young and senescent cells

In parallel with the development of the molecular anti-WRN tool, which posed multiple technical challenges that took a significant time to overcome, we also explored the effect of natural replicative senescence on protein levels within cells in order to ensure that we could analyse young/old cell protein differences within the time frame of the NDA project. To do this required growing cells in the laboratory for over 150 days until they reached senescence. Cells at several stages along the senescence trajectory were harvested and protein composition analysed using a technique known as mass spectrometry. In essence, the cells were burst open to release their contents, proteins were isolated and subjected to controlled breakdown into smaller parts (by an enzyme that cuts proteins at very specific sites), which were then analysed by placing them in a machine that ionises the fragments and then measures their mass. By piecing together all the mass data and comparing with a database of all known and predicted proteins (according to the published sequence of the human genome), we can identify which proteins were present in which cell samples, and obtain a measure of relative levels. Our results suggested that as cells senesce, they activate DNA damage-response pathways; in addition, levels of other stress response factors were also elevated. Furthermore, we saw changes in tissue remodelling factors between young and senescent cells, consistent with previous reported findings that senescent cells damage the tissue in which they exist.

Key findings
- Cell senescence is likely to underlie many age-related deleterious changes seen in the body.
- A novel molecular tool has been developed to selectively remove a key anti-ageing protein from cells. Loss of this protein results in early onset of many of the signs and diseases of normal ageing, together with highly premature cellular senescence.
- The new molecular tool responds to a small chemical switch that allows tight regulation of the protein in cells. This tool should enhance the progress of biochemical research on cell senescence in the laboratory.
- As cells age, they express elevated levels of DNA damage-response proteins and various other stress-response factors. Cellular stress and stress signalling are therefore likely to be involved in driving cellular senescence.
- A potential anti-ageing drug rapamycin significantly affects the rate of onset of senescence, that is, the trajectory of cell senescence can be modulated using a clinically licensed drug.

Conclusions

In conclusion, therefore, we have demonstrated that senescence can be studied in the laboratory (for example, by WRN removal), and that senescence is associated with marked changes in protein composition, highlighting novel pathways of study for altering senescence onset. So what are the immediate next steps and the wider implications for an ageing society?

It is possible that without an understanding of the biological basis of ageing, our aims to describe biological ageing and senescent cells in terms of detriment, and our goal of delaying the appearance of – or even removing entirely – senescent cells from the body may be misunderstood. Our data clearly demonstrate that senescent cells are different at the molecular level from 'young' cells; and these differences are detrimental to overall health. We have followed these findings up since the NDA project by conducting more detailed proteomics analyses and by targeting molecular pathways highlighted in this way. For example, we recently reported reversal of many detrimental phenotypes of senescence using both a commercially available drug (Walters et al, 2016) and newly developed drugs (Latorre et al, 2017).

We argue strongly here that age-related decrease in functionality of parts of the body do not render that person any less valuable to society, and that ageing for many brings with it positive benefits (such as accumulated wisdom and experience), despite inevitable physical decline. What we and other biological gerontologists are trying to do is to tackle the biological deficits of ageing while retaining full regard and respect for the person. A young person with cancer contains detrimental and dangerous cells, which medical science aims to remove or destroy; it is a moral duty of society to develop better treatment and work towards a cure for cancer, and huge resources go into biological and medical research to better understand the enormous range of diseases that comprise 'cancer'. No one would ever consider a patient *with* cancer to be *a* cancer within society. Similarly, older adults contain senescent cells that inflict adverse consequences on the individual; it would be beneficial to remove or destroy such cells. We contest the view (surprisingly widely encountered in the social sciences) that biogerontologists equate the accumulation of detrimental cells in the body to an older person being detrimental to society. This could not be further from the truth. The individual as a person is untainted by the fact that dysfunctional cells are present within them, in ageing as in cancer; biogerontologists simply seek to understand and then treat the diseases associated with older age by understanding the underlying causes of cell and biological ageing and developing novel therapies based on that greater knowledge.

What would be the immediate outcome if we succeed in our goal of treating senescence and hence compressing morbidity? There is a populist fear that enhancing the health of people in later life would markedly increase their lifespan and that the whole structure of society would disintegrate if the balance between young and old were shifted significantly. A quick glance at any demographic study over the past 100 years would show that society has indeed shifted significantly towards an older population (Burger et al, 2012), thanks in large part to improved sanitation, housing, diet and antibiotics. Very few would argue that this societal shift has been of major detriment. If our aim of treating – or better still, preventing – age-related disease becomes a reality through research of the type undertaken on the NDA programme, it *is* likely to have the knock-on effect of increasing the number of years alive (perhaps by as much as 10-12 years); however, such years would be beneficial years, to the individual, their family and society, since that person would be more able to continue to live independently and contribute positively to society.

Evidence supporting this assertion comes from the studies of Nir Barzilai, who is analysing the genetic predisposition to healthy later life in a population of Ashkenazi Jewish supercentenarians in New York (Barzilai, 2014). Such studies have shown clearly that improved health adds years to life; most importantly, however, it also shows that those years can be used productively and positively without an additional cost to society. So increasing longevity does not have to increase the tax burden on the young, or involve longer stays in residential care; it aims, instead, for the opposite situation, where older adults live healthy productive lives until the end. Professor Barzilai's study group did not evade death, simply the morbidities associated with later life in the majority of the population. Thus, increasing healthy ageing can have the required outcome of decreasing the morbid period at the end of life. In order to increase *healthy* ageing, we argue that it is imperative to tackle the issue of senescent cell accumulation.

This NDA-funded project not only achieved its initial aims, but also extended them to provide proof-of-principle that senescence can be modified in human cells by understanding the underlying biochemical pathways. The implications of ageing research and the future development of treatment of age-related diseases are significant: age-related disease could and should be treated and not simply be accepted as a natural consequence of increasing years. Cell senescence is likely to provide a central underlying mechanism that underpins the development of many otherwise dissimilar age-related diseases, and understanding biochemical pathways that contribute to senescence is key to developing novel modes of treatment for senescence. Such research is extremely cost-effective as it tackles a large range of highly deleterious outcomes by treating the cause rather than the symptoms.

Delaying the onset of senescence, clearing senescent cells efficiently from tissues, reversing their deleterious effects or preventing their accumulation at all should therefore have marked health span benefits and increase the health, wellbeing and quality of life in the older population.

References

Aird, K.M. and Zhang, R. (2015) 'Nucleotide metabolism, oncogene-induced senescence and cancer', *Cancer Letters*, vol 356, pp 204-10.

Baker, D.J., Wijshake, T., Tchkonia, T., Lebrasseur, N.K., Childs, B.G., van de Sluis, B., et al (2011) 'Clearance of p16Ink4a-positive senescent cells delays ageing-associated disorders', *Nature*, vol 479, pp 232-6.

Baker, D.J., Childs, B.G., Durik, M., Wijers, M.E., Sieben, C.J., Zhong, J., et al (2016) 'Naturally occurring p16(Ink4a)-positive cells shorten healthy lifespan', *Nature*, vol 530, pp 184-9.

Balajee, A.S., Machwe, A., May, A., Gray, M.D., Oshima, J., Martin, G.M., et al (1999) 'The Werner syndrome protein is involved in RNA polymerase II transcription', *Molecular Biology of the Cell*, vol 10, pp 2655-68.

Barzilai, N. (2014) 'The Longevity Genes Project'. Available at www. einstein.yu.edu/centers/aging/longevity-genes-project/

Bird, J.L.E., Jennert-Burston, K.C.B., Bachler, M.A., Mason, P.A., Lowe, J.E., Heo, S.-J., et al (2012) 'Recapitulation of Werner syndrome sensitivity to camptothecin by limited knockdown of the WRN helicase/exonuclease', *Biogerontology*, vol 13, no 1, pp 49-62.

Bowker, L., Price, J. and Smith, S. (2012) *Oxford handbook of geriatric medicine*, Oxford: Oxford University Press.

Burger, O., Baudisch, A. and Vaupel, J.W. (2012) 'Human mortality improvement in evolutionary context', *Proceedings of the National Academy of Sciences of the USA*, vol 109, pp 18210-14.

Campisi, J. (2001) 'Cellular senescence as a tumor-suppressor mechanism', *Trends in Cell Biology*, vol 11, S27-31.

Castro, E., Edland, S.D., Lee, L., Ogburn, C.E., Deeb, S.S., Brown, G., et al (2000) 'Polymorphisms at the Werner locus: II. 1074Leu/Phe, 1367Cys/Arg, longevity, and atherosclerosis', *American Journal of Medical Genetics*, vol 95, pp 374-80.

Chang, E. and Harley, C.B. (1995) 'Telomere length and replicative aging in human vascular tissues', *Proceedings of the National Academy of Sciences of the USA*, vol 92, pp 11190-4.

Chen, J.H., Hales, C.N. and Ozanne, S.E. (2007) 'DNA damage, cellular senescence and organismal ageing: Causal or correlative?', *Nucleic Acids Research*, vol 35, pp 7417-28.

Chuprin, A., Gal, H., Biron-Shental, T., Biran, A., Amiel, A., Rozenblatt, S. and Krizhanovsky, V. (2013) 'Cell fusion induced by ERVWE1 or measles virus causes cellular senescence', *Genes & Development*, vol 27, pp 2356-66.

Colman, R.J., Anderson, R.M., Johnson, S.C., Kastman, E.K., Kosmatka, K.J., Beasley, T.M., et al (2009) 'Caloric restriction delays disease onset and mortality in rhesus monkeys', *Science*, vol 325, pp 201-4.

Coppe, J.P., Desprez, P.Y., Krtolica, A. and Campisi, J. (2010) 'The senescence-associated secretory phenotype: The dark side of tumor suppression', *Annual Review of Pathology*, vol 5, pp 99-118.

Coppe, J.P., Patil, C.K., Rodier, F., Sun, Y., Muñoz, D.P., Goldstein, J., et al (2008) 'Senescence-associated secretory phenotypes reveal cell-nonautonomous functions of oncogenic RAS and the p53 tumor suppressor', *PLoS Biology*, vol 6, pp 2853-68.

Correia-Melo, C., Hewitt, G. and Passos, J.F. (2014) 'Telomeres, oxidative stress and inflammatory factors: Partners in cellular senescence?', *Longevity & Healthspan*, vol 3, p 1.

Cox, L.S. and Faragher, R.G. (2007) 'From old organisms to new molecules: Integrative biology and therapeutic targets in accelerated human ageing', *Cellular and Molecular Life Sciences*, vol 64, pp 2620-41.

Cox, L.S. and Mason, P.A. (2010) 'Prospects for rejuvenation of aged tissue by telomerase reactivation', *Rejuvenation Research*, vol 13, pp 749-54.

Cox, L.S. and Redman, C. (2017) 'The role of cellular senescence in ageing of the placenta', *Placenta*, vol 52, pp 139-45.

Davaapil, H., Brockes, J.P. and Yun, M.H. (2017) 'Conserved and novel functions of programmed cellular senescence during vertebrate development', *Development*, vol 144, pp 106-14.

Dierick, J.F., Eliaers, F., Remacle, J., Raes, M., Fey, S.J., Larsen, P.M. and Toussaint, O. (2002) 'Stress-induced premature senescence and replicative senescence are different phenotypes, proteomic evidence', *Biochemical Pharmacology*, vol 64, pp 1011-17.

Dimri, G.P., Lee, X., Basile, G., Acosta, M., Scott, G., Roskelley, C., et al (1995) 'A biomarker that identifies senescent human cells in culture and in aging skin in vivo', *Proceedings of the National Academy of Sciences of the USA*, vol 92, pp 9363-7.

Ding, Z., Wu, C.J., Jaskelioff, M., Ivanova, E., Kost-Alimova, M., Protopopov, A., et al (2012) 'Telomerase reactivation following telomere dysfunction yields murine prostate tumors with bone metastases', *Cell*, vol 148, pp 896-907.

Faragher, R.G., Kill, I.R., Hunter, J.A., Pope, F.M., Tannock, C. and Shall, S. (1993) 'The gene responsible for Werner syndrome may be a cell division "counting" gene', *Proceedings of the National Academy of Sciences of the USA*, vol 90, pp 12030-4.

Fumagalli, M., Rossiello, F., Clerici, M., Barozzi, S., Cittaro, D., Kaplunov, J.M., et al (2012) 'Telomeric DNA damage is irreparable and causes persistent DNA-damage-response activation', *Nature Cell Biology*, vol 14, pp 355-65.

García-Prat, L., Martínez-Vicente, M., Perdiguero, E., Ortet, L., Rodríguez-Ubreva, J., Rebollo, E., et al (2016) 'Autophagy maintains stemness by preventing senescence', *Nature*, vol 529, pp 37-42.

Goto, M. (2001) 'Clinical characteristics of Werner syndrome and other premature aging syndromes: Pattern of aging in progeroid syndromes', in M. Goto and R.W. Miller (eds) *From premature gray hair to helicase – Werner syndrome: Implications for aging and cancer*, Tokyo: Japan Scientific Societies Press, pp 27-40.

Goto, M. and Miller, R.W. (2001) *From premature gray hair to helicase – Werner syndrome: Implications for aging and cancer* (Gann Monograph on Cancer Research), Berlin: Karger Publishers.

Gray, M.D., Shen, J.C., Kamath-Loeb, A.S., Blank, A., Sopher, B.L., Martin, G.M., et al (1997) 'The Werner syndrome protein is a DNA helicase', *Nature Genetics*, vol 17, pp 100-3.

Hayflick, L. and Moorhead, P.S. (1961) 'The serial cultivation of human diploid cell strains', *Experimental Cell Research*, vol 25, pp 585-621.

Herbig, U., Ferreira, M., Condel, L., Carey, D. and Sedivy, J.M. (2006) 'Cellular senescence in aging primates', *Science*, vol 311, p 1257.

Huang, S., Li, B., Gray, M.D., Oshima, J., Mian, I.S. and Campisi, J. (1998) 'The premature ageing syndrome protein, WRN, is a $3' \rightarrow 5'$ exonuclease', *Nature Genetics*, vol 20, pp 114-16.

Imanishi, T., Kobayashi, K., Kuki, S., Takahashi, C. and Akasaka, T. (2006) 'Sirolimus accelerates senescence of endothelial progenitor cells through telomerase inactivation', *Atherosclerosis*, vol 189, pp 288-96.

Jaskelioff, M., Muller, F.L., Paik, J.H., Thomas, E., Jiang, S., Adams, A.C., et al (2011) 'Telomerase reactivation reverses tissue degeneration in aged telomerase-deficient mice', *Nature*, vol 469, pp 102-6.

Jeyapalan, J.C., Ferreira, M., Sedivy, J.M. and Herbig, U. (2007) 'Accumulation of senescent cells in mitotic tissue of aging primates', *Mechanisms of Ageing and Development*, vol 128, pp 36-44.

Kelley, A.S., McGarry, K., Gorges, R. and Skinner, J.S. (2015) 'The burden of health care costs in the last 5 years of life', *Annals of Internal Medicine*, vol 163, pp 729-36.

Kenyon, C.J. (2010) 'The genetics of ageing', *Nature*, vol 464, pp 504-12.

Kipling, D. (1995) *The telomere*, New York: Oxford University Press.

Kirkland, J.L., Tchkonia, T., Zhu, Y., Niedernhofer, L.J. and Robbins, P.D. (2017) 'The clinical potential of senolytic drugs', *Journal of the American Geriatrics Society*, vol 65, pp 2297-301.

Kyng, K.J., May, A., Kolvraa, S. and Bohr, V.A. (2003) 'Gene expression profiling in Werner syndrome closely resembles that of normal aging', *Proceedings of the National Academy of Sciences of the USA*, vol 100, pp 12259-64.

Kyng, K.J., May, A., Stevnsner, T., Becker, K.G., Kolvra, S. and Bohr, V.A. (2005) 'Gene expression responses to DNA damage are altered in human aging and in Werner Syndrome', *Oncogene*, vol 24, pp 5026-42.

Latorre, E., Birar, V.C., Sheerin, A.N., Jeynes, J.C.C, Hooper, A., Dawe, H.R., et al (2017) 'Small molecule modulation of splicing factor expression is associated with rescue from cellular senescence', *BMC Cell Biology*, vol 18, p 31.

Lees, H., Walters, H. and Cox, L.S. (2016) 'Animal and human models to understand ageing', *Maturitas*, vol 93, pp 18-27.

Longhese, M.P., Anbalagan, S., Martina, M. and Bonetti, D. (2012) 'The role of shelterin in maintaining telomere integrity', *Frontiers in Bioscience (Landmark Ed)*, vol 17, pp 1715-28.

Lunetta, K.L., D'Agostino, R.B., Sr, Karaski, D., Benjamin, E.J., Guo, C.Y., Govindaraju, R., et al (2007) 'Genetic correlates of longevity and selected age-related phenotypes: A genome-wide association study in the Framingham Study', *BMC Medical Genetics*, vol 8, Suppl 1, S13.

Mallet, F., Bouton, O., Prudhomme, S., Cheynet, V., Oriol, G., Bonnaud, B., et al (2004) 'The endogenous retroviral locus ERVWE1 is a bona fide gene involved in hominoid placental physiology', *Proceedings of the National Academy of Sciences of the USA*, vol 10, pp 1731-6.

Matrix Science (2014) *Mascot proteomics software*. Available at www.matrixscience.com/

Maxwell, C.J., Soo, A., Hogan, D.B., Wodchis, W.P., Gilbart, E., Amuah, J., et al (2013) 'Predictors of nursing home placement from assisted living settings in Canada', *Canadian Journal on Aging*, vol 32, pp 333-48.

Mitchell, C., Hobcraft, J., McLanahan, S.S., Siegel, S.R., Berg, A., Brooks-Gunn, J., et al (2014) 'Social disadvantage, genetic sensitivity, and children's telomere length', *Proceedings of the National Academy of Sciences of the USA*, vol 111, pp 5944-9.

Muñoz-Espin, D., Canamero, M., Maraver, A., Gomez-Lopez, G., Contreras, J., Murillo-Cuesta, S., et al (2013) 'Programmed cell senescence during mammalian embryonic development', *Cell*, vol 155, pp 1104-18.

Nishimura, K., Kumazawa, T., Kuroda, T., Katagiri, N., Tsuchiya, M., Goto, N., et al (2015) 'Perturbation of ribosome biogenesis drives cells into senescence through 5S RNP-mediated p53 activation', *Cell Reports*, vol 10, pp 1310-23.

ONS (Office for National Statistics) (2014) *Life expectancy at birth and at age 65 for health areas in the United Kingdom, 2003-05 to 2007-09.* Available at www.ons.gov.uk/ons/publications/re-reference-tables. html?edition=tcm%3A77-235372

Opresko, P.L., von Kobbe, C., Laine, J.P., Harrigan, J., Hickson, I.D. and Bohr, V.A. (2002) 'Telomere-binding protein TRF2 binds to and stimulates the Werner and Bloom syndrome helicases', *Journal of Biological Chemistry*, vol 277, pp 41110-19.

Opresko, P.L., Otterlei, M., Graakjaer, J., Bruheim, P., Dawut, L., Kolvraa, S., et al (2004) 'The Werner syndrome helicase and exonuclease cooperate to resolve telomeric D loops in a manner regulated by TRF1 and TRF2', *Molecular Cell*, vol 14, pp 763-74.

Paddison, P.J., Caudy, A.A., Bernstein, E., Hannon, G.J. and Conklin, D.S. (2002) 'Short hairpin RNAs (shRNAs) induce sequence-specific silencing in mammalian cells', *Genes & Development*, vol 16, pp 948-58.

Passos, J.F., Nelson, G., Wang, C., Richter, T., Simillion, C., Proctor, C.J., et al (2010) 'Feedback between p21 and reactive oxygen production is necessary for cell senescence', *Molecular Systems Biology*, vol 6, p 347.

Peffers, M.J., Liu, X. and Clegg, P.D. (2013) 'Transcriptomic signatures in cartilage ageing', *Arthritis Research & Therapy*, vol 15, R98.

Pilotto, A., Rengo, F., Marchionni, N., Sancarlo, D., Fontana, A., Panza, F., et al (2012) 'Comparing the prognostic accuracy for all-cause mortality of frailty instruments: A multicentre 1-year follow-up in hospitalized older patients', *PLoS One*, vol 7, e29090.

Pluquet, O., Pourtier, A. and Abbadie, C. (2015) 'The unfolded protein response and cellular senescence. A review in the theme: Cellular mechanisms of endoplasmic reticulum stress signaling in health and disease', *American Journal of Physiology-Cell Physiology*, vol 308, C415-C425.

Rodier, F. and Campisi, J. (2011) 'Four faces of cellular senescence', *Journal of Cell Biology*, vol 192, pp 547-56.

Rodier, F., Campisi, J. and Bhaumik, D. (2007) 'Two faces of p53: Aging and tumor suppression', *Nucleic Acids Research*, vol 35, pp 7475-84.

Rodriguez-Lopez, A.M., Jackson, D.A., Iborra, F. and Cox, L.S. (2002) 'Asymmetry of DNA replication fork progression in Werner's syndrome', *Aging Cell*, vol 1, pp 30-9.

Rodriguez-Lopez, A.M., Jackson, D.A., Nehlin, J.O., Iborra, F., Warren, A.V. and Cox, L.S. (2003) 'Characterisation of the interaction between WRN, the helicase/exonuclease defective in progeroid Werner's syndrome, and an essential replication factor, PCNA', *Mechanisms of Ageing and Development*, vol 124, pp 167-74.

Saffrey, M.J. (2014) 'Aging of the mammalian gastrointestinal tract: A complex organ system', *Age (Dordr)*, vol 9603.

Spalding, K.L., Bhardwaj, R.D., Buchholz, B.A., Druid, H. and Frisen, J. (2005) 'Retrospective birth dating of cells in humans', *Cell*, vol 122, pp 133-43.

Storer, M., Mas, A., Robert-Moreno, A., Pecoraro, M., Ortells, M.C., di Giacomo, V., et al (2013) 'Senescence is a developmental mechanism that contributes to embryonic growth and patterning', *Cell*, vol 155, pp 1119-30.

van Rensbergen, G. and Nawrot, T. (2010) 'Medical conditions of nursing home admissions', *BMC Geriatrics*, vol 10, p 46.

Vasan, R.S., Sullivan, L.M., Roubenoff, R., Dinarello, C.A., Harris, T., Benjamin, E.J., et al (2003) 'Inflammatory markers and risk of heart failure in elderly subjects without prior myocardial infarction: The Framingham Heart Study', *Circulation*, vol 107, pp 1486-91.

Vitlic, A., Lord, J.M. and Phillips, A.C. (2014) 'Stress, ageing and their influence on functional, cellular and molecular aspects of the immune system', *Age (Dordr)*, vol 36, p 9631.

von Zglinicki, T., Saretzki, G., Ladhoff, J., D'Adda di Fagagna, F. and Jackson, S.P. (2005) 'Human cell senescence as a DNA damage response', *Mechanics of Ageing and Development*, vol 126, pp 111-17.

Waaijer, M.E., Parish, W.E., Strongitharm, B.H., van Heemst, D., Slagboom, P.E., de Craen, A.J., et al (2012) 'The number of p16INK4a positive cells in human skin reflects biological age', *Aging Cell*, vol 11, pp 722-5.

Walters, H.E., Deneka-Hannemann, S. and Cox, L.S. (2016) 'Reversal of phenotypes of cellular senescence by pan-mTOR inhibition', *Aging (Albany NY)*, vol 8, pp 231-44.

Walther, T.C. and Mann, M. (2010) 'Mass spectrometry-based proteomics in cell biology', *Journal of Cell Biology*, vol 190, pp 491-500.

Wang, C., Jurk, D., Maddick, M., Nelson, G., Martin-Ruiz, C. and von Zglinicki, T. (2009) 'DNA damage response and cellular senescence in tissues of aging mice', *Aging Cell*, vol 8, pp 311-23.

WHO (World Health Organization) (2014) 'The top 10 causes of death'. Available at www.who.int/mediacentre/factsheets/fs310/en/index1.html

Yu, C.E., Oshima, J., Fu, Y.H., Wijsman, E.M., Hisama, F., Alisch, R., et al (1996) 'Positional cloning of the Werner's syndrome gene', *Science*, vol 272, pp 258-62.

Yun, M.H., Davaapil, H. and Brockes, J.P. (2015) 'Recurrent turnover of senescent cells during regeneration of a complex structure', *Elife*, 5 May, p 4.

Yuan, R., Peters, L.L. and Paigen, B. (2011) 'Mice as a mammalian model for research on the genetics of aging', *ILAR Journal*, vol 52, pp 4-15.

Part Three:
Nutrition in later life

NINE

NANA: a tale of ageing and technology

*Arlene Astell, Elizabeth Williams, Faustina Hwang,
Laura Brown, Sarah Cooper, Claire Timon, Lin MacLean,
Tom Smith, Tim Adlam, Hassan Khadra and Alan Godfrey*

Introduction

Nutrition plays a key role in later life health and wellbeing. Older people face a high risk of nutrient deficiencies and malnutrition that can lead to sarcopenia, loss of skeletal muscle mass and strength. A recent review identified that sarcopenia was associated with functional decline, higher rate of falls, higher incidence of hospitalisations and increased mortality (Beaudart et al, 2017). Understandably severe sarcopenia is extremely disabling as it prevents independent living and places an increasing burden on care providers.

Avoiding late life malnutrition is dependent on a number of factors including physical, mental and cognitive health. However, the relative impact of each of these factors and the relationships between them are not well understood. Physical factors, such as problems with chewing, swallowing and impaired mobility, all contribute towards nutritional decline (Hickson, 2006). Mental health status also plays a part, particularly depression, which has been identified as a predictor of poor appetite in older adults (see Engel et al, 2011). Treating depression can be an effective way of increasing appetite and improving nutritional status, but it is commonly under-diagnosed and under-treated among older people (Allan et al, 2014).

There is also growing evidence of associations between diet and cognitive function. Older people with dementia or cognitive decline have a poorer nutritional status than those without (Atti et al, 2008), with increasing dementia severity related to poorer nutritional status (Riccio et al, 2007). The potential for diet to protect against cognitive decline in older people is not currently well understood as much of the epidemiological research has not been supported in trials, and more research is needed to confirm the impact of changing whole diets on cognitive measures (Smith and Blumenthal, 2016).

To explore the associations and interactions between mental and physical health and diet, new intervention and prospective cohort studies are needed (Psaltopoulou et al, 2008). Such research is challenging to complete with older adults, as both ageing itself and the accompanying cognitive and physical decline are progressive and dynamic. Existing tools for measuring diet, cognition and physical activity typically provide snapshots of the situation and cannot identify rate of decline nor readily distinguish cause and effect.

Traditionally, dietary assessment has used pen–and–paper recall and recording of what participants have eaten (for example, a food log, food diary). Older people, especially those with memory loss or other impairments, may struggle to use these (Bowman and Rosenberg, 1982). Increasingly technology is being used to capture information by participants in their daily lives. Momentary measures can prompt participants to record aspects of their current experience, such as mood or current activity, at different times of the day (Cain et al, 2009). Computer-based dietary assessment methods (Illner et al, 2012) are also being developed, but more so for children or younger adults.

We decided to explore the potential of interactive technology for older adults to record their diet and other aspects of functioning, including mood and cognition, in their own homes. Such multidimensional assessment would enable early detection of change in functioning and effective targeting of interventions (Balducci and Beghe, 2000). The Novel Assessment of Nutrition and Ageing (NANA) project set out to develop and evaluate a touch-screen, computer-based, comprehensive daily assessment toolkit for older adults to use in their own homes. A key aim of NANA was to work with older adults to provide a user-friendly interface that makes it easy to enter data. Touch screens are particularly useful for people with no prior computer experience (Wandke et al, 2012) as they require little training and can be used without a mouse or keyboard. We partnered with older adults in an iterative design approach (Nielsen, 1993) whereby each aspect of the NANA toolkit was refined over multiple versions. The individual components of nutrition, cognition, mood and physical activity were developed and tested separately before combining them and conducting a validation in the home (Astell et al, 2014a).

Developing NANA

To achieve the aims of the NANA project, a multidisciplinary team combining expertise in the psychology of ageing, human nutrition, medical engineering (including mechanical and electrical) and human–computer interaction (HCI) was assembled. The team was based across four sites around the UK (one each in Scotland, the North East, South East and South West England), and included three postdoctoral and one Master's level researchers, two PhD students and four early-career academics. In addition, three Master's level and three undergraduate students joined the project at different times.

Over the course of the project a total of 533 older adults (aged between 65 and 91) participated directly in the NANA studies, and dietary information from another 217 was also included (Forster et al, 2010). In addition, 53 nutritionists, 15 health professionals and 90 adults under the age of 65 took part.

The NANA approach

Our approach to creating NANA comprised three key elements: (1) whole project management; (2) transdisciplinary working; and (3) partnership with older adults. We first took a whole project management approach, whereby every part of the project was seen in its relation to the whole – that is, part of delivering the NANA toolkit – rather than in disciplinary or work package silos. This whole project approach contributed to creating a shared project identity, which is particularly important for multidisciplinary teams (van der Vegt and Bunderson, 2005). We achieved this through (1) shared document management; (2) a two-day kick-off meeting; (3) two-day face-to-face meetings every six months, rotating around the four sites; and (4) a standing weekly meeting for all team members. The weekly meetings covered updates on each aspect of the project, trialling iterations of the software and hardware, sharing data from the studies and decision-making. Each team member took turns taking weekly minutes, and anyone who missed a meeting had a record of what was covered in the shared NANA folder.

Weekly meetings have several benefits for large teams on different sites. One is that team members who are working wholly or mainly on the project can cover a lot of ground in one week, and so meeting less often can slow momentum. Another benefit is that decisions can be made in a timely fashion with as many people as possible involved in reaching them. A third benefit is that problems can also be dealt with in a timely manner, ensuring that things that are not working or going to plan are addressed as quickly as possible.

The second complementary aspect of delivering NANA was the adoption of a transdisciplinary approach that crossed boundaries between the different fields of expertise in the project team. Each discipline brought its own knowledge, expertise and skillset. They also brought their own languages, including jargon terms, and methods. While this skill mix was intended and indeed desired, it also presented a challenge of how to establish shared communication to drive the project forward. From the outset, we teamed up members from across the disciplines to deliver activities and run studies that they may not usually gain experience of. For example, at the start of the project, we ran seven focus groups, three for older adults, two for nutritionists and two for health professionals. Each focus group was co-facilitated by team members from two different disciplines whereby the HCI researcher and mechanical engineer each attended one nutritionist, one health professional and one older people's focus group. This was to ensure that all members of the team had a good grasp of the concerns raised by the older adults and health professionals and of the challenges to be overcome in developing the NANA system. This transdisciplinary approach facilitated discussions about research methods and design, data collection and analysis. These discussions revealed some differences in understanding and approach, but also allowed for fruitful discussion and decision-making.

Partnership with older adults was the third critical element to developing NANA. Building on previous experiences developing technology with older adults, specifically the CIRCA (Computer Interactive Reminiscence and Conversation Aid; see Alm et al, 2004) and Living in the Moment (Astell et al, 2014b) projects, we embedded partnership working into NANA. Our previous experiences highlighted that it is critical to work with older adults as the users of technology in the context in which the technology is going to be used. Also, it is essential to make all design decisions, such as fonts, colours, layouts, and so on, together. This partnership approach influenced the project design and resulted in us carrying out a total of 44 sub-projects ranging from working with two individuals in their own homes to examine the usability of a video camera for recording their daily food and drink to 72 people participating in a dual task experiment with eight conditions, looking at the relationship between gait and cognitive function.

In each of the four sites we advertised NANA through flyers in GP surgeries, outpatient clinics, community centres and places of worship and newspaper advertisements. We visited assisted living facilities and gave talks to community groups for older adults. We also teamed up with Age UK, the UK's largest charity working with older adults, to maximise the relevance on NANA for older adults. An Age UK representative sat on the NANA Advisory Panel along with two older adults, making up one-third of the external experts. The others were one NHS dietitian, the Chair of the National Association of Care Catering, one joint NHS/social services planning officer, the Head of Extra Care and Home Care at our other partner Sanctuary Care, and one academic expert in ageing research.

The NANA Advisory Panel, along with the four project leads who comprised the NANA Management Group, was convened to provide input in four areas: (1) oversight of the running of the NANA project in respect of meeting the key project milestones; (2) oversight of the management of the NANA project in respect of the rules laid down by the funding body for management of research grants; (3) advice and guidance to the Management Group and the wider NANA project group through the Management Group on the direction and development of the NANA project; and (4) expertise and input to support the Management Group in terms of meeting the project aims and objective. As such, the Advisory Panel played a key role in keeping NANA relevant and focused on usability in the real world.

With these pieces in place we set out to develop the holistic NANA toolkit and validate it in people's homes. The process of developing NANA was broken down into three parts, each of which is described briefly below.

Part 1: User needs analysis

The first steps in developing NANA were to meet with older adults to discuss both their views of technology and of dietary assessment. We held three focus groups, one in each of three different sites (Scotland, South West England and South East England). The older people who attended were living in their own homes or in extra care accommodation. The first group session with seven older adults explored their attitudes to new technology generally, as well as to diet and health assessments. The second focus group with another seven older adults explored their attitudes to diet and health assessments, dietary recording inside and outside home, and new technologies, including personal digital assistants (PDAs), mobile phones and tablet PCs. The third focus group with a further eight older adults explored their views of touch screens, mobile phones, digital scales, and dietary recording at home and in public including photographing and audio recording. They also looked at mock-ups of the NANA system and gave their opinions about activity monitoring using technology. The focus groups were video and audio recorded and then transcribed for thematic analysis.

The findings from the first group informed the direction and structure of the second, and likewise the findings from this group in turn informed the focus of the third. These three focus groups with older adults informed the development of the technology in the NANA toolkit and illuminated issues of concern to older adults relating to monitoring and assessment. For example, there was wariness among older adults about being monitored remotely and use of the internet to share data.

In addition to these three groups with older adults, two focus groups were held with nutrition professionals. In total, 11 nutritionists attended the two nutrition focus groups, one held in the South East of England and one in the North East. Most participants were nutrition researchers who were well versed in currently available measures and techniques for collecting dietary information in the community as well as the limitations of these. Thematic analysis identified a focus on current limitations to collecting good nutritional information in the community and generated a 'wish list' that they would like to see from the NANA system.

Two focus groups were also held in Scotland, with 14 health professionals, 7 at each group. These comprised four dietitians, two occupational therapists, one research nurse, one day care service manager, one patient and public NHS representative, one health worker, one social worker, one old age psychiatrist, one geriatrician, one clinical psychologist and one member of staff from a community meals service. These two groups of health and social care professionals also produced a 'wish list' for NANA and highlighted the limitations of current approaches to assessment and support of nutritional concerns in the community. They also noted the importance of interprofessional communication and the need for shared language for supporting people with complex needs living in the community.

Part 1 of the NANA project also included five field studies with older adults. In the first field study eight older adults were supplied with a smartphone to evaluate the feasibility of them using this to take pictures of their food. These photographs were compared with dietary data collected using the existing 24-hour multiple pass recall method (Thompson and Subar, 2008). In the second field study three older adults used a digital camera to take photographs, which were again compared with 24-hour multiple pass recall data. The third field study was a variant of the previous two, with two older adults recording their food and drink with a Flip Video camera. The comparison of these recording methods helped to inform decisions about how to capture visual images of food and drink in the NANA toolkit.

The fourth field study was designed to explore older adults' reactions to early ideas for the NANA interface using mock-ups, and eight older adults partnered in this process. The next field study was carried out in the homes of three older adults who examined three different-sized touch-screen devices and tried them in different locations in their homes. This exploration was video recorded with the older adults providing commentary as they put the devices in different parts of their homes, including on kitchen worktops and dining tables. The pros and cons of portable versus fixed devices were also discussed, all of which fed into the development of the prototype NANA toolkit.

Part 2: Development of the integrated measurement toolkit

This part of the project was informed by findings from Part 1, and comprised three integrated strands: dietary measurement; cognition and mental health measurement; and iterative design and development of the measurement toolkit. These three strands were carried out synchronously to place the NANA toolkit in the context of existing measures of nutrition, physical activity, mental health and cognitive function.

During this phase, the nutrition team worked closely with the technical team to develop the novel tools for monitoring dietary intake (see below) and particularly with the HCI researcher to explore methods of streamlining the entry and analysis of the dietary intake data. The validity and feasibility of the software solutions developed were tested extensively. McCance and Widdowson's Composition of Foods Integrated dataset (see www.bda.uk.com/news/view?id=58?) and the photographic atlas of food portion sizes (Nelson et al, 1997) were used.

While this was taking place the psychology team were working with the technical team on developing and validating novel measures for assessing and monitoring cognitive function and mental health. Traditional measures of cognitive function are one-off assessments that provide a snapshot of a person's performance on the day of the test. Similarly, most existing mood measures require answers that reflect how one has felt over the past week or two, although momentary assessment methods are becoming more widespread in mood studies. Developing cognition and mood measures that could be completed daily was informed by the need for reliability and repeatability. The psychology team also worked with the nutrition team on developing methods for collecting information on physical function, including gait, and with the HCI team on methods to integrate this information with the cognition and mental health measures. The technical team took the lead on developing a means of recording grip strength within the NANA toolkit.

Dietary measurement

This phase of the project comprised 10 sub-projects that together contributed to the development of the novel dietary assessment method in the NANA toolkit. The first of these was a field trial in which seven older adults evaluated the use of a bespoke weighing device to be integrated into the NANA system. The next study looked at the specifics of weighing food at home and involved three older adults who tried an early version of NANA with Kern scales and a barcode scanner. The next study involved two nutritionists entering information from the same food diary to look at repeatability and sources of variation. In the next study a database of foods commonly consumed by older adults compiled by one of the NANA team with data from 217 older adults in South Yorkshire (Forster et al, 2012) was compared with data from a sample of adults aged 40 years and older in Newcastle. This was followed by a study comparing the accuracy of dietary information collected using a Food Frequency Questionnaire (FFQ) compared to an estimated food diary using a subset of data from 40 older adults in the South Yorkshire database. The results of the FFQ studies suggested first, that dietary assessment methods should be specifically designed for the target population and second, that there is major variation between the calculations of food intake between the FFQ and diary method. This suggested that a FFQ-style dietary assessment method is not suitable, and a more detailed method needs to be used for dietary assessment in older adults.

The next study was designed to assist in developing the dietary recording software in NANA. Fifteen older adults generated a hierarchical tree structure containing food and drink items based on a card-sorting task. The resultant dietary recording system was then tested by a further 10 older adults who used it to enter their food and drink. The food tree study enabled us to develop a hierarchical tree structure with a satisfactory number of items suitable for use within the older adult population.

The next two studies looked at portion size, a major challenge for all methods of food recording outside of the laboratory. The first study involved 20 older adults and 15 nutritionists who were asked to judge portion sizes using traditional food photograph methods and the newly developed computer-based software. Older adults' accuracy in judging portion sizes was improved with the computer software, but unsurprisingly, they were less accurate than the nutritionists. In a further study 40 older adults and 41 adults aged between 18 and 40 were asked to assess the portion size of 18 self-served food portions using photographs from the food atlas or on a computer. Both groups over- and under-estimated portions in the same directions, suggesting that the perception of portion size is similar for both older and younger adults (Timon et al, 2018). As in the previous study, 25 nutritionists who carried out the estimation were more accurate than either age group. These portion size studies revealed that estimating portion size is particularly difficult for certain food types, and needed to be addressed by the NANA system.

Cognition and mental health measurement

This phase of the project focused on developing new assessments of cognitive function and mental health in older people. Standardised measures were used to identify tasks that were valid and reliable with repeated use. In addition, the length of the individual measures, time to complete and ease of completion plus acceptability to older adults of a daily assessment of both mood and cognition was considered.

Specific studies conducted in Part 2 included the development of 12 candidate cognitive tasks that were tested with 48 older adults aged between 65 and 89. Over three sessions the repeatability and validity of the new digital measures were compared with existing gold-standard pen-and-paper cognitive tests (Brown et al, 2016). From these the two most sensitive measures were identified for inclusion in the NANA toolkit.

The same 48 older adults also assisted in the development of a novel method for self-reporting mood using a touch-screen computer. Based on a conceptual review of existing measures of mood (Brown and Astell, 2012), we developed a simple reporting method that included five mood states plus appetite. This was also validated against existing pen-and-paper measures in the laboratory and shown to be reliable and acceptable for use at home (Brown et al, 2018).

Development of an integrated toolkit

In addition to the nutrition, cognition and mental health components, we also explored measures of physical activity and function including gait and grip strength. In part this was to explore the possibility of using the NANA toolkit to assess the five physical features – unplanned weight loss, slowed gait, reduced grip strength, low physical activity and self-reported exhaustion – that make up the frailty phenotype (Fried et al, 2001). The intention was to identify elements that are critical for inclusion in a comprehensive assessment that covers physical function as well as cognition and mental health.

This part of the project involved three studies of grip strength. The first involving 16 adults aged between 20 and 60 compared grip strength data from a high-quality hand dynamometer with that collected using a low-cost dynamometer that could be modified for inclusion in the NANA system. The second and third grip strength studies used the same method to look at variance in grip strength over a one- to two-week period. In the first study measures of grip strength in newtons were collected from seven adults aged between 28 and 53. This was repeated with seven older adults aged between 65 and 85.

Further studies were designed to develop methods for collecting accurate data on gait that could be used at home, which presents many challenges in an uncontrolled environment. The first two studies looked at the potential of using beam breakers to measure walking speed. The first testing took place in an office environment where data were collected over several weeks from 17 adults aged between 24 and 63. The second beam breaker evaluation took place in the homes of three adults aged between 25 and 40. From these data an alternate method of gait measurement was sought as it was not possible to accurately distinguish between multiple walkers. The next step was to explore the feasibility of creating a self-powered in-shoe gait sensor using piezoelectric sensors. Unfortunately, there was insufficient funding to pursue this further.

Therefore, the next three studies explored other methods of measuring gait at home. The first was to validate gait data collected by manual analysis of video recording against a mechanical stop-clock. This involved six adults aged between 24 and 37 walking in a controlled environment. The next study compared these data with data collected using 'Bigfoot', a device we designed to capture gait data (Maclean, 2013). In this study six older adults aged between 65 and 88 wore Bigfoot and walked in a controlled environment. Finally, we compared the data from video recording with that captured using

Datagait (Esser et al, 2011), a sensor-based method developed for use in clinical settings. We compared Datagait with video recordings of 36 older adults at home and in a clinical setting. We also carried out two studies looking at the relationship between gait and cognitive function. The first looked at the possibility of steadying gait and the potential impact on cognitive function of 45 older adults aged between 65 and 88 (Maclean et al, 2014). The second examined the impact on older adults' gait of increasing cognitive demands in 72 older adults aged between 65 and 91 (Maclean et al, 2017).

As stated above, an integral and substantial part of the toolkit development was the design and integration of the technology to make in-home measurements of parameters such as nutritional intake, activity levels and grip strength. To ensure the technology fitted closely around the capabilities and preferences of the intended users, an iterative design process was applied. The final four projects described in Part 2 were four iterative studies that took place throughout the development of the components described above, and included building prototypes at an early stage in the development process that were shown to, used and evaluated by a panel of users and professionals in the study sites in the South East and South West of England. Feedback from this panel guided the design of the second and third iterations of the system. The fourth iteration focused less on design and more on integration of the components into a functional system where data can be shared and stored in one place for easy access and analysis. The toolkit development phase concluded with the deployment of sufficient NANA toolkits to support 20 people using the system concurrently.

Part 3: Validation of the NANA assessment toolkit

First validation – diet only

In this first of three validation studies, 40 older adults (over the age of 65) were recruited in one centre in the North of England. Participants recorded their diet using three different assessment methods. Three 24-hour multiple pass recalls were conducted, and participants were then asked to record their diet for three weeks using the NANA system. A fasted blood sample and a 24-hour urine collection were collected from each participant during the second week of recording their diet with the NANA system. Following a three-week period without NANA, the older adults then completed a four-day estimated food diary. Four days of dietary intake data for the NANA and the diary method and three days of intake data for the recall method were entered and analysed using WinDiets (version 2010). Biological samples were used for the analysis of biomarkers of nutrient intake (plasma vitamin C, retinol and carotenoids and urinary urea). This first validation study suggested that NANA is a suitable alternative to estimated food diaries in older adults as the results correlated with a four-day food diary in respect of energy, carbohydrates, protein, fat and vitamin C.

Second validation – diet and cognition

In this second validation study 19 older adults from the North East of England took part, 17 of whom lived in a purpose-built continuing care retirement community. Participants completed a total of three 24-hour recalls, one four-day estimated food diary, and 10 days recording dietary intake using the NANA system. They also completed daily assessment of cognition and mood using the NANA system and a battery of standardised pen-and-paper cognitive tests and a standardised depression scale. Data derived from the NANA system was assessed against that obtained via the estimated food diary method. Acceptability of the NANA system was ascertained via the responses given in a feedback questionnaire. This second validation combining dietary intake and cognitive and mood measures reinforced the findings of the first validation regarding the reliability of the dietary data collection. The cognition and mood measures had high acceptability from the participants, with over 99 per cent of trials completed.

Validation of the full NANA toolkit

Once the NANA components had been completed and validated, the main validation study took place. This was designed to compare the NANA toolkit (see Figure 9.1) with the best pen-and-paper methodologies identified in Part 2 and against independent biochemical markers of nutrient status. Forty older adults aged between 65 and 89, 20 in North England and 20 in Scotland, tried NANA at home. They comprised a cross-sectional group of older people living in their own homes or extra care accommodation in the community. Cross-centre training took place to ensure all methodologies were applied correctly in the two sites where the validation study took place. The older adults were asked to use the NANA toolkit for three separate one-week periods; each one-week period of use was followed by a three-week period without NANA. They used the NANA system to record the

Figure 9.1: The NANA toolkit

food and drink they consumed, their cognitive function, mood and physical activity, plus grip strength. They also provided a fasted blood sample and a 24-hour urine collection during the second week of recording their diet with the NANA system. Following a final three-week period without NANA, the older adults then completed a four-day estimated food diary. They also completed a standardised cognitive test battery, depression scale and physical activity questionnaire at the start and end of the study. Four days of dietary intake data from each method was entered and analysed using WinDiets dietary analysis software.[1] Statistical analysis was carried out using SPSS. Biological samples were used for the analysis of biomarkers of nutrient intake (plasma vitamin C, retinol and carotenoids and urinary urea). The findings demonstrated the suitability of the NANA toolkit for collecting dietary data from older adults with positive correlations both with a four-day food diary and biomarkers for nutrition intake (Timon et al, 2015). Over three months the data demonstrated consistency of nutrient intake by the older adults, with high data recording and no evidence of data collection fatigue (Moore et al, 2013). There was also high acceptability of the cognitive and mood measures and of a simple measure of physical activity (Astell et al, 2014a). The data on grip strength suggested that, like the cognitive and mood data, it is possible to collect these data without a researcher being present.

After the final validation study was complete, a further focus group was held with eight older adults and two staff members from a health and social care service to discuss the potential application of the data collected by the NANA system. This highlighted the possibilities for NANA being used for prospective data collection and early detection of problems emerging in any of the four domains of nutrition, cognition, mood and physical activity.

Policy and practice implications

The complexity and comprehensiveness of the NANA project meant that it yielded large amounts of results, which have implications and relevance for a number of domains. In addition, the multidisciplinary and multidimensional aspects of the NANA project have ensured that the findings are accessible to a wide range of audiences and potential beneficiaries.

The key findings in relation to the main aims of the NANA project to collect data on nutrition, cognition, mood and physical function are that (1) older adults are happy to use new technology in their own homes; (2) older adults are comfortable recording what they eat and drink on a daily basis; (3) older adults are prepared to record their mood on a daily basis; (4) older adults will complete cognitive measures on a daily basis; and (5) older adults will record their physical activity and function using new technology. Furthermore they are willing and interested to do so.

The measures used in NANA were validated against currently available gold-standard measures for diet, cognition, mood and physical activity. The validation studies demonstrated that the data collected in NANA were at least as good as those collected by currently available methods. Another key finding was that reliable cognitive assessment can be carried out every day and be achieved without a researcher being present (Brown et al, 2016). Additionally, an analysis of the NANA data collected in the validation study demonstrated that it is predictive of signs of future depression (Andrews et al, 2017).

The research conducted in the NANA project has demonstrated that it is possible to collect reliable data in people's homes with the potential for early detection of change in any of the NANA domains. The research has also demonstrated that NANA is an accessible and acceptable technology for a wide range of older adults. NANA can be used to collect data that is as good if not better than pen-and-paper methods and reduces the burden on participants, resulting in high rates of data recording. These findings should be of interest to nutritionists and other researchers in the field who wish to collect longitudinal data in older people's homes. The project also generated new knowledge about whole project management, transdisciplinary working and partnering with older adults to create and validate new technology.

In respect of possible practice implications, the findings from the NANA research project highlight the potential for early detection and intervention, not only for older people at risk of malnutrition, but also frailty, cognitive decline and mood disorders. By monitoring over time and looking for changes in functioning, an individual could receive a suggestion to attend their GP, to whom the data could also be sent. Additionally, the data collected by NANA can be fed back to older adults themselves, to facilitate self-management, as many participants expressed a desire to 'see how I am doing'. The data collected could also be shared with family members to form the basis of discussion or provide reassurance. Older adults also saw the benefit of collecting prospective data and like the idea that someone would keep track of them and be alert to any significant changes in their profile.

This latter point links to the policy implications of NANA in respect of the potential for establishing prospective monitoring of older adults, particularly those identified as being at particular risk of health conditions associated with ageing. In addition to the immediate benefits to the current generation of older adults, the information collected would provide a large data set to profile the emergence of some of the major health conditions associated with ageing. Additionally, NANA heralds the way for the functionality of new technology and the availability of holistic assessment to support people to live and age as well as possible.

Key findings
- Older people are happy to use new technology in their own homes.
- Older people are comfortable recording what they eat and drink on a daily basis.
- Older people are prepared to record their mood on a daily basis.
- Older people will complete cognitive measures on a daily basis.
- Older people will record their physical activity and function using new technology.

Conclusions

The primary project output is a validated toolkit for the measurement of nutrition, cognitive function, mood and physical activity of older people (Astell et al, 2014a). Outputs directly related to the toolkit include the data from the user needs analysis, the individual nutrition, cognition, mood and physical activity studies, and the validation studies. Additionally, the technology developed in the project is suitable for measuring the impact of other interventions on physical and mental health. The toolkit could be used to measure the impact of, for example, pharmacological and exercise interventions, or it could be used in a clinical assessment context. It could also be adapted for use with children, people with health needs or used to measure the impact on physical and mental health of assistive technology interventions.

In respect of the next steps in research, the NANA team are working with both food and care providers to develop the outputs from the system and to answer questions about how to integrate the NANA data into services. This includes working with a software development company and a healthcare provider to develop a smartphone app and clinician portal for use in dietary monitoring. We are also seeking major funding to conduct at least one study to assess the efficiency of NANA in detecting change and monitoring an intervention.

Note
[1]   WinDiets dietary analysis software version 2010, WinDiets Research, Robert Gordon University, Aberdeen, UK.

References
Allan, C.E., Valkanova, V. and Ebmeier, K.P. (2014) 'Depression in older people is underdiagnosed', *Practitioner*, vol 258, no 1771 pp, 19-22, 2-3.

Alm, N., Astell, A., Ellis, M., Dye, R., Gowans, G. and Campbell, J. (2004) 'A cognitive prosthesis and communication support for people with dementia', *Neuropsychological Rehabilitation*, vol 14, no 1-2, pp 117-34.

Andrews, J., Harrison, R., Brown, L.J.E., Maclean, L.M., Hwang, F., Smith, T., et al (2017) 'Using the NANA toolkit at home to predict older adults' future depression', *Journal of Affective Disorders*, vol 213, pp 187-90.

Astell, A.J., Alm, N., Dye, R., Gowans, G. M., Vaughan, P. and Ellis, M. (2014b) 'Digital video games for older people with cognitive impairment', in K. Miesenberger, D. Fels, D. Archambault, P. Peñáz and W. Zagler (eds) *ICCHP 2014, Part I. Lecture Notes in Computer Science*, vol 8547, pp 264-71.

Astell, A.J., Hwang, F., Brown, L.J.E., Timon, C., Maclean, L.M., Smith, T., et al (2014a) 'Validation of the NANA (Novel Assessment of Nutrition and Ageing) touch screen system for use at home by older adults', *Experimental Gerontology*, vol 60, pp 100-7.

Atti, A.R., Palmer, K., Volpato, S., Winblad, B., De Ronchi, D. and Fratiglioni, L. (2008) 'Late-life body mass index and dementia incidence: Nine-year follow-up data from the Kungsholmen Project', *Journal of the American Geriatrics Society*, vol 56, no 1, pp 111-16.

Balducci, L. and Beghe, C. (2000) 'The application of the principles of geriatrics to the management of the older person with cancer', *Critical Reviews in Oncology/Hematology*, September, vol 35, no 3, pp 147-54.

Beaudart, C., Zaaria, M., Paleau, F., Reginster, J.-Y. and Bruyère, O. (2017) 'Health outcomes of sarcopenia: A systematic review and meta-analysis', *PLOS One*. Available at https://doi.org/10.1371/journal.pone.0169548

Bowman, B.B. and Rosenberg, I.H. (1982) 'Assessment of the nutritional status of the elderly', *American Journal of Clinical Nutrition*, vol 35(5 Suppl), no 11, pp 42-51.

Brown, L.J. and Astell, A.J. (2012) 'Assessing mood in older adults: A conceptual review of methods and approaches', *International Psychogeriatrics*, vol 24, no 8, pp 1197-206.

Brown, L.J., Adlam, T., Hwang, F., Khadra, H., Maclean, L., Rudd, B., Smith, T., Timon, C., Williams, E.A. and Astell, A.J. (2016) 'Computer-based tools for assessing micro-longitudinal patterns of cognitive function in older adults', *Age*, vol 38, no 4, pp 335-50.

Brown, L.J., Adlam, T., Hwang, F., Khadra, H., Maclean, L., Rudd, B., Smith, T., Timon, C., Williams, E.A. and Astell, A.J. (2018) 'Computerized self-administered measures of mood and appetite for older adults: the Novel Assessment of Nutrition and Ageing (NANA) toolkit', *Journal of Applied Gerontechnology*, vol 37, no 2, pp 157-76.

Cain, A.E., Depp, C.A. and Jeste, D.V. (2009) 'Ecological momentary assessment in aging research: A critical review', *Journal of Psychiatric Research*, July, vol 43, no 11, pp 987-96.

Engel, J.H., Siewerdt, F., Jackson, R., Akobundu, U., Wait, C. and Sahyoun, N. (2011) 'Hardiness, depression, and emotional well-being and their association with appetite in older adults', *Journal of the American Geriatric Society*, vol 59, no 3, pp 482-7.

Esser, P., Dawes, H., Collett, J., Feltham, M.G. and Howells, K. (2011) 'Assessment of spatio-temporal gait parameters using inertial measurement units in neurological populations', *Gait and Posture*, vol 34, no 4, pp 558-60.

Forster, S.E., Jones, L., Sexton, J.M., Flower, D.J., Foulds, G., Powers, H.J., Parker, S.G., Pockley, A.G. and Williams, E.A. (2010) 'Recruiting older people to a randomized controlled dietary intervention trial – how hard can it be?', *BMC Medical Research methodology*, vol 10, no 17, doi: 10.1186/1471-2288-10-17.

Fried, L.P., Tangen, C.M., Walston, J., Newman, A.B., Hirsch, C., Gottdiener, J., et al. (2001) 'Frailty in older adults: Evidence for a phenotype', *The Journals of Gerontology: Series A. Biological Sciences and Medical Sciences*, vol 5, M146-56.

Hickson, M. (2006) 'Malnutrition and ageing', *Postgraduate Medical Journal*, vol 82, no 963, pp 2-8.

Illner, A.-K., Freisling, H., Boeing, H., Huybrechts, I., Crispim, S.P. and Slimain, N. (2012) 'Review and evaluation of innovative technologies for measuring diet in nutritional epidemiology', *International Journal of Epidemiology*, vol 41, pp 1187-203.

Maclean, L. (2013) 'The role of executive attention in healthy older adults' concurrent walking and counting', PhD thesis submitted, University of St Andrews. Available at https://research-repository.st-andrews.ac.uk/bitstream/handle/10023/4435/LindaMacleanPhDThesis.pdf?sequence=3

Maclean, L., Brown, L.J. and Astell, A.J. (2014) 'The effect of rhythmic musical training on healthy older adults' gait and cognitive function', *The Gerontologist*, vol 54, no 4, pp 624-33.

Maclean, L., Brown, L.J., Khadra, H. and Astell, A.J. (2017) 'Observing prioritization effects on cognition and gait: The effect of increased cognitive load on older adults' dual-task performance', *Gait and Posture*, vol 53, pp 139-44.

Moore, C., Timon, C.M., Maclean, L., Hwang, F., Smith, T., Adlam, T., et al (2013) 'Use of NANA, a novel method of dietary assessment, for the longitudinal capture of dietary intake', *Proceedings of the Nutrition Society*, vol 72, OCE4, E267.

Nelson, M., Atkinson, M. and Meyer, J. (1997) *A Photographic Atlas of Food Portion Sizes*, London: Food Standards Agency.

Nielsen, J. (1993) 'Iterative user-interface design', *Computer*, November, vol 26, no 11, pp 32-41.

Psaltopoulou, T., Kyrozis, A., Stathopoulos, P., Trichopoulos, D., et al (2008) 'Diet, physical activity and cognitive impairment among elders: The EPIC-Greece cohort (European Prospective Investigation into Cancer and Nutrition)', *Public Health Nutrition*, vol 11, no 10, pp 1054-62.

Riccio, D., Solinas, A., Astara, G. and Mantovani, G. (2007) 'Comprehensive geriatric assessment in female elderly patients with Alzheimer disease and other types of dementia', *Archives of Gerontology and Geriatrics*, vol 44, Suppl 1, pp 343-53.

Smith, P.J. and Blumenthal, J.A. (2016) 'Dietary factors and cognitive decline', *Journal of Prevention of Alzheimer's Disease*, vol 3, no 1, pp 53-64.

Thompson, F.E. and Subar, A.F. (2008) 'Dietary assessment methodology', in A.M. Coulston and C.J. Boushey (eds) *Nutrition in the prevention and treatment of disease*, San Diego, CA: Academic Press, pp 5-6.

Timon, C.E., Cooper, S.E., Barker, M.E., Astell, A.J., Adlam, T., Hwang, F. and Williams, E.A. (2018) 'A comparison of food portion size estimation by older adults, young adults and nutritionists', *Journal of Nutrition, Health and Ageing*, vol 22, no 2, pp 230-36.

Timon, C.M., Astell, A.J., Hwang, F., Adlam, T.D., Smith, T., Maclean, L., et al (2015) 'The validation of a novel method of dietary assessment for older adults (The NANA study)', *British Journal of Nutrition*, vol 113, no 4, pp 654-64.

Van der Vegt, G.S. and Bunderson, J.S. (2005) 'Learning and performance in multidisciplinary teams: The importance of collective team identification', *Academy of Management Journal*, vol 48, no 3, pp 532-47.

Wandke, H., Sengpiel, M. and Sonksen, M. (2012) 'Myths about older people's use of information and communication technology', *Gerontology*, vol 58, pp 564-70.

TEN

Combating malnutrition in hospitals

Paula Moynihan, Lisa Methven, Gemma Teal,
Claire Bamford and Alastair S. Macdonald

Introduction

According to Age UK, over 3 million people across the UK are either malnourished or at risk of malnourishment, of which over 1 million are over the age of 65 (Age UK, 2017). Over 30 per cent of adults are malnourished on admission to hospital, increasing hospital stay, risk of complications and likelihood of being discharged into care (BAPEN, 2003; Stratton et al, 2004; Age Concern, 2006; Brotherton et al, 2010; Elia, 2015). Malnutrition in people aged 65 and older costs healthcare in England almost £10 billion per year (Elia, 2015). Age UK highlighted the problem of impractical eating environments for many older patients, and made seven recommendations to tackle malnutrition in older hospital patients, which focus on assistance at mealtimes and identification of patients at nutritional risk.

The Better Hospital Food programme launched in 2001 was successful in improving the quality of hospital food, although it did not specifically address older patients' needs, for example, reduced sensory perception, smaller appetites and in some instances, eating difficulties. Approximately 12 per cent of older hospital patients have intermittent swallowing difficulty, which is of concern as the sensorial quality of foods for such patients is poor and does little to stimulate the appetite of those at particular nutrition risk.

The Department of Health (DH) and National Health Service (NHS) devised a Joint Action Plan for improving nutritional care in hospitals with five priorities for action: raising awareness of the link between good nutrition and health; ensuring accessible guidance; encouraging nutritional screening; nutrition training; and improving standards of inspection (DH, 2007). The DH Dignity in Care campaign (DH, 2006) recognised that delivering adequate food is 'a fundamental human right' and stressed the need for maintaining dignity and providing older people with the assistance they require at mealtimes. The Care Quality Commission's Dignity and Nutrition Inspection Programme highlighted concerns over nutritional care, including patients not being given the help they needed to eat, meaning that they struggled to eat or were physically unable to eat meals; patients being interrupted during meals, meaning they could not finish their meal; accurate records of food and drink not being kept so progress was not monitored; and many patients were not able to clean their hands before meals.

The Council for Europe Alliance (UK) stated that a key characteristic of good nutritional care in hospitals should be that hospital facilities be designed to be flexible and patient-centred, with the aim of providing and delivering excellent experience of food service and nutritional care. Despite numerous guidance and malnutrition screening tools, a holistic approach to the provision of adequate nutrition to older people in hospital that exploits state-of-the-art technologies with respect to products, people, places and procedures has not previously been considered. To date, the solution to hospital malnutrition in older patients has not been found by isolated interventions focusing on specific areas of food provision.

To fully address the problem, all stages of the food journey, from preparation to consumption, must be considered, including the type of food product and its preparation, the journey of the food from production to patient (maintenance of quality), the patient's eating environment and their nutritional management including monitoring food and nutrient intake and nutritional status. In view of this, the aim of the mappmal project was to develop a prototype for a new food provision service for older hospital patients in a multidisciplinary, user participative, proof of concept study. The aim was to find a potential solution to the problem of hospital malnutrition in older people using a holistic, multidisciplinary approach.

The mappmal project

The overall objectives of the mappmal project were:

- to explore and define the current interactions between food, people and procedures in elderly care hospital settings, and to identify areas within this for intervention to prevent malnutrition;
- with input from users and stakeholders, to devise novel approaches to food products for older patients (sensorial quality of food), mobile food preparation, delivery, the older patient's eating environment

and monitoring of food and nutritional intake, exploiting current and new technologies;

- to conduct a proof of concept in each of the defined areas collecting qualitative data on feasibility and acceptability from stakeholders and users;
- to collect qualitative data from the food family on the perceived effectiveness and application of the new prototype to other settings, for example, care homes;
- to design a new prototype for food products, people and procedures that, based on qualitative evidence, is amenable to becoming embedded in practice, thereby reducing malnutrition.

A diverse group of researchers from the disciplines of nutrition and dietetics, food science, design, sociology, computer science, speech and language therapy, medicine and ergonomics, worked collaboratively to radically rethink food provision and nutritional management for older people in hospital.

The research questions that the project addressed were:

1. Based on current interactions between food, people, places and procedures in the provision of food to older patients (with fractured neck of femur, stroke and/or dementia), where do opportunities for intervention to minimise malnutrition lie?
2. In particular, what are the opportunities with respect to specific foods for older patients?
3. What are the opportunities for optimising the food journey to minimise deterioration in food quality?
4. What are the opportunities with respect to the older patient's eating environment to maximise enjoyment of meals and food intake (for example, food choice, quality, portion size, encouragement)?
5. What are the opportunities for facilitating monitoring of the older patient's food intake and nutritional status?

We aimed to explore novel innovations in design and technology that could be exploited to address the identified opportunities for intervention. We wanted to explore how novel food ingredients, products and preparation could be developed to address the needs of the older patient. We also wanted to gain insights into how interactions between people, products, places and procedures could be optimised in order to maximise patient benefit.

Methods

Defining current interactions between food, people, places and procedures in elderly care wards

An ethnographic study of the meal services at five hospital sites across two regional locations, focusing on older patients admitted for stroke, fractured neck of femur or with dementia, was carried out. This included hospitals that used in-house and those that used cook-chill systems of food provision. Ethnography included non-participative observations of the meal services (catering through to older people's wards) and semi-structured interviews with 47 NHS staff on current systems for food provision and the nutritional management of older patients, to identify potential areas for intervention, that is, to identify potential solutions to problems.

The users involved in the project were named and referred to as the 'food family', the group of people involved in the food journey from preparation to mouth. The food family comprised hospital caterers, dietitians, nursing staff, ward volunteers, carers, patients, speech therapists, occupational therapists and doctors involved in elderly care. Semi-structured interviews were also conducted with key stakeholders including representation from Age UK, the National Patient Safety Agency, Royal College of Nursing, the Care Quality Commission, Hospital Caterers Association, National Association of Care Catering, British Geriatrics Society, British Dietetics Association and BAPEN (British Association for Parenteral and Enteral Nutrition). A focus group with former patients and carers designed to generate 'solutions' to malnutrition was also held.

Qualitative data generated were analysed using the Normalisation Process Theory (NPT) (May, 2006; May and Finch, 2009), an empirically derived theoretical framework for understanding the embedding of new healthcare interventions into practice. Understanding processes of the design, negotiation, implementation and operation of the food family was informed using NPT as a theoretical framework that informs the analysis of: (1) the *relationships* between a complex intervention and the context in which it is implemented; (2) the *processes* by which implementation proceeds, including interactions between people, technologies and organisational structures, and the work that proceeds from these; and (3) a process-oriented assessment of outcome that also considers the potential and actual workability and integration of a complex intervention as *accomplishments* of its users. This methodology has been used successfully for process evaluations of complex interventions (Finch et al, 2003, 2007; May, 2003). Interviews were audio-recorded, transcribed and data subjected to framework analysis (Ritchie and Spencer, 1999). Analytical themes were identified from field notes arising from non-participant observation in hospitals (Anderson, 1996).

Review of existing technologies and design in the hospital food service

Taking into account safety, hygiene, comfort, privacy and dignity, an in-depth appraisal of existing systems and novel technologies was conducted to gather information on technologies for enhancing and preserving the quality and delivery of food; the use of digital technologies for interfaces and interactions; improving the environment and ambience where eating takes place (spatial layout, colour, lighting) for a more enjoyable eating experience; and design of products such as trolleys, trays, crockery, utensils and chairs. Scenarios of existing daily food lives for the specified patients were mapped including environments, product systems (for example, beds, trays, cutlery), technology systems (heating, preparation, monitoring of temperature) and 'soft design' factors for the quality of the environments of preparation, delivery and consumption of foods (colours, smell, room temperatures).

Impact of current ward practices on the perception of food served to older hospital patients

Impact of catering systems on the sensorial quality of food

Data on the changes in sensorial quality of existing hospital food between point of production and point of consumption were obtained by treating example meals in the same way as for the hospital setting and recording changes in sensorial quality. A trained sensory panel assessed sensorial descriptors of a series of foods that had or had not gone through the usual food journey as it occurs in the in-house and cook-chill systems. The findings informed whether changes to the way food is delivered to hospital patients had an impact on the sensorial quality of food.

Liking of meals, waste at lunchtime, and the impact of ward odour

A four-week trial was carried out on one elderly care ward, two control weeks interspersed with two intervention weeks where carbon-based adsorbent mats were used to adsorb any odours. Odours on the ward were trapped and analysed. Patient participants were asked daily about their liking of their lunchtime meal, whether there was anything about the environment that had affected their appetite, and whether they had noticed any pleasant or unpleasant smells. Total food waste on the ward was measured each week. The results informed whether negative or positive odours were likely to have an impact on food consumption, and should be included within future designs.

Participative co-design approach

A novel approach that employed both qualitative and workshop-based co-design methods was used to identify core opportunities for service improvement and to elicit feedback from the food family and stakeholders. Through these methods an understanding of the existing expectations, means and quality of food provision and nutritional management within a food delivery service for older patients was gained. The methods were also used to facilitate radical questioning and rethinking of these systems, and thus the prototype for a new food service was designed and developed using an iterative process (Macdonald et al, 2012). This involved the use of mixed methods including ethnography, semi-structured interviews, mapping of ideas, development of personas, storyboarding, role-play, enactment and the development of narratives to demonstrate convincing scenarios of the new service in operation, that is, how the new system might work in the everyday clinical setting. At all key stages in the development of the prototype, workshops were held with the food family and stakeholder representatives to elicit feedback on the developing ideas. Moreover, throughout the design and development process, a rolling programme of semi-structured interviews was undertaken with the food family and stakeholders. The novel iterative and multidisciplinary design process used is summarised in Table 10.1.

Concepts emerging from the evidence base were developed with the assistance of users and stakeholders' experiences and insights. A set of key service principles for a new food service were defined and validated (see Table 10.3). 'Co-design' conditions were created through the workshops using specially designed tools and techniques to engage the researchers and food family. An iterative concept development process with repeated access to the food family was required to determine which were the essential, desirable and workable features and components of the system, and to ensure concepts and designs were acceptable to, and workable for, end users.

Table 10.1: Key stages (1–5) in the development of a new service prototype for food provision for older hospital patients

Activity undertaken	People involved
1. Identifying issues with the status quo and opportunities for improvement	
• Ethnographic study in five NHS hospitals	• Sociologists, nutritionist, designers
• Sensory testing of existing hospital foods	• Food scientists
• Mapping of food journey	• Food scientists, sociologists, designers
2. Analysing, visualising and validating findings	
• Thematic analysis and visualising of issues	• Designers, sociologists
• Mapping of existing food journeys	• Food scientist, designers
• Validation of findings in workshop with food family	• Food family, stakeholders and research team
3. Conceptualisation and co-design	
• Identifying opportunities and stimulating new thinking in a food family workshop research team to define key service principles. Further development of ideas at food family workshop	• Nutritionists, sociologists, food scientists, designers, technologist, ergonomist, food family and stakeholders
4. Iterative co-design and development	
• Determining core elements by research team	• Nutritionist, food scientist, designers, sociologist
• Research team develop concepts for new system, building narratives to make ideas tangible	• Nutritionist, food scientist, designers, sociologist
• Development of new interface application	• Nutritionist, computer scientists, designers, sociologist, food scientist
• Development of nutrient-dense mini-meals	• Food scientist, nutritionist, food family, stakeholders and whole team
• Evaluating early systems concepts at food family workshop	• Food scientist, nutritionist, food family, stakeholders and whole team
• Evaluating early food supply and delivery system concept at food family workshop	• Food scientist, nutritionist, food family, stakeholders and whole team
• Continual qualitative evaluation of concepts through semi-structured interviews with food family	• Sociologists, designers
5. Communication through demonstration prototype	
• Demonstration prototype – working simulation of key elements	• Nutritionist, food scientist, designers, sociologists
• Exhibition design – dissemination to key audiences	• Designers
• Project specific symposia at major conferences	• Nutritionist, sociologists, food scientist, consultant physician
• Website design	• Designers, nutritionist, food scientist, sociologist

Developing a concept for new food products

An aim of the project was to design food with improved sensorial quality and nutritional quality for older patients known to be at risk of malnutrition (stroke, dementia, fractures) by use of appropriate ingredients and processes. The project also specifically developed specifications and guidelines for foods and beverages for those with swallowing difficulties. Information on the perceived quality of food for older patients obtained from the food family and stakeholders through the qualitative interviews and workshops informed the development of new products, as did the findings of the ward trials (see 'Impact of current ward practices' above). Existing information on sensory decline and taste preferences of older people was collated to inform product development. Nutrient-dense foods were developed, both macro- and micro-nutrient-fortified, with high flavour impact but within familiar food formats and names. Feedback on the sensorial quality of the new food products was obtained from quantitative sensory profiling using a trained sensory expert panel and preference information obtained from a taste panel of older volunteers using questionnaires and qualitative methods. Feedback on the prototypes for products was also obtained from the food family and stakeholders through the workshops. During all elements of the qualitative research with the food family and stakeholders, feedback on the potential application of the new concepts to other settings (for example, care homes) was investigated.

Findings

Factors that contribute to low food intake

An ethnographic study of current practice with respect to hospital food provision for older patients identified the main factors that contributed to inadequate food intake (see Table 10.2). These varied from broad organisational and structural issues, to patterns of work and priorities on individual wards. Centrally, respondents regarded assistance at mealtimes as fundamental to adequate nutrition, although the activities that constitute this work were conceptualised differently across occupational, individual and policy contexts. Ward-based staff explained the tacit, technical and nuanced nature of interpersonal 'food work', yet attributed their own proficiency to 'common sense'. However, in policy documentation potential solutions to malnutrition focus on resources, structures and procedures operating beyond the '30-

Table 10.2: Core factors contributing to poor nutritional care

Factor identified	
Inefficient and inflexible food ordering	Ordering systems designed for processing by catering rather than to tempt appetite
Poor mealtime ambience	Cluttered and multi-purpose and non-adjustable eating surfaces
Inflexible meal service	Three main meals a day: patients were overwhelmed by portion size, with limited provision for meals outside set times
Dysphagia	Recognised as contributing to malnutrition
Shortcomings in screening and monitoring	Screening generally took place, but review was more variable. Food intake was not accurately monitored
Assistance at mealtimes	On busy wards those requiring assistance were not always identified and assisted
Lack of accountability for nutritional care	Nobody is solely responsible and nobody is held to account

40cm' between patient, feeding assistant and plate (Heaven et al, 2012). While help with eating is recognised as being fundamental to adequate nutrition for older patients, investment in this work is often overlooked.

Systems used for ordering meals in hospital were inefficient and inflexible, with paper-based systems requiring food to be ordered long before the time of consumption. Food ordering systems were designed for processing by catering as opposed to the older person's needs, and did little to tempt patient appetite. Other factors included a poor mealtime ambience on many wards, with patients eating their meals on cluttered, multipurpose, non-adjustable surfaces. On busy wards, those who needed help with mealtimes were not always identified and assisted. Food provision services in hospitals were inflexible and usually based around the provision of three main and large meals a day. However, it was found that older patients prefer to eat little and often, and so they were often overwhelmed by the large portion sizes at mealtimes. Outside main mealtimes there was limited provision for meals and snacks.

Shortcomings in systems in place for screening for malnutrition and for monitoring of patient food intake were identified. Although nutritional screening generally took place, regular review was more variable. Food intake was not accurately monitored because the end of bed charts used to record intake do not provide very useful or accurate information on food intake and no information on nutrient intake.

Without reliable information on patients' nutrient intake, shortfalls can go unnoticed. Furthermore, no one was solely responsible for the nutritional care of a patient, and the provision of an adequate intake of nutrients was an unaccountable part of care. Current systems do not facilitate good nutritional care with respect to providing an overview, prompting appropriate actions and ensuring these actions have been taken.

Table 10.3: mappmal service principles for a new food system for older patients

A new system for food provision for older patients should:
• Consider food provision as a treatment (as opposed to hospitality services)
• Consider all older patients to be at risk of malnutrition until screening shows otherwise
• Provide nutritionally superior foods that meet the specific needs of older people
• Personalise the food service to older people's needs and preferences
• Stimulate patient appetite and maximise patient comfort and enjoyment of eating
• Facilitate better communication between catering, patient and the food family
• Provide food on demand – little and often access to food

Impact of current ward practices on the perception of food served to older hospital patients

Impact of catering systems on the sensorial quality of food

The investigation of the impact of the food provision systems on food quality indicated that although some deterioration was found in specific foods, the problem was not widespread across many food types. The results showed that the food journey had an impact on only a small number of sensorial descriptors related to flavour, appearance and mouth feel. The majority of these effects were due to temperature changes, which caused dehydration or condensation that had an impact on food sensorial quality (Mavrommatis et al, 2011). An observed day-to-day variation in sensorial descriptors was, in some cases, greater than the effects of the food journey. So the changes that occur in the sensory quality of hospital food due to the processes involved in delivering the food to patients were relatively small. These do not substantially contribute to the acceptability of food to patients and therefore to malnutrition.

Liking of meals, waste at lunchtime, and the impact of ward odour

The ward odour trial showed that on average 36 per cent of plated food was wasted despite the mean 'liking rating' for meals by patients being high (median 8/10). However, hunger ratings were low (median 2/5, where 2 represented not very hungry and 3 neutral). Where lunch was disliked, the most frequent comments were about portion size being too large, food not matching that which had been ordered, temperature too cold or lack of taste/flavour.

The carbon mats decreased the concentration of odour on the ward. Of the 78 daily questionnaires that were recorded (from the 29 patient participants), only 7 recorded positive smells and 12 reported negative smells. Comments (by six patients) related to negative smells concerned 'toilets' or related issues. Ten of the negative smells were reported on control weeks and only two on intervention weeks. There was no difference in measured food waste levels between control and intervention weeks. The findings show it is possible to reduce odour levels on wards. Some, but not the majority of, patients noticed negative odours, and this did not have a measurable effect on food consumption.

Developing new foods for older hospital patients

Development of mini-meals

The need for wider access to nutrient-dense foods of smaller portion sizes was addressed through the development of 'mini-meals'. Nutrient-enriched biscuits (Tsikritzi et al, 2014), ice cream, savoury sauces, soups and cakes were developed through macro- and micro-nutrient fortification. Macro–nutrient fortification focused on both energy as well as protein fortification. Whey protein was utilised for protein fortification as the protein source known to be most effective in muscle mass synthesis. Micro-nutrient fortification utilised vitamin and mineral blends appropriate to the requirements of older adults in residential care.

Foods for older patients

Our research found that the physical properties, perceived mouth feel and ease of swallowing of commercial texture-modified 'puree category' foods for patients with dysphagia varied in physical properties, nutrient density and perceived mouth feel and ease of swallow. Further research is needed in order to determine both optimum physical characteristics of puree meals as well as optimum portion size with associated nutritional composition.

Drinks for patients with dysphagia

Our research found that the thickened drink consistency received by patients with dysphagia varied considerably from that recommended (Payne et al, 2010). Reasons included differences in physical properties between hot and cold drinks, drink types and individual preparation methods (Payne et al, 2012). Mappmal guidance for practitioners for the preparation of drinks for patients with dysphagia was devised (Payne et al, 2011), including the recommendation that pre-weighed thickener drinks are a safer option.

The final prototype: hospitalfoodie

The final prototype for a new food provision service for older hospital patients that emerged from the research was the 'hospitalfoodie' system, a nutritional management and food provision system that facilitates increased engagement by all staff in the process of providing adequate nutrition to patients, and embeds a chain of accountability for nutritional care. The system is based on a set of interactive, interlinked patient and staff interfaces at the bedside, nurses' station and the offices of relevant healthcare, management and catering staff (see Figure 10.1). Each patient has a bedside touch screen for their nutritional management. The multidisciplinary team can access and act on patient nutrition information remotely and at the bedside.

Hospitalfoodie comprises two core elements, nutritional management systems and food products and delivery. The core components and functions of the system are as follows:

- *Nutritional screening:* hospitalfoodie prompts and facilitates staff to complete a patient's nutritional screening on admission and weekly thereafter. It calculates and adjusts the patient's nutritional requirements in real time.

- *Tailored menus:* The system facilitates patient-tailored food choices by enabling recording of preferences. Staff can enter requirements (for example, specialised diets, textural requirements) so that food choices presented to the patient always suit their needs. The patient orders their food/drink through the bedside interactive touch screen.

- *Setting the scene:* The system promotes an environment that is conducive to eating. Before each meal, the bedside interface

Figure 10.1: Illustrations demonstrating elements of the hospitalfoodie prototype: bedside touch-screen interface, remote interfaces tailored to professional requirements, the hospitalfoodie trolley designed to deliver mini-meals.

Source: Image Copyright © Peter Baynton Radish Pictures

presents the patient with a picture of the food they have ordered and a pre-meal checklist for staff including guidance on helping the patient into a safe and comfortable position, necessary help for safe eating, offering hand-wipes and any equipment required (for example, spectacles, dentures, assistive cutlery).

- *Monitoring food and nutrient intake:* The system facilitates more accurate monitoring of a patient's nutrient intake. A unique feature is a bedside touch screen application that allows staff to more accurately measure food intake based on what the patient consumes as opposed to what they ordered (see Figure 10.1). Amounts of nutrients consumed are automatically calculated and tracked against individual targets. This provides more accurate information on nutrient intake and how this compares with the patient's individual requirements. The system alerts ward staff when a patient's daily nutritional requirements are not met, and prompts appropriate remedial action for which the staff are then accountable.

- *Mini-meals:* The system provides patients with six smaller energy and nutrient-dense meals per day. Central catering continues to provide smaller portions of breakfast, lunch and dinner. In addition, ward-based mini-meals are provided during normal snack times. A range of nutrient-dense, micro-nutrient-fortified mini-meals, including ice cream, biscuits and cakes and soups, have been developed that can be provided at a ward level at any time throughout the day. To facilitate the delivery of ward-based mini-meals and to increase flexibility in access to food for patients outside set mealtimes, a purpose-designed hospitalfoodie ward food trolley concept has been designed.

• *Information exchange:* The hospitalfoodie system includes a series of interlinked staff and management interfaces tailored to the needs of different professional groups. This will improve communication between members of the team and will inform resource management, for example, increasing staffing levels on wards with high numbers of patients requiring assistance with meals. The system also generates a patient discharge summary of their nutritional care to assist in information exchange between care settings – that is, when a patient is discharged or readmitted, a history of their nutritional status, needs and preferences is transferred with them. The system is designed to enable hospital-wide nutritional performance to be tracked and audited.

Applications to other care settings

Through the qualitative methodologies employed, we explored the potential relevance of the hospitalfoodie system to community care. Many of the factors identified in the qualitative study contributing to inadequate food intake in older patients in hospital, including poor mealtime ambience, lack of necessary mealtime assistance, inflexible meal provision, lack of monitoring of nutrient intake and absence of accountability in nutritional care, are also relevant to older people living in the community (Moynihan et al, 2012).

Residential care home staff were confident that clients at risk of malnutrition were identified, but formal nutritional screening practices varied. A standard approach to regular nutrition screening for older people in all care settings, such as the Malnutrition Universal Screening Tool (MUST) in the hospitalfoodie system, was seen as a positive step to improving nutritional care in the community.

Personalisation and choice were central to community care services, but information available on client preferences varied, particularly for people with communication difficulties. Systems for ordering food simply involved a discussion with a member of staff. For people with dementia there was an emphasis on deciding at the point of consumption rather than making a choice in advance. Picture menus were only used in one of the homes.

Community care staff saw a key aspect of setting the scene to be company at mealtimes, and the homely nature of dining rooms in residential care homes was emphasised. Staff described eating with clients to encourage consumption, and recognised the importance of setting the scene and ensuring that sufficient help was available. Views on the applicability of the hospitalfoodie touch-screen monitoring system to community care varied. The visual nature of the task and speed with which intake could be recorded appealed, but an obvious barrier to use was dealing with variable portion sizes and non-standard menus. Issues were also raised about the potential intrusiveness of monitoring in the non-clinical setting.

The introduction of nutrient-dense foods as a potential alternative to oral nutritional supplement drinks was welcomed by many and fitted the ethos of 'food first' (before artificial nutrition).

Community care staff unanimously welcomed the idea of a nutrition discharge summary for patients leaving hospital. They reported currently receiving little information, and thought the more detailed reports proposed by the hospitalfoodie system would minimise delays in optimising nutritional care after discharge. The ability of the system to facilitate communication between staff was seen as important because shift patterns meant that staff were not always be able to passed on nutritional information in person. The scope of the system to alert managers and the community dietitian to clients at greatest risk was welcomed.

Policy and practice implications

The findings of the project were widely disseminated through publications, presentations and a purpose-designed exhibition. Findings have provided nutritionists, social scientists, food scientists, academic speech and language therapists, nurses and medical practitioners with insights on how to apply multidisciplinary co-design methods to develop new healthcare solutions. This is of particular value for increasing engagement of the public, patients and stakeholders in research. By presenting our multidisciplinary approach to researchers in design they have also gained insights into how to apply their expertise in the field of health research, and also how a more multidisciplinary approach encompassing qualitative techniques can enrich their work.

This unique methodological approach has led to the development of a novel and transferable synergistic methodology encompassing qualitative and design techniques in a suite of methods that can be applied to user-led healthcare research that is now being applied to other studies. Our findings suggest that there are advantages to including designers/design researchers as core members of the multidisciplinary team and to integrating design methods into the overall research methodology. The involvement of design approaches and the integration of these methods with methodologies from other disciplines assisted in the development of potentially workable solutions. For example, the visualisation of ethnographic and scientific data allowed these to be more easily shared among all members of the team and food family, and for processes, concepts and possible service solutions to be more easily understood. A rich mix of design methods, including visualisation, 'narratives' and prototyping workshops enabled the team to understand and discuss how the hospitalfoodie system would work, and to facilitate communication of this to the food family for their feedback. These made ideas and concepts more tangible, and facilitated the iterative and participative development. To achieve innovative solutions required particular techniques to enable speculative thinking 'outside the box' and for the 'rapid prototyping' and testing of concepts.

The mappmal project aimed to define current practice with respect to food provision to older hospital patients to clarify areas that may contribute to malnutrition and, with user engagement, to develop a new food provision service prototype to optimise the nutritional care of older patients. The results have produced original qualitative and ethnographic data that provide insights into the factors that contribute to hospital malnutrition, and have identified new service principles to optimise food provision and nutritional management that informed the development of a new service prototype for food provision for older hospital patients. The results have produced insights into the required rheological, textural, sensorial and nutritional properties of foods for older patients, including those with dysphagia, and have increased technical knowledge of valid computerised means of monitoring and tracking patient food intake against nutritional requirements.

The findings have increased the knowledge of many academic disciplines on the causes of malnutrition in older patients and, moreover, their knowledge of multidisciplinary approaches that offer potential solutions. The findings have had an impact on the knowledge base and potentially the practice of hospital catering staff, dietitians, nurses, speech and language therapists, healthcare assistants, care home managers and clinicians. By considering solutions to malnutrition from the perspective of all professions simultaneously, each profession gained knowledge and understanding of the issue relating to the food and nutritional care of older patients, from the perspective of all the professions involved. This also resulted in the potential solution that hospitalfoodie offers being better than what could have been achieved through working with each profession in isolation. Through dissemination of the findings to older people, their knowledge and understanding of the importance of good nutritional care to wellbeing and on the complexity of factors that contribute to hospital malnutrition will have increased.

The outcomes from the mappmal study have resulted in expressions of interest from several companies (for example, food producers and software companies) and care home providers who are interested in developing products based on our prototype. To date we have non-disclosure agreements in place with companies who have seen the potential for commercially viable products to arise from the mappmal outputs.

Hospitalfoodie was conceived as a unified system comprising nutritional management software/interfaces, a 'mini-meals' food trolley and nutrient-dense foods. However, each element is capable of being developed independently, and each is being pursued. The hope for the future is for a commercially viable nutritional management software system derived from the project's outputs.

The hospitalfoodie prototype is the end point of the mappmal project, and further research and investment is required to test the feasibility of the hospitalfoodie interfaces in a simulated clinical environment prior to ward-based pilot trials and full-scale implementation and evaluation trials. A longer-term aim of the mappmal team is to develop a sister system for care homes that is compatible with that designed for the acute setting. This could potentially facilitate improved transition of nutritional care across acute and primary healthcare and community settings. Many of the issues identified in hospital were also relevant to community care. While some aspects of hospitalfoodie are easily transferable to a community setting, other aspects will require modification.

Key findings

- A novel prototype for food provision and nutritional management of older hospital patients has been developed in a multidisciplinary iterative process involving users and stakeholders.
- The prototype was informed by ethnography that identified the core factors contributing to malnutrition, which were: inefficient and inflexible food

ordering/provision systems; poor mealtime ambience; lack of required assistance at mealtimes; poor monitoring of patient nutritional intake; and lack of accountability for nutritional care.

• The involvement of designers, and the integration of design methods and approaches with more traditional social science methods, enhanced user and stakeholder engagement and optimised project outcomes.

• The iterative development and participative co-design process facilitated user engagement, and innovative design approaches made ideas and opportunities tangible through mock-ups and prototyping methods.

• To address an identified need for smaller nutrient-dense foods for ward-level food provision, a range of mini-meals were developed including nutrient-enriched biscuits, ice cream, savoury sauces, soups and cakes.

Conclusions

A novel prototype for food provision and the nutritional management of older hospital patients has been developed in a multidisciplinary iterative process involving users and stakeholders. The prototype was informed by ethnography that identified the core factors contributing to malnutrition that were inefficient and inflexible food ordering/provision systems; poor mealtime ambience; lack of required assistance at mealtimes; poor monitoring of patient nutritional intake; and lack of accountability for nutritional care. The involvement of designers, and the integration of design methods and approaches with more traditional social science methods, enhanced user and stakeholder engagement and optimised project outcomes. The iterative development and participative co-design process facilitated user engagement, and innovative design approaches made ideas and opportunities tangible through mock-ups and prototyping methods. To address an identified need for smaller nutrient-dense foods for ward-level food provision, a range of mini-meals were developed including nutrient-enriched biscuits, ice cream, savoury sauces, soups and cakes. The hospitalfoodie prototype is the end point of the mappmal project, and further feasibility, pilot and implementation studies are required to realise the full potential of the prototype.

Acknowledgements

The mappmal project was conducted by Newcastle University, the University of Reading and the Glasgow School of Art in collaboration with the University of Loughborough. It was funded through the UK Research Councils' New Dynamics of Ageing programme. The authors acknowledge the contributions of the mappmal team – Ian Bell, Robert Coomber, Carol Fairfield, Margot Gosney, Ben Heaven, Martin Maguire, Yiannis Mavrommatis, Carl May, Patrick Olivier, Clare Payne, Elsie Richardson, Roussa Tsikritzi and Jack Weeden – and of the older people's representatives, food family and stakeholders, without whom the research would not have been possible.

References

Age Concern (2006) *Hungry to be heard: The scandal of malnourished older people in hospital*, London: Age Concern.

Age UK (2017) The Malnutrition Task Force Programme. Available at www.ageuk.org.uk/health-wellbeing/doctors-hospitals/campaign-against-malnutrition-in-hospital

Anderson, B. (1996) *Work, ethnography and system design*, Vol EPC-1996-103, Cambridge: Rank Xerox Research Centre.

BAPEN (British Association for Parenteral and Enteral Nutrition) (2003) *The MUST report: Nutritional screening of adults a multidisciplinary responsibility*. Available at www.bapen.org.uk

Brotherton, A., Simmonds, N. and Stroud, M. (2010) *Malnutrition matters. Meeting quality standards in nutritional care*. Available at www.bapen.org

DH (Department of Health) (2006) *Our health, our care, our say*, White Paper, London: DH.

DH (2007) *Improving nutritional care. A joint action plan from the Department of Health and Nutrition Summit Stakeholders*, London: NHS/DH.

Elia, M. (2015) *The cost of malnutrition in England and potential cost savings from nutritional interventions*. Available at www.bapen.org.uk/pdfs/economic-report-short.pdf

Finch, T.L., Mair, F.S. and May, C.R. (2007) 'Teledermatology in the UK: Lessons in service innovation', *British Journal of Dermatology*, vol 156, pp 521-7.

Finch, T.L., May, C.R., Mair, F.S., Mort, M. and Gask, L. (2003) 'Integrating service development with evaluation in telehealthcare: An ethnographic study', *British Medical Journal*, vol 327, pp 1205-9.

Heaven, B., Bamford, C., May, C.R. and Moynihan, P. (2012) 'Food work and feeding assistance on hospital wards', *Sociology of Health and Illness*, vol 35, pp 628-42.

Macdonald, A.S., Teal, G., Bamford, C. and Moynihan, P.J. (2012) 'Hospitalfoodie: An inter-professional case study of the redesign of the nutritional management and monitoring system for vulnerable older hospital patients', *Quality in Primary Care*, May, vol 20, no 3, pp 169-77.

Mavrommatis, Y., Moynihan, P.J., Gosney, M.A. and Methven, L. (2011) 'Hospital catering systems and their impact on the sensorial profile of foods provided to older patients in the UK', *Appetite*, vol 57, pp 14-20.

May, C.R. (2006) 'A rational model for assessing and evaluating complex interventions in health care', *BMC Health Services Research*, vol 6, p 86.

May, C.R. and Finch, T. (2009) 'Implementing, embedding, and integrating practices: An outline of normalization process theory', *Sociology*, vol 43, pp 535-54.

Moynihan, P., Macdonald, A., Teal, G., Methven, L., Heaven, B. and Bamford, C. (2012) 'Extending an approach to hospital malnutrition to community care', *British Journal of Community Nursing*, vol 17, no 12, pp 614-17.

Payne, C., Bell, A., Methven, L. and Fairfield, C. (2010) 'Consistently inconsistent – Commercially available starch-based dysphagia products', *Dysphagia*, vol 26, pp 27-33.

Payne, C., Methven, L., Bell, A.E., Fairfield, C. and Gosney, M.A. (2011) 'Reducing variable consistency in thickened drinks for patients with dysphagia', *Nursing & Residential Care*, 1 October, vol 13, no 10, pp 469-73.

Payne, C., Methven, L., Fairfield, C., Gosney, M.A. and Bell, A. (2012) 'Variability of starch-based thickened drinks for patients with dysphagia in the hospital setting', *Journal of Texture Studies*, vol 43, pp 95-105.

Ritchie, J. and Spencer, L. (1999) 'Qualitative data analysis for applied policy research', *Analysing Qualitative Data*, pp 173-94.

Stratton, R.J., Hackston, A., Longmore, D., Dixon, R., Price, S., Stroud, M., et al (2004) 'Malnutrition in hospital outpatients and inpatients: Prevalence, concurrent validity and ease of use of the "Malnutrition Universal Screening Tool" ("MUST") for adults', *British Journal of Nutrition*, November, vol 92, no 5, pp 799-808.

Tsikritzi, R., Moynihan, P.J., Gosney, M.A., Allen, V.J. and Methven, L. (2014) 'The effect of macro and micro-nutrient fortification of biscuits on their sensory properties and on hedonic liking of older people', *Journal of the Science of Food and Agriculture*, vol 94, no 10, pp 2040-8.

ELEVEN

Migration and nutrition

Janice L. Thompson, Joy Merrell, Barry Bogin,
Hannah Jennings, Michael Heinrich, Vanja Garaj,
Diane Harper, Bablin Molik and Jasmin Chowdhury

Introduction

The Bangladeshi population is one of the fastest growing ethnic groups within the UK. In 2011 the Bangladeshi population resident in England and Wales was 447,201, or 0.8 per cent of the total UK population; this is an increase of just over 50 per cent from the previous census in 2001 (ONS, 2012). Additionally, this group is reported to be one of the most deprived populations in the UK, having high rates of unemployment, social deprivation and low rates of education (Brice, 2008; Alexander et al, 2010). This group also has poorer self-reported and measured health status indicated by higher rates of disability, centralised obesity and chronic diseases such as type 2 diabetes and cardiovascular disease (Sproston and Mindell, 2006). Older Bangladeshi women are particularly affected as they play a lead role in caretaking for multiple generations within relatively large extended families, and many struggle to cope with the complex challenges of ageing, poverty, racism and social exclusion.

The migration of Bangladeshis to the UK has a long history, with the majority of those migrating originating from the Sylhet region in northeast Bangladesh (Gardner, 2002). Research has been dedicated to understanding how to improve the health of Bangladeshi residents in the UK; however, the majority of this research has concentrated on the Tower Hamlets region of London, limiting the amount of knowledge about those communities living outside of the London area (Brice, 2008). Findings from these studies may not be generalisable to other UK communities, so more research is needed to expand our understanding of this minority ethnic group and how to improve their health and wellbeing and reduce existing health inequalities.

MINA was a three-year project that examined ageing, migration and nutrition across two generations of Bangladeshi women living in

Cardiff, UK and Sylhet, Bangladesh. The 2011 Census indicates that the Bangladeshi population living in Cardiff is 4,838, or approximately 45 per cent of the Bangladeshis living in Wales (ONS, 2012). This research builds on the existing literature focusing on migration and ageing among UK Bangladeshis (Gardner, 2002; Phillipson et al, 2003), providing new insights into specifically food, nutrition and their interactions with ageing and migration among UK Bangladeshi families who are living in communities outside of Tower Hamlets, London.

As in the general population, nutrition plays a crucial role in the health status of the Bangladeshi population. Despite this, there is no clear understanding of how eating patterns and migration affects this group's nutritional status and experiences of ageing. Without this information we cannot develop effective, culturally tailored interventions. The MINA project addressed these gaps using interdisciplinary approaches, integrating methods and combined expertise not used in previous research to gain an in-depth understanding of Bangladeshi women's nutritional status, food practices, beliefs and experiences of ageing in the UK and Bangladesh.

Aims and methods

The aim was to investigate migration, nutrition and ageing via an intergenerational and transnational project incorporating multidisciplinary methodologies. The intergenerational component included recruiting a sample of older women who migrated from Bangladesh to the UK and their adult daughters, who were either UK-born or migrated to the UK in childhood. The transnational component included recruiting women of the same two age groups and familial relationship living in Sylhet, Bangladesh, providing a continuum to understand the influence of migration, nutrition and eating patterns on ageing. Participants in both countries were purposively recruited across the range of deprivation. The project's multidisciplinary component is based on the diverse disciplines of the MINA research team, providing expertise in public health nutrition and exercise, biological anthropology, health psychology, public health nursing, ethnobotany, environmental and media design, social gerontology and social anthropology. We integrated these components via a bio-cultural perspective that gives equal importance to the physical/biological and social/psychological aspects of food, nutrition, migration and ageing.

MINA addressed the following research questions:

1. Does migration impact on nutritional status, food practices and health among first-generation Bangladeshi women aged 45 and older? If so,
2. How does migration affect the nutritional status, food practices and health of the successive generation of women living in the UK? and
3. How does migration affect changes in nutritional status, food practices and health compared with non-migrating women of the same ages and familial relationships in Bangladesh?

These questions were addressed through four integrated work packages using a participatory, mixed-methods approach to gather and analyse data. Ethical approval was granted by the Ethics Committee of the College of Human and Health Sciences at Swansea University, Wales. All participants were provided with written information in Bangla and English about the study and written, or where there were literacy issues, recorded verbal consent was obtained. A purposive sample of 40 Bangladeshi women (target age 45+) who migrated to the UK and were residing in Cardiff, 37 of their daughters (target age 18-35) and 44 women of the same age groups living in Sylhet, Bangladesh were recruited. The total sample size was therefore 121 women. In addition, a sub-sample of 54 mothers and daughters from the total MINA sample (24 in Bangladesh and 30 in Cardiff) participated in a qualitative interview. Inclusion criteria for this sub-sample included age at migration, evidence of chronic health conditions, marital status and age. The research conducted within Work Package 3 (WP3) also included additional participants independent of the main MINA sample who were recruited from London and Sylhet; ethics approval for the research conducted for this work package was granted by University College London and Brunel University.

A Community Advisory Committee (CAC) was established in Cardiff, which was comprised of men and women from the Bangladeshi community in Cardiff, as well as Cardiff-based health and local authority representatives who advised on the entire research process. Eleven Bangladeshi women residing in Cardiff and Swansea were recruited and trained as community researchers and participated in all aspects of the study. Their participation enhanced access and recruitment of participants and the quality of data generated, as participants were able to complete the questionnaires and interviews through their preferred language, that is, Bengali, Sylheti or English.

As a token of appreciation a £10 supermarket voucher was provided to participants who agreed to participate in the qualitative interview.

In Cardiff data collection was organised through hosting five community events in a local leisure centre, which included a range of physical and social activities, and lunch, and provided curtained facilities for the anthropometric measurements, ensuring participants' privacy. In Bangladesh, data collection occurred in a host's house in rural villages as well as in urban areas across the Sylhet region. Participants in Bangladesh were given a basket of fruit equivalent to the UK value of £10, which, after local enquiries, was deemed an appropriate token of appreciation.

The following measurements were used to quantify nutritional status: height, weight, sitting height, knee height and waist circumference. Physical function was assessed by the Guralnik Short Physical Performance Battery (SPPB) (Guralnik et al, 1994), a standardised set of tests for leg muscle strength, walking speed and standing balance that can be validly and reliably conducted in the field in older adults. Questions were also asked about age at marriage and age at birth of first child, total number of pregnancies and number of living children. Differences between life course experiences and the typical 'food environments' of the Bangladeshi community in the UK and in Bangladesh were assessed using a semi-structured questionnaire, in-depth interviews, participant observation and photo-ethnography. Detailed accounts of migration and biographical experiences were gathered using a semi-structured questionnaire and qualitative interviews to assess their impact on nutritional status, health behaviours and transmission of nutritional knowledge cross-generationally and transnationally. Additionally the influence of cultural beliefs on nutrition, health and health-seeking behaviours and how this has changed across the lifespan and between generations was examined. The impact of social inequalities on nutrition and health status, changes in the roles, position and responsibilities of women in the household and the impact on their nutrition, the family unit and wider community were also assessed.

Quantitative data were analysed using IBM-SPSS (version 16). All data were double-entered and verified for accuracy. Descriptive statistics were calculated for all variables by the categories of generation (mother or daughter), country of birth and current country of residence. Descriptive statistics (means, standard deviations, ranges, frequencies) were calculated for all quantitative variables. Statistical significance of comparisons between generations, locations, place of birth and other contrasts were assessed by Mann–Whitney U Tests,

Kruskal–Wallis Tests, Student's t-test, analysis of variance, multiple regression and similar non-parametric and parametric statistics. All interviews were transcribed verbatim and translated. A sub-sample of interviews ($n=4$) was back-translated to ensure accuracy of the translation. Thematic analysis was used to analyse the qualitative data in order to identify key patterns and themes, which were linked and categorised in order to make inferences (Bowling, 2002). Two researchers coded and categorised the data that was then compared, and any discrepancies discussed and categories revised accordingly to facilitate inter-rater reliability. Deviant cases were identified and reported and the findings were compared with the literature.

Findings

The findings presented here are organised into the four work packages for ease of reporting. We follow these with an overview of implications for policy, practice and product development, and conclude with a brief discussion highlighting areas needing further exploration in future research.

WP1: Community engagement and conceptual development

The aims of this work package were to develop a common conceptual framework, to review the existing evidence and to develop methods for community engagement. These aims were achieved via: (1) the successful establishment of a Community Advisory Committee (CAC) that included local Bangladeshi people and other key stakeholders as members; (2) the establishment of a Scientific Advisory Committee (SAC) including experts in migration/social anthropology (Professor Katy Gardner, Sussex University) and social gerontology (Professor Christina Victor, Brunel University); (3) frequent meetings (face-to-face and conference calls) to exploit the synergy of the different disciplines and maintain cohesion within the research team; (4) recruitment and training of two Bangladeshi research assistants, one Bangladeshi postdoctoral fellow, and 11 Bangladeshi community researchers from the Cardiff and Swansea areas; and (5) a thorough review of existing secondary data sets from the UK Data Archive that include health information on Bangladeshis, and are summarised in the MINA data map for health information among Bangladeshis (Harper et al, 2011).

WP2: Nutritional status and physical function

The aims of this work package were to assess the nutritional status and physical function of two generations of Bangladeshi women. The underlying premise for the proposed biological and functional measures is based on the Intergenerational Influences Hypothesis (IIH) proposed by Emanuel (1986, p 27), and defined as, '... those factors, conditions, exposures and environments experienced by one generation that relate to the health, growth and development of the next generation.' In the context of this study, the IIH relates to the existence of a non–genomic mechanism (that is, not inherited via classic genetic inheritance) in which the nutritional status of the mother during her early development may have health and ageing consequences for not only the mother and her offspring, but even for subsequent generations who do not experience the same exposures and environments.

The descriptive characteristics of all participants are reported in Table 11.1. Cardiff and Bangladeshi mothers ranged in age from 40-70, while Cardiff and Bangladeshi daughters ranged in age from 17-36. All participants were short in stature (mean height: mothers = 148cm, daughters = 153cm, no significant difference between age groups, $p>0.05$). Cardiff mothers were older, and Cardiff mothers and daughters were shorter and had higher levels of overweight and obesity than the general UK-Bangladeshi population, as assessed in the Health Survey of England (Sproston and Mindell, 2006). As expected, UK-residing women had higher rates of overweight, obesity and centralised obesity than women residing in Bangladesh. Obesity was particularly high in Cardiff mothers, with 65 per cent having body mass index (BMI) values indicative of obesity compared to 27.3 per cent of Bangladeshi mothers using definitions for South Asians (WHO, 2004). Similarly, 42.5 per cent of Cardiff daughters had BMI values indicative of obesity as compared to 13.6 per cent of Bangladeshi daughters. Conversely, about one-fifth of all women living in Bangladesh were underweight, whereas none of the UK-residing participants were underweight.

In addition to high rates of overweight and obesity in the Cardiff participants, the Cardiff mothers exhibited average physical function scores indicative of an increased risk for frailty, with eight unable to perform most elements of the SPPB test. Physical function in Cardiff mothers was significantly lower than in Bangladeshi mothers. Even the Bangladeshi mother participants of higher socioeconomic status who did not engage in physical work and had servants assisting

Table 11.1: Descriptive characteristics of project MINA participants

	Cardiff mothers (*n*=40)	Bangladesh mothers (*n*=22)	Cardiff daughters (*n*=37)	Bangladesh daughters (*n*=22)
Age (years)	55.3 (8.1)	51.9 (8.8)	27.4 (5.5)[a]	22.8 (5.1)[a]
Height (Cardiff mothers)	147.7 (6.2)	148.8 (5.7)	153.2 (5.8)	152.7 (6.0)
Sitting height (Cardiff mothers)	77.4 (3.7)	76.4 (3.4)	81.4 (2.4)[a]	78.2 (3.0)[a]
Knee height (Cardiff mothers)	45.9 (2.4)	46.9 (2.4)	46.7 (2.5)	48.2 (2.3)
Weight (kg)	66.0 (13.4)[b]	53.5 (15.2)[b]	64.5 (14.5)[a]	50.8 (10.6)[a]
Waist circumference (Cardiff mothers)	97.9 (9.6)[b]	82.5 (14.0)[b]	82.4 (13.0)[a]	72.4 (8.3)[a]
Body mass index (BMI) (kg/m²)	30.1 (5.2)[b]	24.1 (6.4)[b]	27.5 (5.7)[a]	21.8 (4.4)[a]
BMI category[c]				
Underweight	0%	13.6%	0%	22.7%
Acceptable risk	5%	40.9%	25.0%	40.9%
Increased risk	30%	18.2%	22.5%	22.7%
High risk	65%	27.3%	42.5%	13.6%
Physical function score[d]	6.3 (3.0)[a]	9.4 (1.9)*	10.8 (1.1)	11.2 (0.8)
Age at marriage (years)	16.3 (2.7)	16.5 (3.3)	18.7 (2.3) *n*=24	18.4 (3.8) *n*=7
Age when first child was born (years)	20.8 (4.2)	23.2 (5.5)	21.3 (2.2) *n*=20	20.5 (2.6) *n*=6
Total pregnancies	6.6 (2.0)	5.6 (2.1)	2.9 (1.0) *n*=20	2.9 (2.3) *n*=7
Number of living children	5.6 (1.8)	4.9 (1.6)	2.6 (0.9) *n*=20	2.7 (1.5) *n*=7

Notes: Values represent mean (standard deviation) or percentages.

[a] Differences between daughters are statistically significant (*p*≤0.01).

[b] Differences between mothers are statistically significant (*p*≤0.01).

[c] World Health Organization BMI cut-off categories for South Asians: Underweight < 18.5; increasing but acceptable risk 18.5-23; increased risk 23.1-27.5; high risk >27.5.

[d] Score on the Short Physical Function Battery, maximum score = 12.

with household activities achieved higher physical function scores than the Cardiff mothers. The cultural norm to honour one's elders by encouraging limited physical movement was described by both Cardiff mothers and daughters, in addition to many Cardiff mothers reporting being socially isolated (discussed later in this chapter). Previous research indicates that limited engagement in physical and social activities outside of the home is associated with low physical function in older adults (Davis et al, 2011). Physical activity levels were not measured in the MINA project, but during qualitative interviews participants were asked about types of activities they participated in during a 'typical day'. Cardiff mothers described lifestyles that were much more sedentary and less socially engaged than Bangladeshi mothers; limited opportunities for Cardiff mothers to get 'out and about' on a daily basis likely contributed to their low levels of physical function. Cardiff daughters described leading busy lives focusing on family duties, work and education, but few reported participating in physical activities that promote health.

All mothers (Cardiff and Bangladeshi) were married or widowed; according to their demographic history all had completed fertility (defined as age over 45 and at least five years since last birth). Mothers in both countries had, on average, an equal number of pregnancies, number of live born children, pregnancy loss and relatively high fertility. Data on age at marriage and number of children for the daughters (Cardiff and Bangladeshi) indicate that 24 of the 37 Cardiff daughters were married or divorced, and only 7 of 22 Bangladeshi daughters were married at the time of data collection. The lower number of married Bangladeshi daughters reflects their younger age and our decision to interview the Bangladesh-residing women who lived in the same geographic region of Sylhet; in Bangladesh, married daughters typically live with their spouse and parents-in-law, and in this study most of the married daughters did not live in close proximity to their mothers.

WP3: Food ethnobotany and 'food environments' – A comparative study between the UK and Bangladesh

Initial research related to food ethnobotany was conducted in Cardiff to provide a formative assessment and to allow for the piloting of questions for subsequent focus groups and interviews. The food ethnobotany-related research questions examined in this work package were:

1. What foods and medicines are used therapeutically among Bangladeshis in the UK and Bangladesh?
2. How do food and medicine overlap?
3. What is the nature of global links (and exchange between families) and their contribution to the therapeutic foodscape of the home?
4. What impact do these links have on the plants and foods consumed therapeutically in the homes of families in the UK and Bangladesh?
5. What is the nature of knowledge transfer across the two generations regarding plants and food?

Research took place in both Sylhet and London exploring the above questions, and comparisons were made between the two places. Some of the key findings of our research were (Jennings et al, in press):

- Various plants are taken as medicine or 'healthy' food among Bangladeshis in the UK and Bangladesh. Therapeutic plant use is more common among older Bangladeshis in the UK, with both older and younger Bangladeshis engaging in therapeutic plant use in Bangladesh. However, use also depended on family dynamics as well as individual preferences and beliefs related to medicinal plant use.
- In the UK, plants are most frequently used to promote general health, and to treat minor upper respiratory ailments and type 2 diabetes. Most of the plants used therapeutically are considered 'Bangladeshis', and medicinal plant use is strongly identified with Bangladesh.
- UK-based links and exchanges with Bangladesh, through word of mouth as well as physical exchanges of foodstuff and seeds, are important to maintaining existing food medicine knowledge.
- Transnational links play out in each place differently. In the UK, Bangladesh is viewed as the source of medicinal plant knowledge and food related to home. In Bangladesh, foods associated with wealth and pleasure are sent from the UK.
- The conceptualisations of 'food' and 'medicine' are used interchangeably across countries and generations. What plant is consumed as well as how it is prepared, and the reasons for its consumption, helps determine whether it is taken as a food or a medicine, and the boundary between the two is often blurred.
- Knowledge transfer between generations is complex. While daughters in both countries learn from their mothers about food medicine, there are other important knowledge sources including peers, other family members, local and global networks, formal education, books and practitioners. The acquisition and transmission

of knowledge is also part of much larger processes, with age/ ageing, power structures, access to different forms of healthcare and migration all being important contributors.

In addition to exploring food ethnobotany, another aim of this work package was to document, analyse and compare the typical 'food environments' used by the Bangladeshi communities in Cardiff and London with those used in Bangladesh. The term 'food environments' implies four domains: (1) the types of food in the diet; (2) the environment in which food is acquired (for example, supermarket, allotment); (3) the environment in which food is prepared (for example, kitchen); and (4) the environment in which food is consumed (for example, dining room). Focusing on women across two generations, but also considering the society at large, the research employed the methods of photo-ethnography and qualitative interviews. The findings were summarised in a collection of 69 photographs and accompanying short stories; these provide an overview of the food habits in the two countries (see Figure 11.1) (Garaj et al, 2012). The photographs and the stories (Garaj, 2012) have been presented to the Bangladeshi community and general public through numerous exhibitions in different locations across the UK. These include a month-long exhibit that took place between 15 November and 15 December 2011 in 'The Cardiff story – The new museum of Cardiff history' (BBC News Southeast Wales, 2011; Chamberlain, 2011), and the New Dynamics of Ageing and Age UK dissemination 'Event of the Decade' held on 23 October 2013 in London at the Business Design Centre, Islington, London (New Dynamics of Ageing programme, 2013).

The final aim of the work package was to establish the best ways of using digital media to promote the importance of healthy food habits among the Bangladeshi women living in the UK. The questionnaire-based study involved 28 women of Bangladeshi origin residing in London and Cardiff and focused on the distribution language/s, media format/s and content types needed and preferred when presenting nutritional information. The results suggest that print and digital resources should be made available. Participants also want information provided digitally on the internet and in DVD format, emphasising the need for information that is presented in the spoken word format, using the oral dialect of Sylheti to accompany English and Bengali print information. This flexibility is to ensure that the health promotion content reaches the widest possible pool of targeted users and their family members (Garaj et al, 2010).

Figure 11.1: Two examples of photos and short stories of 'food environments' from the project MINA

Photo A: Bishwanath, Sylhet Division, Bangladesh: Bengali food is traditionally cooked over a wood fire, and the vast majority of Bangladeshi women still prepare food this way. It's not only a matter of tradition, but of economic status – cooking with gas is not an option for families in the countryside, and wood remains the cheapest and most readily-available fuel, providing over 60% of the country's energy. The downside is constant exposure to wood smoke, which can damage the lungs. Salma, aged 22, says she suffers constant headaches, but does not regard this as a sign of illness.

Photo B: 'Londoni' diet in the UK reflects the mingling of the two cultures – a mixture of traditional food, with Bangladeshi herbs and spices, alongside Western snacks and fast food. Traditional Bangladeshi cuisine includes fatty ingredients like oil and ghee, but is generally balanced by fresh fish, fruit and vegetables. When migrants come to the UK, they often end up eating the worst of both worlds – the Western portion of this diet and low physical activity contribute to obesity and heart disease, especially among older women.

WP4 – Migration, nutrition and ageing: Health beliefs, health behaviours and health status

The aims of this work package were to explore the influence of migration on health beliefs, health behaviours and health status across the lifespan and in two generations of Bangladeshi women. Using methods described previously, we (1) obtained detailed accounts of the women's migration and biographical experiences and explored the impact on nutritional status, health behaviours and transmission of nutritional knowledge; (2) explored the influence of cultural beliefs on nutrition, health and health-seeking behaviours and how this has changed across the lifespan and between generations; (3) examined the impact of social inequalities on nutrition and health status; (4) explored changes in the roles, position and responsibilities of women in the household and the impact on their nutrition, the family unit and wider community; (5) obtained detailed accounts of the women's perceptions and expectations of an older person in their community; and (6) gained an understanding of the extent and nature of transnational ties and their influence on issues related to nutrition and ageing.

Results indicated that the majority of participants migrated from villages in the Sylhet region to Cardiff during the 1980s, although due to the age range of participants, the period of migration ranged from 1972 to 2005. This migration pattern is consistent with other published studies (see, for example, Gardner, 1995; Phillipson et al, 2003) that have reported Bangladeshi women's migration to the UK. Similar to these studies, most of our participants migrated not as individuals but as members of transnational communities and households, and over two-thirds had resided in Cardiff for more than 21 years. In contrast to Burholt's (2004a) study conducted in Birmingham on Bangladeshi women's migration patterns, most of the MINA participants migrated directly to Cardiff rather than experiencing several moves within the UK before finally settling. The main reasons for migration were to accompany family (58 per cent), economic reasons (26 per cent) and for marriage (14 per cent). The Cardiff mothers' mean age at migration was 30 (SD=9.4), and most had born and were raising children in Sylhet prior to migration. Seventeen (46 per cent) of the Cardiff daughters were born in Bangladesh, and as the mean age at migration was 8.2 (SD=6.8), accompanying family was their main reason for migration. The majority reported regular contact with family in Bangladesh maintained through frequent phone calls and regular visits. The varied migration histories of participants exert differential effects on nutritional and health status (both in childhood and adulthood), personal food preferences, the role that traditional food and cooking practices plays in one's daily life and perspectives on ageing.

In terms of cooking practices, the Bangladeshi mothers and daughters were more likely to report following the cooking practices of their mothers than the two generations of women living in Cardiff, although the Cardiff daughters were the least likely to cook like their mothers. While some Cardiff and Bangladeshi mothers were adapting their cooking to promote health (for example, reducing fat and salt content), they consistently emphasised that this had a negative impact on the taste, and for some family members this raised issues of palatability:

> 'In this country [Wales] you need to put a bit more oil in cooking. In our country you need less oil. In this country if you don't put a bit more oil, everything tastes bland.' (Cardiff mother 13)

Adding salt to cooking was the norm among participants. There was evidence of behaviour change by some Cardiff mothers as, for example, five out of the seven who reported reducing their salt intake had self-reported being diagnosed with hypertension. Their daughters had not been influenced by this behaviour change to the same extent, despite reporting wider access to a range of nutritional information sources, including school-based education and the internet. While addition of spices were acknowledged as enhancing taste, several of the Cardiff mothers reported reducing spice content because of gastrointestinal problems.

All participants recognised that food is crucial to promoting good health and understood the importance of good nutrition. However, a diagnosis of a risk factor or disease was a key motivator or 'a cue for action' (Glanz et al, 2002) for behaviour change. For example, participants diagnosed with type 2 diabetes were more likely to report eating fewer ready meals, savoury snacks and sweet foods and were less likely to use salt or add sugar to hot drinks. Our findings suggest that participants were more likely to alter food choices or modify their cooking habits as a result of the diagnosis of disease rather than as a preventative measure.

Consumption of fruit was low for all groups, with the highest consumption reported by Cardiff daughters, of whom just over a quarter (27 per cent) ate fruit more than three to four times a day. Just under a fifth of participants in Bangladesh rarely or never ate fruit. Although widely available, the cost of fruit in Bangladesh was a barrier to its consumption. Vegetable and rice consumption was lower in Cardiff-residing participants than their counterparts in Bangladesh. Cultural factors also influenced food consumption, as indicated in the following:

> 'Never to waste anything away, I think that's a cultural thing, never throw anything away, eat everything that you got on your plate, I think that's a cultural thing. They [parents] would say, "there are poor people and we left Bangladesh to have all this food", and I think that's the key. Culturally, the social eating means you eat more. We grew up in a large family and we all ate more. There was always somebody making different things and it's almost rude not to eat when somebody offers you something.' (Cardiff daughter 14)

While avoidance of waste is not specific to Bangladeshi culture, the practice of cooking and eating communally tends to be more common in Asian than Western cultures. However, this practice is now changing as the roles of second-generation Bangladeshi women are expanding due to wider opportunities outside the home becoming accessible to them. In an environment of communal cooking and food consumption, participants emphasised that trying to introduce changes in dietary habits was challenging, as it had an impact on all family members. This approach to cooking and eating is also quite challenging for researchers and participants in monitoring individual food intake. Consistent with the findings from WP3, participants reported frequent exchange of nutritional and health information, especially from Wales to Bangladesh. For older Cardiff mothers, health professionals, especially doctors, were the main source of nutritional information, while their daughters accessed wider information sources. In this sample, 75 per cent of the Cardiff mothers and daughters reported receiving healthy eating advice; however, a fifth of Cardiff mothers and one of the Cardiff daughters reported that this information was not helpful. As previously discussed, Cardiff-residing participants emphasised that there is a need for health promotion information in oral Sylheti, and for bilingual information sources, placed side-by-side on the same page in both Bengali and English, as this aids intergenerational exchange of information.

Distinct differences were evident in self-reported health, emotional wellbeing and level of social participation between generations and transnationally. Both generations residing in Bangladesh reported better health status than Cardiff-residing mothers and daughters, who were more likely to report their own health as poor or very poor. Cardiff mothers were also more likely than Bangladeshi mothers to report poor emotional wellbeing. Conversely, Cardiff daughters reported better emotional wellbeing than their counterparts in Bangladesh. Many of the Cardiff mothers reported feelings of isolation and loneliness, as reported by others (Victor et al, 2012; Phillipson et al, 2003), although only one Cardiff mother reported living alone. Lack of English proficiency, a paucity of culturally acceptable social activities and community spaces, and concerns regarding cold weather, physical safety, vulnerability and racism severely limit many older women's social connectivity and engagement with wider society. For Cardiff daughters, particularly those who are bilingual, most have benefited from gaining a UK-based formal education, and engage fully in paid or voluntary work, further education and in social activities connected with their children and the wider community. Bangladeshi daughters who had also been provided with such educational opportunities acknowledged the benefits in terms of enhancing social mobility, connectivity and life opportunities, but these opportunities were not accessible to all living in Bangladesh.

All participants residing in Sylhet lived in large, multigenerational households. Half of the Cardiff mothers and 61 per cent of Cardiff daughters lived in nuclear or sub-nuclear structured households. These findings contrast with studies of Sylheti elders residing in Birmingham (Burholt, 2004a, b; Burholt et al, 2000) and London (Phillipson et al, 2003), where multigenerational households were the most common arrangement. Changes in household structure have important implications for the availability of support and future care of ageing Bangladeshi women in Cardiff. Additionally, adult daughters as opposed to traditionally sons and daughters-in-law are increasingly assuming responsibility for the care of ageing parents as a result of changing family structures, due to the global migration of children and grandchildren. As the majority of Cardiff mothers reported they would stay in the UK for the remainder of their lives, even though this had not been their intention when they initially migrated, some participants expressed concerns about their future care needs, as they may not have adult children living nearby who can provide care at home as they age.

Policy and practice implications

Our findings indicate the importance of health and social care practitioners and policy-makers being aware of the complexity of factors that influence Bangladeshi women's food behaviours, practices and health status. Cardiff-residing mothers and their daughters were making dietary changes, but often in response to a disease diagnosis rather than as a preventive measure. The diagnosis of disease or a related risk factor acted as the trigger for making dietary changes, often following medical advice. The roles of doctors and other members of the primary healthcare team in providing culturally tailored nutritional information need to be more clearly defined and enhanced; there is also a need to provide accessible public health nutrition information in non-clinical, community-based settings. Family members are also an important source of health-related, cooking, food/plant and nutrition information in both countries, and exert a strong influence on older women and their ability to make dietary changes. This finding emphasises the need for family members across all generations to have access to accurate nutrition information in culturally tailored and accessible formats, and to be involved in research that is conducted with their older Bangladeshi family members.

Applying dietary advice developed for the general population to the Asian diet was also reported by participants to be challenging. The Western ethnocentric concept of the Eatwell plate (NHS, 2013) is inappropriate for cultures whose food practices include serving multiple dishes, with individuals filling and refilling their plate several times throughout one meal. It is also the case that social eating can result in eating more, as individuals are less aware of the amount they are eating. These findings support the need for explicit guidance with respect to portion sizes. Providing recommendations with respect to portion sizes for males and females of different ages in ways that are easily implemented and better reflect eating behaviours, such as using 'handfuls', may be more relevant. Portion size-focused recommendations may also be appropriate for the general population, as portion sizes have been steadily increasing, and this trend is especially noticeable in countries such as the US (US Department of Health and Human Services et al, 2013), which also has high levels of obesity.

Within the next decade the number of Bangladeshi elders will significantly increase (Burholt, 2004a, b). In Cardiff, daughters are assuming primary responsibility for the care of elderly parents. However, with wider opportunities available to women, changing family and household structures and greater geographical mobility of family members, it cannot be assumed that all families will be able to care for their elderly parents. Planning and provision of healthcare and social services need to take account of the diverse care needs of this growing ageing Bangladeshi population. This may be particularly challenging for cities such as Cardiff, where there is a smaller population density of Bangladeshis than in other areas of the UK (for example, Tower Hamlets and Birmingham, where culturally tailored services have been mainstreamed). Innovative strategies including the co-design and co-production of services (Joyner, 2012), which build on the knowledge, skills and resources of the Bangladeshi community, may enhance the planning and provision of culturally acceptable health and social care services.

Key findings

- High levels of obesity were found among Bangladeshi mothers and daughters living in Cardiff, which are associated with frequent consumption of high-fat savoury and sweet foods and low levels of physical activity.
- Low levels of physical function are common among Bangladeshi mothers living in Cardiff, which are associated with low physical activity levels and increased risk for frailty.
- Bangladeshi mothers and daughters living in Cardiff report poorer health status than their counterparts in Bangladesh.
- The exchange of health and nutrition knowledge is dynamic and spans across generations and countries through a range of mediums, including word of mouth, the internet, formal education and health professionals.
- There is a need for health promotion and public health campaigns and materials tailored for the Bangladeshi community that actively engages them, uses oral Sylheti information, and provides health and social care services designed to meet the diverse needs of this increasingly ageing population.

Conclusions

The results of project MINA indicate that varied migration histories and changing family structures play an important role in influencing nutritional status, perceived and actual health status and the future health and social care needs of ageing Bangladeshis in the UK. There is a clear need for greater access to leisure facilities, day centres and other social opportunities that can consistently offer culturally appropriate physical and social activities. Providing a social component in conjunction with a physical activity may promote engagement, particularly for older UK-residing Bangladeshi women. There is a clear and critical need for further culturally relevant health promotion, disease prevention and public health campaigns for the Bangladeshi community, provided through a range of media and incorporating oral Sylheti. Nutrition-related health promotion messages and materials need to focus more on portion sizes, as opposed to the concept of the Eatwell plate that has limited relevance for communities who eat communally. Changes in family structures, wider employment opportunities for women and increased geographical mobility means that not all families may be able to care for their elderly parents.

Future research should focus on the development of validated culturally and linguistically tailored research tools to assess the dietary intake and eating behaviours within this population. Additionally, more research needs to be conducted with family members and other key influences to gain a better understanding of the complex interplay between family dynamics, cultural norms and social influences that have an impact on the ability of older Bangladeshi adults to eat more healthily and to engage in physical and social activities that promote healthy ageing.

References

Alexander, C., Firoz, S. and Rashid, N. (2010) *The Bengali diaspora in Britain: A review of the literature*, London: London School of Economics. Available at www.banglastories.org/uploads/Literature_review.pdf

BBC News Southeast Wales (2011) 'In pictures: Vanja Garaj's lives of Bangladeshi women', 20 November [Online Photo Gallery]. Available at www.bbc.co.uk/news/uk-wales-south-east-wales-15765782

Bowling, A. (2002) *Research methods in health. Investigating health and health services* (2nd edn), Buckingham: Open University Press.

Brice, J. (2008) 'Migrants and the second generation: Health inequalities in Bristol's Bangladeshi community', *Durham Anthropology Journal*, vol 15, no 1, pp 59-105.

Burholt, V. (2004a) 'The settlement patterns and residential histories of older Gujaratis, Punjabis and Sylhetis in Birmingham, England', *Ageing and Society*, vol 24, pp 383-409.

Burholt, V. (2004b) 'Transnationalism, economic transfers and families' ties: Intercontinental contacts of older Gujaratis, Punjabis and Sylhetis in Birmingham with families abroad', *Ethnic and Racial Studies*, vol 27, no 5, pp 800-29.

Burholt, V., Wenger, C., Scott, A., Yahya, B. and Roy, S. (2000) 'Bangladeshi immigration to the United Kingdom: Older people's support networks in the sending and receiving countries', *Quality in Ageing and Older Adults*, vol 1, no 2, pp 18-30.

Chamberlain, L. (2011) 'Photography exhibition explores Bangladeshi community', *BBC Wales Arts Blog*, 25 November. Available at www.bbc.co.uk/blogs/walesarts/2011/11/photography_exhibition_explores_bangladeshi_community_cardiff_story.html

Davis, M.G., Fox, K.R., Hillsdon, M., Coulson, J.C., Sharp, D.J., Stathi, A. and Thompson, J.L. (2011) 'Getting out and about in older adults: The nature of daily trips and their association with objectively assessed physical activity', *International Journal of Behavioral Nutrition and Physical Activity*, vol 8, p 116. Available at www.ijbnpa.org/content/8/1/116

Emanuel, I. (1986) 'Maternal health during childhood and later reproductive performance', *Annals of the New York Academy of Sciences*, vol 477, pp 27-39.

Garaj, V. (2012) 'Wales and Bangladesh', *Planet – The International Magazine for Wales*, vol 205, pp 124-32 [Photo Essay].

Garaj, V., Hunt, N. and Thompson, J.L. (2012) *Project MINA: Migration, nutrition, ageing.* Available at projectmina.org

Garaj, V., Thompson, J.L., Merrell, J., Meier, P., Bogin, B., Heinrich, M. and Basher, J. (2010) 'Project MINA: Designing multimedia resources to improve the nutrition of Bangladeshi immigrants in the United Kingdom', *Proceedings of the 2nd International Conference for Universal Design*, Hamamatsu, 30 October-3 November, Japan: International Organisation for Universal Design.

Gardner, K. (1995) *Global migrants, local lives: Travel and transformation in rural Bangladesh*, Oxford: Open University Press.

Gardner, K. (2002) *Age, narrative and migration: The life course and life histories of Bengali elders in Britain*, Oxford: Berg.

Glanz, K., Rimer, B.K. and Lewis, F.M. (2002) *Health behavior and health education. Theory, research and practice*, San Francisco, CA: Wiley & Sons.

Guralnik, J.M., Simonsick, E.M., Ferrucci, L., Glynn, R.J., Berkman, L.F., Blazer, D.G., et al (1994) 'A Short Physical Performance Battery assessing lower extremity function: association with self-reported disability and prediction of mortality and nursing home admission', *Journal of Gerontology*, vol 49, M85-M94.

Harper, D., Bogin, B., Merrell, J., Heinrich, M., Garaj, V., Chowdhury, J., et al (2011) *Data map for health information amongst Bangladeshis from the United Kingdom Data Archive (UKDA)*. Available at www.bris.ac.uk/mina/reports/

Jennings, H.M., Heinrich, M. and Thompson, J.L. (in press) 'Bengali-British food journeys: Exploring the movement of food and plants across transnational landscapes', in P. Howland, C. Rey Vasquez and H. Macbeth (eds) *Food, globalization and human diversity*, Oxford: Berg.

Joyner, S. (2012) 'Co-production in social care: A practical exercise', in E. Loeffler, D. Taylor-Gooby, T. Bovaird, F. Hine-Hughes and L. Wilkes (eds) *Making health and social care personal and local. Moving from mass production to co-production*, Birmingham: Governance International, pp 15-20.

NHS (National Health Service) (2013) *NHS Choices. Live well. The Eatwell Guide.* Available at www.nhs.uk/Livewell/Goodfood/Pages/eatwell-plate.aspx

New Dynamics of Ageing programme (2013) 'A new dynamic of ageing: The NDA Programme and Age UK research showcase of the decade'. Available at www.newdynamics.group.shef.ac.uk/showcase.html

ONS (Office for National Statistics) (2012) 2011 Census. Available at www.ons.gov.uk/ons/guide-method/census/2011/index.html

Phillipson, C.R., Ahmed, N. and Latimer, J. (2003) *Women in transition: A study of the experiences of Bangladeshi women living in Tower Hamlets*, Bristol: Policy Press.

Sproston, K. and Mindell, J. (2006) *Health Survey for England 2004: The health of ethnic minority groups*, NHS Digital, pp 1-22. Available at www.ic.nhs.uk/pubs/hse04ethnic

US Department of Health and Human Services, NIH, National Institute for Heart, Lung and Blood (2013) 'Larger portion sizes contribute to US obesity problem', *We Can!® Community News Feature.* Available at www.nhlbi.nih.gov/health/public/heart/obesity/wecan/news-events/matte1.htm

Victor, C.R., Burholt, V. and Martin, W. (2012) 'Loneliness and ethnic minority elders in Great Britain: An exploratory study', *Journal of Cross Cultural Gerontology*, vol 27, pp 65-78.

WHO (World Health Organization) (2004) 'Expert consultation. Appropriate body-mass index for Asian populations and its implications for policy and intervention strategies', *Lancet*, vol 363, pp 157-63.

Part Four:
Representations of old age

TWELVE

Representing self – representing ageing

Lorna Warren

Introduction

Thirty years ago Barbara Macdonald published a collection of essays with contributions by her partner Cynthia Rich on 'old women, ageing and ageism' (1984). It took a first-person feminist approach to exploring experiences of marginalisation and inequality that was unfamiliar in the field of social gerontology at that time. Macdonald provided candid self-descriptions of her grey hair, deeply lined face, liver-spotted hands, loose-skinned arm that seemed disconnected from her and, ultimately, of the young women who could not look her in the eye, who could talk about her but not to her. The book's front-cover portrait, with Macdonald's uncompromising gaze fixed directly on the reader, represented the writer's desire to challenge her embodied sense of 'otherness' and was echoed by the rallying title of the book, *Look me in the eye*.

Nearly 20 years later, the Madrid International Plan of Action on Ageing, drawn up at the Second World Assembly on Ageing, identified as one of its objectives the need to 'facilitate contributions of older women and men to the presentation by the media of their activities and concerns' (UN, 2002, p 45). The importance of promoting positive images of older women was highlighted as of particular concern. In the intervening years, research had shown that older women, more than older men, were heavily under-represented within an increasingly image-saturated society (Woodward, 1999), a trend that continues across the world (Zhang et al, 2006).

Visual images have, in fact, defined women's age through history (Botelho and Thane, 2001; Richards et al, 2012) and, in turn, been used by women to aid their political campaigns (Parkins, 1997). However, while the contemporary digital world opens the door to increasingly diverse visual representations of middle-aged and older women, cultural pressure to remain youthful has led to the misrepresentation of women through digital enhancement or airbrushing (Hurd Clark, 2010). Women are increasingly the target of a rapidly expanding anti-ageing industry. The dominant image of women in popular Western society is as a 'living doll' (Walters, 2010): a youthful, sexualised body is the route to success for women (Bartky, 1990; Bordo, 1992) and their task is to learn 'how not to get old'.[1] Under the growing influence of anti-ageing discourses (Calasanti, 2007; Hurd Clarke, 2010), the physical signs of ageing for women are framed by negative stereotyping and deprecating humour, or are hidden from view. Women report becoming 'invisible' in everyday life as they reach their 40s and 50s (Bates, 2014, p 299), and rather than bucking trends, the current vogue of employing older (female) fashion models tends instead to reinforce the sociocultural celebration of youthfulness: older models are typically thin, classy but never age-neutral (Twigg, 2013; Karpf, 2014).

The 'double standard' of ageing (Sontag, 1979) has intensified with the growth of cosmetic enhancements, and women are 'straight-jacketed' by stereotyped ideals of beauty (Twigg, 2004; Hurd Clarke, 2010) promoted via newspapers, magazines, films and TV (Gill, 2006). In this context, the assignment of social value, resources and opportunities contingent on appearance (Clarke and Griffen, 2008) remains a crucial issue for older women (cf *Guardian*, 2013). In order to influence these expectations of ageing and old age, new sets of images need to be presented to the media that counteract current ageist preoccupations and first-person counter-stories that instead reflect the 'contributions, strengths and resourcefulness' of older women (UN, 2002).

Aims and methods

The aim of the 'Representing self – representing ageing' (RSRA) project was to involve 'ordinary' older women – women who were neither celebrities nor professional artists – in the creation of visual images, equipping them with a novel means of critiquing and challenging persistent media stereotyping and invisibility. The study asked how media and cultural representations framed later life, conveying ideas and expectations about age and gender. The original goals were to:

• enable older women drawn from different community settings to create their own images of ageing using a variety of participatory visual methods;

- explore the relationship between cultural and creative activity and later-life wellbeing;
- reflect on the contribution of visual methods to participatory processes;
- demonstrate the contribution of arts and humanities to critical gerontology;
- enhance recognition, by policy-makers and the wider public, of the authority, wisdom and productivity of older women.

A team of researchers from backgrounds in the social sciences and arts and humanities worked in collaboration with 41 women, aged 43-96, using a range of qualitative visual methods to elicit knowledge and understanding of older women's everyday experiences. In recruitment literature, 'older' was left to be self-defined due to the multiple ways in which ageing and old age are understood. Participants in both the art therapy and photo therapy workshops were self-selected. All had an interest in ageing and some, although by no means all, applied to the project because they had prior experience of or an interest in the creative arts. Participants in the community-based workshops were recruited from pre-existing groups.

Community arts-based workshops

Eventus, an established community arts organisation in Sheffield, took a community-led approach engaging participants from priority neighbourhoods, in this case:

- nine volunteers (aged 60–74) and the volunteer coordinator at the historic Manor Lodge site, managed by environmental social enterprise Green Estate;
- nine residents (aged 77–96) and one key worker at an Extra Care housing scheme called Guildford Grange.

In turn, representatives from each group helped to recruit professional photographers, Laura Pannack and Monica Fernandez, to work alongside them and the other older women participants and to develop ideas in collaboration with the group. The groups helped to write the photographer's brief and were actively involved in deciding what form the workshops would take. Each photographer spent 6-10 days taking photographs with their respective group. Images were disseminated by Eventus at two local exhibitions to which all participants were invited, and each woman was given a certificate and a framed print of their favourite image.

Art therapy workshop

Art therapist Susan Hogan ran a workshop for two hours a week over eight weeks. Self-selected older women were invited to discuss images of older women found in the media, art books and other popular sources. They then created their own artworks (sculptures, drawings and paintings, textiles, collage, photographs) based on their personal experiences of ageing, which were subject to further discussion in the group. Nine women, aged 43-75, completed the workshop. Artistic ability was not a requirement, only a stated interest in creating new images of old age. Facilitation was needed to maintain group focus on the research themes and to offer basic instruction in how to use the art materials. While some participants struggled with what they felt to be a lack of structure, the therapeutic underpinning to this workshop series encouraged participants to feel personally invested in the process and its outputs.

Photo therapy workshop

Artist/photographer and therapist Rosy Martin used phototherapeutic techniques developed over a number of years (cf Martin and Spence, 1986) to explore women's ageing identities. Twelve self-selected women, aged 47-60, were recruited. The workshop ran for five full days over a four-week period, with a subsequent session held three months later to review the images and to assess any lasting impacts. These sessions were highly structured and precisely timed. Initially, the women were asked to create photo diaries about their lives, as homework, which they shared within the group. They then worked in pairs to select specific scenarios, that *might* have occurred in the past or that *might* occur in the future, to 're-enact' in front of the camera. Each woman performed her stories using a variety of clothes and props while their partners offered support and took the photographs. The roles were then reversed.

Like the art therapy workshops, the photo therapy approach had a strong participatory element involving the women in an intense process of self-reflection over a number of sessions. The image-making used their own creative skills and imagination, guided by only very broad research themes. The images produced captured highly personal experiences and reflections on a sensitive topic and were made immediately available for discussion and interpretation among the groups who reflected on the process of making them.

Exhibitions

The climax of the project was the exhibition of the women's artwork. Titled 'Look At Me!', the curated exhibition presented 63 images, as artwork and as an electronic installation, with accompanying text and video documentation. 'Look At Me!' ran in three diverse venues in Sheffield: the Workstation in the city's cultural quarter; city centre shop windows on the Moor, and the brand new Jessop West Exhibition Space at Sheffield University. Targeted audiences included participants and their family and friends, academics and researchers, local politicians and policy-makers, practitioners and service providers, older people's organisations and representatives, and members of the public.

Documentation, evaluation and analysis

The project was documented and evaluated by a variety of means comprising 'before and after' interviews with participants, observation of workshops, questionnaires completed by visitors to the exhibitions, and filming of all stages of the research process. The combination of interviews and filming elicited detailed narratives from participants both about specific photographs or pieces of artwork and motives for creating that work, and also about the process of involvement. Participants' interpretations of the images they produced featured centrally in the analysis, as did the images themselves. Qualitative data was coded thematically (Braun and Clarke, 2006), analysed interpretively (Rabinow and Sullivan, 1987) and understood within a critical gerontological framework informed by feminist theories (Achenbaum, 1997; Formosa, 2005). A project website (www. representing-ageing.com) was developed to showcase the images and films and to disseminate information about the project, its publications and other outputs, and its ongoing impact.

Findings

A range of visual media, including photography, fine art, sculpture and textiles, was used across the different workshops. Together they produced a diverse collection of images engaged with various critiques of representations of ageing.

Collaborative images

In the two community arts-based workshops, the professional photographers worked collaboratively with the participants, although inevitably the style of each set of images generated bore the stamp of the photographer, their vision of old age and their interpretation of the brief. Photographer Monica Fernandez and the Guildford Grange residents chose to satirise the pervading makeover format through a series of 'before' and 'after' photographs (see Photograph 12.1). In their 80s and 90s, the participants lampooned youthful glamour wearing 'big hair' wigs, bright lipstick and celebrity-style sunglasses. The images were the antithesis of the 'grumpy old woman' stereotype: they captured older women at play and 'having a laugh': "I were a bit cheeky and I felt 'do something different!'"

Inspired by pictures of their mothers from family albums brought into early sessions by a number of the participants, photographer Laura Pannack took a series of photographs of the Green Estate participants modelled on the formal portraiture of the early 20th century (see Photograph 12.2). These images were taken using natural light and have muted colours, bestowing on them a more sombre and wistful tone, a notable contrast to the 'over the top, mutton dressed as lamb' look to which some women made critical reference. An additional set of tableau shots on the historic Manor Estate where the women

Photograph 12.1: Sheila Congreves from the 'before and after' series by Monica Fernandez (Eventus workshop)

Photograph 12.2: Elizabeth Templeman taken by Laura Pannack (Eventus workshop)

volunteer and, in another case, at a skating rink where one participant refereed children's ice hockey matches (see Photograph 12.3) show the women in a more humorous vein, communicating the fun they have together and with others. However, the formal portrait shots, in which the participants appear more reflective, break the common photographic convention of capturing people smiling:

Photograph 12.3: Ice rink taken by Laura Pannack (Eventus workshop)

'You look at yourself and you see the creases and you see the wrinkles and everything like that but inside I feel about 30, 35 so I reckon everybody has a time-stop, at a different period in their lives. I think what happens in your life is that you get periods where something really major happens and you learn from it, or there's grief from it and I think that is like a mental age for you, that you stop there.'

Over half of the Green Estate women were widowed, and Laura Pannack's images created space among the mainstream for representations of grief and loss.

Self-created images

In the workshops drawing on approaches from art and photo therapy, participants directed and created their own images. The art therapy workshops began with group discussions about media images. Participants were uniformly critical of 'false images' presented through the surgical or digital enhancement of media personalities, identifying the subsequent pressure this put on them to deny their own ageing. However, there was dissonance between the desire to see images of older women 'looking good for their age' and the awareness that such statements reduced older women to the status of their physical appearance. A number of participants therefore expressed a preference for images of older women that highlighted their character and purpose, and showed their continuing engagement in the world.

Exploration of their own feelings of ageing, identified in these group discussions, was the springboard for most of the women's artwork. Their images were testament to how women experience ageing at the site of the body, focusing commonly on ageing hair and skin (see Photograph 12.4), but also including other body parts typically used in the representation, if not the denoting, of women, including the mouth/teeth, vagina and breasts, as well as the tools for maintaining the ageing body. Other themes that were depicted in the artwork were: dealing with pressures to conform to societal expectations; narrowing horizons and increasing invisibility; transitions and changing self through the life course; family history; and inner feeling/outside perception. Sheila plotted her female family tree (see Photograph 12.5) and dressed in a Victorian outfit that she made herself:

Photograph 12.4: Colleen Penny, 'Varicose veins' (art therapy workshop)

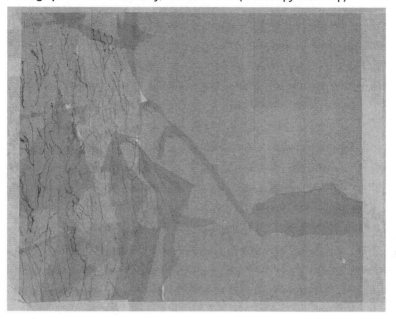

Photograph 12.5: Sheila Carter, 'Female family tree' (art therapy workshop)

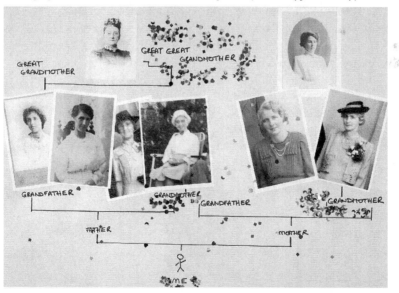

'Granny was old when I was born, she was a Victorian but now I realise that she was not much older than I am now. Now I am going to become a grandmother, what kind of Granny will I be?'

Participants in the photo therapy workshops recognised older women to be differently framed according to context. The media, in which a premium was placed on youthful, sexualised female bodies and older women were generally not valued, stood in contrast to the communities in which they lived where currency was about involvement in giving and sharing, and women were therefore 'the main traders'. Participants were asked to keep individual photo diaries at the start of the workshops, prompting them to think about their lives in a visual way. The diaries yielded a mix of self-portraits, images of familiar scenes and scenery, and records of everyday objects and activities. The re-enactment sessions that followed were similarly varied in their focus. Working with their photography partner, some women chose to recreate childhood images or poses (see Photograph 12.6), thereby illuminating the ways in which their early life stories had influenced their experiences and expectations of growing older:

'The re-enactment wasn't actually from pictures, it was more like what wasn't going on in the pictures. Memories that I had that weren't portrayed in the family album. And deep, dark, difficult stuff in the middle. The first one was me dancing as a little girl and the last one was me dancing now, almost identical but in different clothing.'

Photograph 12.6: Jen Greenfield in collaboration with Barbara Harriott (photo therapy workshop)

Photograph 12.7: Laura Richardson as 'Madame Bijou', in collaboration with Chris Herzberg (photo therapy workshop)

Other women assumed specific characters as inspiration for their role-playing, such as Lady Gaga and Brassaï's 'Madame Bijou' (see Photograph 12.7). In many of the images, the women appeared in bold and colourful dress, appearing invigorated, playful and uninhibited. Each participant shared a selection of her images with the others after her re-enactment. The experience of talking about the images together and identifying common themes is provided in one woman's words:

'… so much positive reinforcement about ourselves as ageing women … one of the images of older women that we get is women who've, in inverted commas, "let themselves go"… whereas there were a lot of women there who were just saying "look at me, I'm glorious!", well, by the end anyway!'

The women enjoyed a strength of closeness and intimacy that led to a sense of solidarity and enduring bonds.

Findings across the workshops

A comparison of findings across the workshops highlighted the general trend for participants in the third age of life to be far more conscious of older women being stereotyped, misrepresented or absent from media images and to feel the accompanying pressures on their baby-boomer generation to look a certain way compared with participants in the fourth age, who discussed ageing largely in the context of health and mobility. Across all ages, participants wanted to see more images that talked directly to them and their experiences (Warren and Richards, 2012): images of 'ordinary', 'real' or 'natural' older women who had not been surgically or digitally enhanced. Alongside different body shapes, they also identified the importance of representing older women of power, independence and voice, and older women still 'making a contribution', volunteering or 'being as active as they can' so that 'younger people won't feel that fear of getting old'.

In terms of methods, the chosen participatory visual approach engaged women in the aims of the project by giving them a sense of ownership of the research process. Participation does not necessarily follow automatically from recruitment, however: it has to be well facilitated and enabled, and can be intensive. Sustaining involvement in the RSRA project required ongoing communication and constant checking with participants that they were happy with the research methods and use of the artwork. A handful of women withdrew due to a perceived lack of structure in the respective workshop – they felt unsure about how they fitted into the group or about the end outcomes of the workshop activities – or because changes to individual circumstances were in tension with the demands of participation. For most women, the sense of personal investment in research that had demonstrable visible outcomes (multiple public exhibitions, city-wide advertising, media coverage etc) increased the impact on their wellbeing and sense of public validation:

'I've got images now and I've seen myself, it's lovely to see because, you know, life has never been around me, it's always been around other people.'

Findings from the 'Look At Me!' exhibition questionnaires (n=242) and vox pop recordings not only provided important evaluative data but also helped to capture the multifaceted ways in which images of older women may be seen and framed. General tick-box questionnaire rankings showed that 87 per cent of visitors judged the exhibition either 'good' or 'very good'; 83 per cent found it 'thought-provoking' and 88 per cent wanted to see more images of older women, like those in the exhibition, displayed in public. Open comments captured a more nuanced viewer engagement (Murray et al, 2014). For example, a 33-year-old woman wrote in the visitors' comments book:

It made me smile, and later it made me think, and later it made me sad, and later it gave me a little bit of hope that I'm still a little bit young, and later it made me feel scared about me and my life decisions and later … confused and … more confused … WEIRD!!

A male artist, sculptor and potter in his 60s who usually observed people thinking 'I hope I don't look as old as they do' said that after viewing the exhibition, he was going to "look at people shopping in a much more positive way – aware that no one is as they seem at first glance".

Implications

Participatory visual methods

Sociologists have understood that ageing takes place at the site of the body (Hockey and James, 2003). By bringing arts-based practices into the social sciences, the experience of this – and the subsequent distortion, exaggeration, misrepresentation and invisibility of ageing female bodies – can be demonstrated in a way that is both visceral and tangible. The power of visual methods lies in the opportunity they give to research participants to *show* how they perceive the world, rather than just *telling* researchers (Richards, 2011), and thereby to reach out to audiences at a number of different levels.

'There's something empowered in that art, they're not just objects ... there's a lot of feeling and emotion there.' (Art therapy participant)

As a young woman I find this very moving. It made me consider my mother and grandmother differently. I wonder how men would respond in similar workshops and the loss of masculinity would interest me. I feel: CARPE DIEM! (Woman aged 21, exhibition comments book)

Participation is key to the success of this interdisciplinary marriage. The participatory nature of the approach means handing over control of image-making to some degree. The many ways of producing data in visual form – for example, painting and drawing, sculpture, textiles, filming and photography – makes it important to tailor the chosen methods to suit the needs of individual participants; to provide guidance and support, as appropriate; and, potentially, to involve participants in the recruitment of facilitators/professional artists.

Images are often more accessible, to participants and audiences alike, than dense academic text, and offer the potential to keep people engaged, in and with the research, through their novelty factor. Sustained involvement in accompanying aspects of the research needs to be thought about in advance and, typically, negotiated as the project progresses. It should be facilitated by agreed ground rules that respect confidentiality, and explicit processes for delivering and acting on feedback. In the RSRA project, participants' interpretations of the images they produced, as well as those generated by/of others in the project, were solicited and incorporated into the process of analysis wherever possible.

Involvement of participants in the dissemination of outputs from a project using a visual approach will also require facilitation. Participants are likely to have different views on the format of an exhibition, as well as varying degrees of relevant experience and desire and ability to commit time. The employment of a curator brings a sense of cohesion and gives an exhibition a professional look. In the RSRA project participants contributed centrally to the planning of the Sheffield-based exhibitions through a day-long meeting giving them an opportunity to say how they wanted their images displayed and revisiting consent forms. They continued to be involved through writing or amending the labels accompanying their images, featuring in press-related activities, and attending a private viewing of the installations with their friends and relatives.

The benefits of maximising and sustaining involvement in the different aspects of the research include the increased likelihood of participants producing revealing, heartfelt images benefiting the research by increasing the insights gained and participants themselves through an enhanced sense of wellbeing:

> 'Something really personal came out of everybody's work and I think if we'd have just sat there and talked about women and ageing generally ... it wouldn't have been as deep and it wouldn't have been as personal and we probably wouldn't have got as close to each other.' (Photo therapy participant)

Participants may subsequently be more willing to continue their involvement through follow-on activities. In the RSRA project, participants have been co-presenters at conferences and have taken part in post-project activities in schools (see below).

While the emphasis in a study concerned with contesting dominant social representations of gender ageing should be on the participation of older women, it should not be forgotten, however, that by their very nature, visual methods extend involvement beyond participants to include the wider viewing audience. Pursuing the relationship between image and viewer by gathering structured feedback gives insight into the complex ways in which the meaning and effects of representations depend on how audiences 'see' the visual representations and reflexively elaborate on them (Fairhurst, 2012), with important implications for policy and practice/effecting change.

Policy and practice

The enhanced sense of wellbeing that participatory arts-based initiatives can offer has already been indicated above. The therapeutic approaches that underpinned two of the project workshops significantly altered the attitudes of some women towards their own ageing in a positive direction and beyond the duration of the workshop. Indeed, two participants have gone on to become members of a theatre group set up to explore the performance of age and ageing. In the community-based workshops, the concentrated gaze of a professional photographer, on each of them as individuals as well as on their wider activities as a group, made participants feel celebrated. Their quality of life was boosted for the lifetime of the initiative through fun, creative activities as well as focused attention. These essentially collaborative arts-based practices can generate lasting relationships: a number of women from the photo therapy workshop continue to meet as friends and to engage in arts activities, and while witnessing first-hand the benefits of participating together, a group led two of the Green Estate volunteers to set up a new lunch club for over-55s. One resident's comment that, "when I came in here I thought it was the end, now I've done [the project] I know that's not true", highlights the potential for using creative arts in Extra Care schemes.

The critical contribution that can be made by visual arts practices also extends to their power to present and raise questions about social diversity, attested to by the numerous and continuing requests to display and use the project outputs in diverse ways. The five project films, available on the website (see www.representing-ageing.com), have been shown at the Showroom Cinema in Sheffield to hundreds of cinema-goers. The 'Look At Me!' exhibition – the climax to the RSRA project – was deliberately housed in a range of Sheffield venues in an attempt to reach different audiences but also to represent older women in spaces both where they were typically seen and also under-represented. The exhibition was billed as part of the City Council International Women's Day Centenary celebrations. Its success led to invitations to show images at events/locations UK-wide, including the Royal College of Art, University of Plymouth, City Screen York, the University of Derby and the NDA showcase. Images from the project are now on permanent display at Age UK Sheffield and at Swansea University where they have formed part of an arts-based Coming of Age Trail (see http://www.swansea.ac.uk/media-centre/news-archive/2013/comingofageexhibitionofartworksaimstoboost researchintoageingatswansea.php).

> 'They always get a reaction…. Once people understand what they're about they either love them or hate them – depending how they feel about being challenged. The images make people feel uncomfortable; they open our minds to the possibility that there is beauty in old age.' (Rosalind Eve, Chief Executive, Age UK, Sheffield, 10 June 2013)

They also feature as book covers on two international texts concerned with representations of ageing (Dolan and Tincknell, 2012; Ylänne, 2012). In addition, the project is being used in postgraduate research in diverse ways: for example, as a case study and as a source of images for presentations in theses looking at gender and later life, and as a source of participants for the above-mentioned theatre group, Passages, created by student Bridie Moore, among other things 'to confound expectations of "elder theatre" by engaging with experimental practice and contemporary theatre forms' (Moore, 2014).

Viewing figures for exhibitions have varied from 416 visitors at the Sheffield venues where visitors could be counted to footfall figures for public 'thoroughfares' of 1,918 at City Screen York, 14,447 (average daily estimate) at the Moor shops, and 30,000 for the entire Swansea Coming of Age Trail. The most recent follow-on activities, in which images from the project were projected on to the walls of well-known buildings in Sheffield and then discussed the next day on BBC Radio Sheffield (www.newdynamics.group.shef.ac.uk/now-can-you-see-me-images-of-older-women-in-sheffield.html), broadened audiences to include younger people occupying night-time city centre spaces and potentially housebound individuals who are an important constituent of radio listeners.

Nevertheless, what is clear is that no matter how iconoclastic the representation or diverse the venues or channels for its display, images by themselves are unlikely to transform attitudes and practices towards ageing in the same way that the infirmities of old age cannot necessarily be resisted solely through body work. Because of this, the RSRA project has attempted to build on the strength and extent of responses to its findings and outputs and, in a number of cases in collaboration with the NDA programme, to push for more tangible policy change. This is where the opportunities to achieve influence may sometimes be unpredictable or serendipitous, but researchers have to remain consistently dogged in their efforts to secure impact.

During the funded period of RSRA (2011), concerns about heavily airbrushed and distorted images in the media found a political voice in the formation of the All-Party Parliamentary Group (APPG) on Body Image and an international platform in the form of the Endangered Bodies campaign. The RSRA project submitted written evidence to a public inquiry into body image dissatisfaction set up by the APPG (2012). Coordinated by the YMCA and with support from the Government Equalities Office, the campaigning activities are being taken forward in the Be Real: Body Confidence for Everyone initiative (www.berealcampaign.co.uk/home/), with signs of increasing efforts to extend the gaze beyond the predominant focus on the effects of distorted imagery on younger women's attitudes to their bodies.

A year after the formation of the APPG, but nevertheless unreferenced by it or the Be Real initiative despite the shared concern with issues of representation, the Labour Party established a Commission on

Older Women Working, led by Harriet Harman. RSRA findings were submitted to its call for evidence and subsequently cited in its interim report (2013, p 31). In the same year, Birmingham Policy Commission invited the project to submit evidence to its review, published in 2014, of *Healthy ageing in the 21st century*. Locally, RSRA also contributed to Sheffield City Council's Strategy for an Ageing Population, including loaning images for display at a seminar for councillors on commissioning services for older people.

Working under their own academic steam, the RSRA project and the NDA programme, with Age UK support, mounted a half-day event in 2012 for media professionals, policy-makers and researchers to discuss the major issue of ageism and sexism in the media. One of the outcomes was the strongly expressed need for a new agenda to combat this issue, supported and evidenced by first-person accounts as well as data from women working in media industries (Women in Journalism, 2012). At a follow-up event a year later, the Charter against Ageism and Sexism in the Media (ChASM) was launched. A public pledge developed in collaboration with Women Ageing and Media (WAM), the National Union of Journalists (NUJ) and Women in Journalism (WiJ), it calls for the media to recognise the important role they play in shaping perceptions of women and ageing and to take action to better represent the diversity, complexity and potential of women aged 50 and over (www.newdynamics.group.shef.ac.uk/petition.html).

At the same time, RSRA has made efforts to raise awareness that ageism and sexism are not issues that only concern women aged 50 and over. A number of participants in the project stressed the importance of exploring ageing issues early on in children's education. Post-project activities, again, run in collaboration with the NDA programme, have therefore also included the initiation of Act Your Age! workshops. Run in a local primary school, they have brought together older individuals from the project, as well as the NDA Older People's Reference Group, with pupils aged 10-11, to unpack children's understandings of ageing and later life (ESRC, 2013).

Key findings
- Women in their 50s–60s feel more pressure from media and advertising imagery compared with participants in their 80–90s.
- Eighty-eight per cent of visitors to the project exhibitions want to see more images of older women, like those created through the project, displayed in public.

- Participants captured various experiences from continued public involvement, friendships and fun to fears of increasing limitations and invisibility. Images challenged stereotypes such as the 'grumpy old woman', and reflect rarely represented grief and loss.
- Participants want to see more images of 'ordinary' older women who are still 'making a contribution'.
- Images produced by participants show that women experience ageing at the site of the body, for example, in the form of wrinkles and greying hair.
- Participatory visual methods give women a sense of solidarity and ownership of the research process, impacting on wellbeing and a feeling of public validation.

Conclusions

RSRA confirmed the 'overshadowing' power of visual images (Bytheway, 2011, p 79) and the complex and subtle role they play in shaping and communicating the experience of older age in everyday life. The project identified how representation can affect older women's self-image and quality of life and the need to raise awareness of the combined effects of ageism and sexism earlier in the life course to avoid potential intergenerational alienation. At the same time, having followed Barbara Macdonald's clarion call to look older women 'in the eye' (1984), 'Look At Me!' has also confirmed that knowledge and imagery that originate through lived experience can provide a powerful challenge to traditional understandings of age, incorporating a reflective stance with transformative potential (Cotterell and Moriss, 2001). The project's innovative, multidisciplinary methods have generated widely displayed, iconoclastic images, and ensured participants' central involvement in unpacking and challenging stereotypes and invisibility, thereby foregrounding older women's 'contributions, strengths and resourcefulness' (UN, 2002). The creation of these various images in a group context, grounded in shared experiences of ageing, was a validating experience for the women, and fostered a collective spirit and a shared, in some cases enduring, desire to challenge conventional representations. Together, the ethos, structure and outputs of the project have demonstrated what visual approaches and creative activity can offer to participatory processes and wellbeing, adding to a growing body of research evidence and UK policy drivers supporting the usefulness of initiatives in the arts for health (Hogan and Warren, 2013).

Participants captured a range of experiences framing their ageing, commonly relating to the ageing body but also, and powerfully, their continued involvement in public life, whether through employment or volunteering, and an enjoyment of life and friendships (Richards et al, 2012). A number of images portrayed aspects of ageing, typically centring on life course transitions – menopause, grandparenthood and bereavement – which participants critiqued as seldom seen or discussed in limited ways in mainstream media, while others dealt directly with fears of contracting horizons, increasing limitations or of fading away (Warren and Richards, 2012; Hogan and Warren, 2013). That some of the photographs fell foul of reproducing hegemonic perceptions of ageing as carnivalesque/melancholic has been called into question (Richards et al, 2012), as has the associated idea that the some of the women were degrading themselves, potentially through age-inappropriate behaviour (Hogan and Warren, 2012). Crucially the images have initiated encounters with and conversations about representations of ageing which, as a previous NDA publication has evidenced (Murray et al, 2014), highlight 'the complex negotiation of the relationship between the image, accompanying text or video, different cultural narratives of ageing (Gullette, 2004), and the contexts within which individual viewers experienced their own ageing or interest in representations of ageing (Bytheway, 2011)' (p 104).

Efforts to further unpack and understand the implications of that complex negotiation, and older women's involvement in it, have been made post-project. Findings have been shared with and/or located as important evidence in campaigns and policy commissions relating to body image, older women in public life and healthy ageing. They have been the focus of numerous wide-ranging and successful public engagement activities, audience members of which have signalled an appreciation of this 'celebration of the ordinary' and called for 'more truthful images of older women in the media'. ChASM has additionally called for a more accurate representation of women aged 50+ in the media professions channelling those representations. Ageism awareness workshops have initiated new conversations on age, selected images from the 'Look At Me!' exhibition stimulating primary school children's appraisal of older women, some their classroom collaborators, as 'super cool', 'jazzy', 'funky', 'chilling out' and 'having fun'.

Suggestions regarding the next steps for research, but also tackling ageist stereotyping more broadly, follow from the key areas of impact achieved by the RSRA project, and include:

- Continuing the development of cultural gerontological understandings of the framing of age that highlight transition and the importance of dynamic understandings of transition and change for individuals, as well as across societies. Indeed, a female visitor to the exhibition suggested that there was "more work to be done around transition, maybe around adolescence to womanhood." Representations of age are clearly not fixed but may be open to negotiation and revision across the life course. Empirical research is still at a relatively early stage in comparing and contrasting these 'highly nuanced processes' (Botelho and Thane, 2001, p 3) and their social, economic, historical and cultural embedding.
- Extending participatory visual approaches to capture experiential knowledge of aspects of, or transitions in, ageing defined by participants as taboo or literally 'unspeakable' areas – the visual death and dying is a key example here.
- Achieving a more systematic and comparative scrutiny of media representations of gender and ageing across different cultural and ethnic groups as well as societies.
- In collaboration with schools and through knowledge exchange-funded research, taking forward arts-based intergenerational approaches to age-awareness education, identifying key lessons for curriculum development nationally and Europe-wide.

Note

[1] See the Channel 4 television programme, 'How Not to Get Old' (www.channel4.com/programmes/how-not-to-get-old).

References

Achenbaum, W.A. (1997) 'Critical gerontology', in A. Jamieson, S. Harper and C. Victor (eds) *Critical approaches to ageing and later life*, Buckingham: Open University Press, pp 16-26.

APPG (All-Party Parliamentary Group) on Body Image (2012) *Reflections on body image*. APPG on Body Image and Central YMCA. Available at www.berealcampaign.co.uk/help-and-resources/2014/09/19/appg-reflections-on-body-image/

Bartky, S.L. (1990) *Femininity and domination: Studies in the phenomenology of oppression*, New York: Routledge.

Bates, L. (2014) *Everyday sexism…*, London: Simon & Schuster.

Birmingham Policy Commission (2014) *Healthy ageing in the 21st century: The best is yet to come*, Birmingham: University of Birmingham. Available at www.birmingham.ac.uk/Documents/research/policycommission/healthy-ageing/Healthy-Ageing-Policy-Commission-Report.pdf

Bordo, S. (1992) *Unbearable weight: Feminism, Western culture and the body*, London: University of California Press.

Botelho, L. and Thane, P. (eds) (2001) *Women and ageing in British society since 1500*, London: Longman.

Braun, V. and Clarke, V. (2006) 'Using thematic analysis in psychology', *Qualitative Research in Psychology*, vol 3, pp 77-101.

By15theway, B. (2011) *Unmasking age: The significance of age for social research*, Bristol: Policy Press.

Calasanti, T. (2007) 'Bodacious berry, potency wood and the aging monster: Gender and age-relations in anti-ageing ads', *Social Forces*, vol 86, no 1, pp 335-55.

Clarke, L. and Griffin, M. (2008) 'Visible and invisible ageing: Beauty work as a response to ageism', *Ageing and Society*, vol 28, no 5, pp 653-74.

Cotterell, P. and Morris, C. (2011) 'The capacity, impact and challenge of service users' experiential knowledge', in M. Barnes and P. Cotterell (eds) *Critical perspectives on user involvement*, Bristol: Policy Press, pp 57-69.

Commission on Older Women, The (2013) *Interim report September 2013*, Labour Party. Available at www.yourbritain.org.uk/uploads/editor/files/Commission_on_Older_Women_-_Interim_Report.pdf

Dolan, J. and Tincknell, E. (2012) (eds) *Aging femininities: Troubling representations*, Cambridge: Cambridge Scholars Publishing.

ESRC (Economic and Social Research Council) (2013) 'Act Your Age!', *Britain in 2013: Annual Magazine of the Economic and Research Council*, p 117.

Fairhurst, E. (2011) 'Positive images and calendars', in V. Ylänne (ed) *Representing ageing: Images and identities*, Basingstoke: Palgrave, pp 189-206.

Formosa, M. (2005) 'Feminism and critical educational gerontology: An agenda for good practice', *Ageing International*, vol 30, no 4, pp 396-411.

Gill, R. (2006) *Gender and the media*, Cambridge: Polity Press.

Guardian, The (2013) 'Datablog: TV presenters after 50: Which channels hire older women?'. Available at www.theguardian.com/news/datablog/2013/may/16/broadcasters-over-age-50-women

Gullette, M. (2004) *Aged by culture*, Chicago, Il: University of Chicago Press.

Hockey, J. and James, A. (2003) *Social identities across the life course*, Basingstoke: Palgrave Macmillan.

Hogan, S. and Warren, L. (2012) 'Dealing with complexity in research findings: How do older women negotiate and challenge images of ageing?', *Journal of Women and Aging*, vol 24, no 4, pp 329-50.

Hogan, S. and Warren, L. (2013) 'Women's inequality: A global problem explored in participatory arts', *International Perspectives on Research-Guided Practice in Community-Based Arts* in Health Special Issue, UNESCO Observatory, vol 3, no 3, pp 1-27. Available at http://education.unimelb.edu.au/__data/assets/pdf_file/0011/1067429/008_HOGAN_PAPER.pdf

Hurd Clarke, L. (2010) *Facing age*, Lanham, MD: Rowman & Littlefield.

Karpf, A. (2014) *How to age (School of life)*, Basingstoke: Macmillan.

Macdonald, B. with Rich, C. (1984) *Look me in the eye: Old women, aging and ageism*, London: Women's Press.

Martin, R. and Spence, J. (1986) 'Photo therapy: New portraits for old', in J. Spence, *Putting myself in the picture: A political, personal and photographic autobiography*, London: Camden Press, pp 172-93.

Moore, B. (2014) ' "Old people can have ideas, dreams and can move gracefully": Re-inscriptions of the ageing body in performance', Paper presented at the 8th International Symposium on Cultural Gerontology/2nd Conference of the European Network in Aging Studies, National University of Ireland Galway, Galway, Ireland.

Murray, M., Amigoni, D., Bernard, M., Newman, A., Rickett, M., Tew, P. and Warren, L. (2014) 'Understanding and transforming ageing through the arts', in A. Walker (ed) *The new science of ageing*, Bristol: Policy Press, pp 77-112.

Parkins, W. (1997) 'Taking Liberty's, breaking windows: Fashion, protest and the suffragette public', *Continuum*, vol 11, no 3, pp 37-46.

Rabinow, P. and Sullivan, W.M. (1987) *Interpretive social science: A second look*, London: University of California Press.

Richards, N. (2011) *Using participatory visual methods*, Toolkit 17, Manchester: University of Manchester. Available at www.socialsciences.manchester.ac.uk/morgan-centre/research/resources/toolkits/toolkit-17/

Richards, N., Warren, L. and Gott, M. (2012) 'The challenge of creating "alternative" images of ageing: Lessons from a project with older women', *Journal of Aging Studies*, vol 26, no 1, pp 65-78.

Sontag, S. (1979) 'Double standard of ageing', in J. Williams (ed) *Psychology of women*, New York: W.W. Norton, pp 462-78.

Twigg J. (2004) 'The body, gender, and age: Feminist insights in social gerontology', *Journal of Aging Studies*, vol 18, no 10, pp 59-73.

Twigg, J. (2013) *Fashion and age: Dress, the body and later life*, London: Bloomsbury Academic.

UN (United Nations) (2002) *Second World Assembly on Ageing: Madrid international plan of action on ageing*, New York: UN.

Walters, N. (2010) *Living dolls: The return of sexism*, London: Virago.

Warren, L. and Cook, J. (2005) 'Working with older women in research: benefits and challenges of involvement' in L. Lowes, L. and I. Hulatt (eds) *Involving Service Users in Health and Social Care Research*. London: Routledge, pp 171-189.

Warren, L. and Richards, N. (2012) '"I don't see many images of myself coming back at myself": Representations of women and ageing', in V. Ylänne (ed) *Representing ageing: Images and identities*, Basingstoke: Palgrave, pp 149-68.

Woodward, K. (2006) 'Performing age, performing gender', *Feminist Formations*, vol 18, no 1, pp 162- 89.

Women in Journalism (2012) 'Seen but not heard: How women make front page news'. Available at Womeninjournalism.co.uk

Ylänne, V. (2012) (ed) *Representing ageing: Images and identities*, Basingstoke: Palgrave.

Zhang, Y.B., Harwood, J., Williams, A., Ylänne-McEwan, V., Wadleigh, P.M. and Thimm, C. (2006) 'The portrayal of older adults in advertising: A cross-national review', *Journal of Language and Social Psychology*, vol 25, pp 264-80.

THIRTEEN

Ageing, fiction, narrative exchange and everyday life

Philip Tew and Nick Hubble

Introduction

This chapter focuses on the development, engagement with respondents and analytical results of the 'Fiction and Cultural Mediation of Ageing' project (FCMAP) that was part of the New Dynamics of Ageing (NDA), a UK cross-Research Council initiative. From its inception FCMAP sought novel ways to access the opinions of older subjects about the facts and experiences of ageing in a manner that radically diminished any influence over (or implicit guidance given to) its selected respondents, and that could thereby generate interesting and informative qualitative data, which was self-reflective on the part of those older people who formed a broad sample approached through various strands, as described below. The FCMAP team of researchers came from areas of scholarship concerned with a combination of literary studies, history and social narrative, and so our initial set of questions set out to explore how, with regard to older people within such a research project, one might address:

- Thinking about narratives of ageing, considering issues regarding their social exchange and influence through attitudinal research rather than researcher opinion (or presumptions).
- Developing methods of engagement with, and analysis of, such narratives in their social context while in circulation without recording or transcription by the research team itself (again, which method might potentially introduce at least implicit bias).
- How to obtain robust and significant qualitative data concerning such active narratives where respondents were as uninfluenced as possible (apart from each other in discussion groups on which they could reflect).

The primary aims of FCMAP were to seek to comprehend how representations of ageing circulate in culture and society and were reflected on by older subjects (being the subject of such narratives on the part of others). In one strand the research team considered that elective readership of relevant contemporary fiction *and* the respondents' own diary entries might facilitate a purposeful critical interaction undertaken by older subjects concerning such symbolic representations and life experiences simultaneously. The team sought to develop locations or sites where this might take place. We next considered that a close analysis *en masse* of records of such interactions might potentially facilitate some radical thinking about current social attitudes and behaviour with regard to ageing and its attitudinal reception (how people perceived both themselves and how others regarded them), both on the part of the respondents and the research team.

FCMAP adopted two main approaches (with three strands): Volunteer Reading Groups (VRGs) organised over 10 months in conjunction with the University of the Third Age (U3A) in and around London, where participants were asked to keep reflective diaries concerning novels they were asked to read (all of which dealt variously with topics and contexts concerned with ageing); and also through a directive issued by the Mass Observation (MO) Archive at the University of Sussex to various existing diarists with a long track record of diary-keeping (whose responses could be compared longitudinally across time with the responses to earlier directives on ageing and related topics held in the archive). FCMAP was designed to be especially responsive to the following key NDA areas of concern (published before FCMAP was developed), which, in summary, were:

- the forces driving ageing and influences shaping them (cultural, historical and social);
- the dynamic interplay between ageing individuals and their changing cultural and social environments, providing insights;
- how individual patterns of ageing respond to and are produced by social factors;
- the dynamics of transformations in the meaning, understanding and experience of ageing;
- how in-depth qualitative data concerning such issues might contribute to policy and practice.[1]

In practice, diaries proved methodologically a most useful tool for gathering the required data because they are a familiar format for recording interactions and personal views on such engagements, and, as Sheble and Wildemuth specify (2009, p 1), of all the ways of recording experience, 'diaries are distinct in that time structures their creation, layering text and objects into a chronological composite of snapshots and reflections a few minutes, a day, or a week at a time.'

FCMAP adopted a consciously interdisciplinary approach in its attempt to reveal the complexity and variety of certain attitudinal processes in contemporary culture, since patterns emerged when such diaries were collected in large numbers, thus producing big or large-scale data when combining the data submitted by respondents in both diary formats; those from MO and the U3A. During analysis, respondents were identified anonymously to ensure freedom of thought and expression. One of the founders of MO, Tom Harrisson (1940, p 368), details in 'What is public opinion?' his objections to 'Crude stratification', pointing out that genuine public opinion inevitably represents huge numbers of people, and may require particular approaches and understanding processes that will inevitably concern:

> ... one with a private opinion, with private prides and prejudices, personal antagonisms and loyalties. This is the stuff of Britain, tough, solid, stolid stuff – the rhythm essentially slow. When we talk about public opinion, we should mean the top level in this great conglomeration of private opinions. There is not, anywhere, a separate entity called public opinion. Public opinion only comes from the minds and the tongues of the people. But there is an important distinction between the two areas of existence – the area of the minds and the area of the tongues. In the mind is the private thought; and on the tongue, the public statement. Logically, a person's "real opinion" is the opinion he holds privately. He will not necessarily voice publicly, as public opinion, certain parts of his private opinion, which is a complex of feelings, often conflicting. (Harrisson, 1940, p 369)

In light of such contexts indicated above, FCMAP sought to access a broad range of such private thoughts, for as Elliott (1997) says of this narrative diary format, 'the log and the intimate journal are essentially private documents, written primarily for the diarist themself. They are therefore constructed within the diarist's own frame of reference and can assume a forgiving, understanding reader ... for whom there is no need to present a best face.' Moreover, diaries offer evidence of everyday life practices, and as Gubrium and Holstein (2006, p 9) state, 'Everyday life and its world of meanings are too complex, socially mediated, and locally differentiated to be adequately captured by a quantitative approach….' Additionally, as Raoul Vaneigem says in *The revolution of everyday life* (1994, p 7), 'I conjectured that the examination of my own subjectivity, far from constituting an isolated activity, would resonate with other, like endeavours…', adding that 'There are more truths in twenty-four hours of a man's life than in all the philosophies' (p 21). It can therefore be seen that the data in the FCMAP diaries might well be regarded as being qualitatively relevant to more than a single subject (ageing), and they reflect other aspects of identity and culture, especially when a mass of such data is subjected to intense qualitative analysis. At all levels, the research incorporated Gubrium and Holstein's (2006, pp 9, 5) concern with a qualitative approach being able to capture socially formulated meanings, since what is produced is:

> The body of knowledge formed around the stories told by older people in their own right. Aging and everyday life features what older people themselves make of who and what they are, as well as how they view their worlds. (Gubrium and Holstein, 2006, p 3)

Moreover, narrative is central to human culture and identity, much as Fisher indicates in *Communication as narration: Toward a philosophy of reason, value, and action* (1987, p xi), where he also argues that it is essentially irreducible in terms of its processes and practices, and needs to be considered as a social practice *in situ*, stating:

> I propose (1) a reconceptualisation of humankind as *Homo narrans*; (2) that all forms of human communication need to be seen fundamentally as stories – symbolic interpretations of aspects of the world occurring in time and shaped by history, culture, and character; (3) that individuated forms of discourse should be considered as "good reasons" – values or value-laden warrants for believing or acting in certain ways; and (4) that a narrative logic that all humans have natural capacities to employ ought to be conceived of as the logic by which human communication is assessed. The basic principles of that narrative logic are coherence and fidelity. (p xi)

The concerns outlined above influenced the structure at all levels of the three primary strands that made up the data collection phase of FCMAP and additionally the analysis of the three areas that took place in an integrated and comparative process.

The first strand involved, as indicated above, collaboration with the MO Archive, that was commissioned to issue a new directive in Spring 2010 to the MO panel concerning ageing and representation (51 per cent of respondents to the Spring 2007 directive were over 60). Framed broadly (and written by Nick Hubble of the FCMAP team), it elicited a wide variety of reflections on changing representations of ageing and their relationship to self-understanding.[2] Respondents explored the influence of particular representations on their own and others' images and expectations of ageing, often making social and generational comparisons from personal experience. The resultant material not only complemented the data produced by the second, smaller reader group strand (see below) but was further comparable with the responses to earlier MO directives concerning ageing in 1992 and 2006 and thus enabled longitudinal study.

In the second strand district associations in and around London of the Third Age Trust or U3A organised nine VRGs as a Shared Learning Project (SLP). Participants explored the changing representations of ageing stimulated by a series of British novels concerned with ageing-related themes published from 1941. VRG members kept MO-style diaries recording responses to each novel during and after the reading process and again after subsequent group discussions of the book. In the order of reading, the books were as follows (groups were allowed to substitute one novel on the A list with one from the B list):

A list
- David Lodge, *Deaf Sentence* (2008)
- Jim Crace, *Arcadia* (1992)
- Caryl Phillips, *A Distant Shore* (2003)
- Hanif Kureishi, *The Body* (2003)
- Trezza Azzopardi, *Remember Me* (2003)
- Angela Carter, *Wise Children* (1991)
- Barbara Pym, *Quartet in Autumn* (1977)
- Norah Hoult, *There Were No Windows* (1944)
- Fay Weldon, *Chalcot Crescent* (2009)

B list
- B.S. Johnson, *House Mother Normal* (1971)
- Muriel Spark, *Memento Mori* (1959)

- Angus Wilson, *Late Call* (1964)
- Elizabeth Taylor, *Mrs Palfrey at the Claremont* (1971)
- Margaret Forster, *The Seduction of Mrs Pendlebury* (1974)
- Jonathan Coe, *What a Carve Up!* (1994)
- Mark Haddon, *A Spot of Bother* (2006)
- Anita Brookner, *Strangers* (2009)

The third strand (in essence intersecting the second VRG strand) involved four major literary events featuring six contemporary novelists (five of whose novels featured among those sent to the VRGs). In this series entitled 'Ageing Re-imagined' authors discussed publicly the representation of ageing in their work with both the general public and specifically VRG members at open events: Jim Crace and David Lodge (3 February 2010, Brunel University London) had 300+ participants; Caryl Phillips (19 March 2010, London School of Economics and Political Science) 150+ participants; Trezza Azzopardi (10 June 2010, Brunel University London) 50+ participants; and Will Self and Fay Weldon (8 April 2011, Brunel University London) 450+ participants. Each discussed their representational strategies with both readers and researchers. Drawing on both the authors' own literary practices and output as well as FCMAP's central research questions, a series of semi-structured interviews were conducted with four of these novelists (Azzopardi, Crace, Lodge and Phillips), asking them to consider ageing as both as a fictional theme and as part of their professional and life experiences. Resultant data from the all three strands, including the author participations, informed both a co-authored Demos policy report, *Coming of age* (Bazalgette et al, 2011), and Hubble and Tew's *Ageing narrative and identity: New qualitative social research* (2013), which discusses the methodology of FCMAP in detail and provides extensive analysis of the data.

From the start the team decided that public and social policy ought to be a priority. Hence the team decided on collaboration with researchers from the think tank Demos from the very first phase of planning before the project was finalised and well before funding was awarded (with seed funds provided by Brunel University London Research Support and Development Office), and eventually, again, extensively after data analysis to undertake further background research on policy issues and initiatives on ageing, following which researchers from both FCMAP and Demos wrote a policy report, *Coming of age* (Bazalgette et al, 2011). It was decided that to have genuine policy impact required a robust methodology and a large number of respondents producing valuable and relevant data. Three main methods of collecting data (as described above) were devised precisely to create a large cohort of respondents to underpin such relevance.

Aims and methods

Among the other primary research questions that informed both the aims and methods were:

- How older people respond to and reflect on changing (sometimes challenging) representations of ageing.
- Whether such responses produce further self-reflection that shed light on the changing cultural contours of ageing in Britain during the period from 1941.
- Whether either fictional representation or self-reflection in diaries reflects and/or resists commonplace assumptions and stereotypes concerning ageing in this period.
- Whether such responses and reflections illuminate the role played by representation in the shaping of both individual and group self-image and broader social attitudes.
- Whether the data produced might potentially inform new ways of thinking about ageing and if could it offer insights to policy-makers and stakeholders.

As discussed above, the team adopted an approach designed to minimise any contamination of the opinions and views expressed by respondents with the researchers' underlying assumptions.

As it transpired, many of FCMAP's findings reflected a set of opinions quite divergent from the team's particular range of personal and ideological commitments, but the team decided that a legitimate researcher ought to be prepared to incorporate such attitudinal preferences however uncomfortable they might feel these to be, given their own set of innate beliefs (which at times were contradicted variously by the views expressed). Naturally in everyday life influences do abound, and in the considered opinion of the FCMAP team, they largely do so through the circulation of a mass of intersecting (sometimes contradictory) social narratives, and this perspective underpinned the FCMAP methodological approach. From the start the team realised that a method would be required that could draw on this larger social process, as indicated above, with a minimum of shaping or influencing with regard to the views and opinions expressed by respondents. Citing Bourdieu on narrative as profoundly structuring the social world, in a book written by the authors of this chapter after

FCMAP entitled *Ageing, narrative and identity*, we add that 'Narrative impulses, propensities and modes of understanding (or processing) are not just conduits, but together constitute a whole that is in itself one of those "profound structures"' (Hubble and Tew, 2013, p 48). Moreover, such a process needed to be situated not just in terms of simply a sense of the power of language tied to essentialist notions of identity, but as an embodied framework of social narration of various intersecting selves where, as Marco Caracciolo indicates (2011), the fact is that 'our fleshy, living body is as much a product of our cultures as a constraint on them', producing an ongoing interplay. To achieve its goals, FCMAP deployed a 'methodological bricolage', adapting the mixture of elements suggested by Holstein and Minkler (2007, p 22) as follows:

> Methodological bricolage means not ruling out knowledge that is gained from personal narratives, fiction, poetry, film, qualitative investigations, philosophical inquiries, participatory action research and any other method of inquiry we my discover that yields insights into fundamental questions about how, and why, we experience old age in very particular ways. We need to worry less about large-scale generalisations and more about getting the story right.

FCMAP treated both fiction and narrative self-reflection as first, parts of a public space of narrative exchange and second, as incorporating a complex knowledge of and response to such exchanges (people know that opinions circulate and that such interactions mutate accordingly), and this approach hinged on a notion of active readership as one dimension of social engagement, drawing on such narratives to reflect on both fiction and life, which, in the U3A VRGs, became a subject for active discussion and reflection. FCMAP drew on and radically extended Hepworth's (2000) application of Symbolic Interactionism to ageing studies, combining methodologies drawn from both sociology (Bourdieu, 1993; Savage, 2007) and literary studies (Waugh, 1995; Stevenson, 2005; Tew, 2007; Tew et al, 2008).

The research also drew on various theoretical perspectives, including Bourdieu's concepts of symbolic capital, the *habitus* and the space of possibles (1990, 1993, 1996) and Bennett's account of culture's action on the 'working surfaces of the social' and his examination of the impact of cultural research on Australian social policy (2007). FCMAP was much influenced by Savage and Burrows (2007), who identify the need to rethink methodological techniques such as the sample survey and the in-depth interview, and to explore fresh types of social description that resist replicating the 'representative' categories of consumer research. Such modes of critical reflection inflect existing humanities research and, indeed, were a significant feature of the work of the generation of British sociologists who researched class and community in the 1960s. With a pleasing symmetry, FCMAP involved collaboration with organisations established by two of the senior members of that generation: Charles Madge, co-founder of MO, and Michael Young, co-founder of the U3A.

Following the example of Savage's (2007) MO study on the changing narration of social class in Britain between 1948 and 1990, material from all strands of the project was coordinated to shed fresh light on the changing cultural contours of ageing during particularly the post-war period, and to provoke reflection on some of the policy implications of those changes. By collaborating with existing and well-established organisations – MO, DEMOS and the U3As – which employ tried and tested structures and practices, rich data emerged for analysis, generated by subjects who understood themselves as active participants in the research process. These organisations also offered FCMAP excellent conduits for disseminating the research findings.

Findings

In terms of general findings, FCMAP established that older people's capacity to control their own personal narratives was central to 'good ageing' (and essential for effective social agency), for it is precisely at the point of becoming deemed older when older people lose control variously of their personal narrative and find that any concept of 'good ageing' is diminished or ceases. A woman in her 70s from the Highgate VRG said, "it is others who are old not ourselves … though I must be very different in nearly every way I, in fact, still feel 'me', ie, not old but timeless and ageless." A woman in her 60s from the Banstead group observed that, "part of the ageing process is that we don't see it in ourselves." For some, "ageing is something that is always on the horizon, rather than imminent." As another respondent said, "I think of the elderly as someone 20 years older than me." In *Coming of age* a VRG participant was quoted as reflecting when approaching 65: "'[T]here was a great deal of pressure from my family and friends to retire, but I supposed I felt this would be admitting that I was "old". I think many of us define ourselves by our work to a certain extent…'" (pp 72-3). *Coming of age*'s joint authors reflected that: 'Ageism and stereotyping were viewed as a significant problem by those who took part in the volunteer reading groups and the Mass Observation study' (2011, p 55).

Extensive and intensive narrative analysis of all three types of data revealed widespread agreement on the shortage of positive older characters in fictional narratives – written or filmed – while certain stereotypes of passive dependency and an inability to manage were readily identified. Even more significantly, the research revealed how the dominant socio-narrative associations of the word 'old' as pejorative interact with older respondents' narrative understanding of their own lives. A contrast is discernible in both MO and U3A respondents concerning attitudes that self-define as 'old' and the imposition of the term – there exists an intense antipathy regarding the latter. Opinions are also seen as being conditioned by the fact that the 'third age' is most often defined against a perceived 'fourth age' of 'decay, decrepitude and death' – all of which demonstrates in rich detail how difficult, but nonetheless essential, it is for older subjects to prevent dominant narratives shaping their own sense of identity.

The general wish was demonstrated of wanting to self-define against the grain of public opinion of other generations. In particular, the reading diaries show how literary fiction, which tends to foreground the cultural conventions that underpin everyday thought and actions, assists critically reflective readers to question such conventions when they encounter them in society, while the MO directive responses testify to the capacity of sustained narrative life-writing itself to provide practitioners with a space to particularise their own experience against the generalising and stereotyping force of dominant cultural values. Overall, the research establishes the central importance to older people of continued control over their personal narratives in maintaining social agency. Self-expression tends to empower people. Certainly engagement with such narratives was seem as beneficial by participants, as giving them voice in a significant fashion. Participation in of itself was seen as positive.

FCMAP data and findings were regularly shared with the think tank Demos, culminating in an intense collaborative drafting of a 200-page report, *Coming of age*, which made recommendations on five policy areas: work and finances, housing and independence, health and social care, active ageing, and end of life. *Coming of age* was published as a paperback and available as a free online download from the Demos website (www.demos.co.uk/publications/comingofage). The Executive summary focused on the following points:

- At the centre of our vision is the need for long-term strategies to support people to experience good health, social inclusion and financial resilience across the life course.
- Older people are a highly heterogeneous group, and therefore we need to move away from one-size-fits-all policy approaches and services to offer older people choice and flexibility in how they live.
- We need to challenge all forms of age discrimination, including patronising stereotypes about older people's dependency and vulnerability, and to find better ways to target state support towards those who actually need it.
- Older people are feeling increasingly alienated by policy rhetoric that presents them as a social or financial burden. We cannot meet the challenges posed by an ageing society without the support of older people themselves. Therefore, we need a shift of mindset to recognise the extremely valuable social roles that are already fulfilled by older people, and increase opportunities for older people to use their skills to make a positive contribution to society.

In *Ageing, narrative and identity*, we wrote that, 'Even those suffering some diminishment are capable of interaction and involvement at a societal level with the right frameworks' (Hubble and Tew, 2013, p 201), the reality of which is becoming ever more significant as people grow old with sufficient technological expertise to sustain communication despite disabilities brought on by ageing. In specific policy terms, as detailed in *Coming of age*, the research revealed clearly that ageing cannot be treated as a single, solvable social problem, or an experience that is uniform. For instance, one man in his 70s from the South East London VRG rejected attempts to categorise people by their age group altogether, insisting, "I am an individual and I wish to be treated as an individual. I suspect all older people feel the same." The experience of ageing varies vastly between individuals and groups. It is not only influenced by immediate concerns such as health and financial security, but by experience and outlook developed over the whole of the life course. *Coming of age* cites a 72-year-old MO respondent as saying, "'Thinking about ageing has changed; people have a more active social life these days to a more advanced age than 20 or 50 years ago'" (p 64).

Many respondents resented the prevalence of contrasting ageist policy narratives that emphasise the costs posed by an ageing population and that do not adequately recognise the wide variety of contributions that older people make, from taxation through to voluntary work and caring. In particular, the research questioned a number of assumptions such as that older people are disproportionately concerned with crime and disproportionately prone to feelings of isolation and loneliness. Such staple media representations, which frequently inflect on public and policy debate, were demonstrated to reside in the circulation of a set of culturally dominant narratives, and shown to return to levels in line with the rest of the population in cases where older people were able to separate their personal narratives from those surrounding them. As we argued in *Ageing, narrative and identity*, 'People never simply live out old age in cultural isolation. They live it through culturally and historically specific frameworks that are mostly a synthesis of public and private understandings that both draw upon and sustain cultural representations of ageing' (2013, p 201). As such they can be radically amended.

Policy and praxis: the implications

Coming of age considered the changing cultural contours of ageing in the UK and the implications of such changes for public policy, drawing directly on the data produced both in the VRGs and from responses to the MO directive, as well as the authors who were interviewed and took part in the public literary events that were key to the exchange of views at the heart of the project. As indicated above, Demos participated in the research even before the funding was awarded, and later set up and hosted a high-level policy seminar to launch the *Coming of age* report, which was discussed at a 'Roundtable', held on 16 May 2011 at Demos' London headquarters in Tooley Street, where the research was welcomed as 'excellent' by a former Head of Pensions, Ageing Strategy and Analysis Division at the Department for Work and Pensions. Three key stakeholders then responded to the report under Chatham House rules (which encourage anonymity to speakers while encouraging openness and the sharing of information), all engaging with the implications of the research and all praising the innovative nature of the research. As one said, "It's a really fantastic, very detailed report. I thought there were several particularly useful aspects of this research. I found the use of narratives as a research method particularly helpful, in providing a rich, bottom-up take on issues that are often dealt with in a very top-down way." Subsequent policy dissemination of the report findings include reviews, summaries and links in such influential locations as *Social Policy Digest*, the Department for Environment, Food and Rural Affairs Sustainable Development in Government website, the Centre for Policy on Ageing website, the Local Government Chronicle, and other bodies, including in Ireland.

On 15 November 2011, the Liberal Democrat Health Committee, chaired by Paul Burstow, former Minister for Care Services, on policy proposals for a 'healthier old age' considered the FCMAP findings. Since then the research has been further discussed and cited in various *fora* concerned with policy.

Given its methodological synthesis and its public policy orientation, the investigators anticipated an additional range of beneficiaries who may wish to engage with this underlying methodology, with its capacity over a period of time to record nuanced opinions and attitudes, and to offer detailed analysis from resulting data in a manner that will be penetrative and insightful. Clearly this approach could potentially be applied to a wide range of other issues and contexts. And beneficiaries of such research would include organisations and individuals dedicated to giving voice to older people and their concerns; older people themselves who wish to engage in deliberative democracy; those involved in the commercial provision of goods and services to older people in the commercial, public and voluntary sectors; those concerned with public policy as regards older people; private bodies with an interest in policy provision; scholars, researchers and academics in literary studies, humanities and the social sciences, particularly gerontologists; local authorities; charities; political parties and organisations; volunteer groups; ethnic interest groups; and faith groups.

More generally, to paraphrase the terms adopted by the European Parliament report, *The demographic future of Europe*, FCMAP should help provide, as part of the NDA 'family', a generally better understanding of older people as complex actors or social agents who 'are always involved in, and can never act outside of, the multiplicity of social relations in which they are enmeshed' (Ortner, 2006, p 130), and further, how they can contribute positively to the public sphere. The results should contribute to a more nuanced view of the potential role of the older citizen in public and political processes, in the 'silver economy' as consumers of goods and services (including leisure, care and welfare services) and as part of the workforce beyond the age of 65. FCMAP offered ways in which to also foster a more holistic view of older people that may well contribute towards social cohesion, helping provide both a dialogue and data that can help to encourage the physical wellbeing of older people and provide a positive context to enhance solidarity between generations by developing a better informed sense of what Bourdieu and Wacquant (1992, pp 120-1) offer as a practical and socially constituted sense of the game or habitus, in this case, as regards ageing.

The policy directions outlined in *Coming of age* were about finding a vision for an effective policy approach to ageing as much as making specific recommendations for changes to policy or service provision. Its executive summary identified four key principles for broadly improving policy responses based on recognition that older people are a highly heterogeneous group, and one cannot meet the challenges posed by an ageing society without the support of older people themselves, which implies that one needs:

• long-term strategies to support people to experience good health, social inclusion and financial resilience across the life course;
• to reject one-size-fits-all policy approaches and offer choice and flexibility in services offered to older people reflecting their lifestyles;
• to challenge all forms of age discrimination, including patronising stereotypes about older people's dependency and vulnerability, finding better ways to target state support towards those who actually need it;
• to equally challenge policy rhetoric that presents older people as a social or financial burden, which increasingly alienates older people; to develop a shift of mindset to recognise the extremely valuable social roles that are already fulfilled by older people; and to increase opportunities for older people to use their skills to make a positive contribution to society.

In response to the findings, FCMAP proposed in detail a range of changes of emphasis nationally regarding specific policy areas, outlined in summary below.

Later life working: To realise its ambitions of retaining an older workforce, the government should work with employers to explore opportunities for developing more flexible career pathways for older workers that offer a greater choice of job roles, use older people's skill sets, support a phased approach to retirement, and combat institutional ageism. However, working in later life should be a matter of choice, not compulsion, and the default retirement age should be abolished. To facilitate such later life working, the demands of the job should be subject to reasonable adjustment (including working remotely from home) appropriate to the individual's capabilities.

Pensions and finances: The overall opinion was expressed by respondents that it would be beneficial to reduce complexity in the pensions system, and it was strongly suggested by many in terms of future generations that the government needs to provide a firm basis for people to save towards their retirement; our research suggested strong support for proposals to introduce a single-tier pension, reducing complexity in the state pensions system and thereby tackling pensioner poverty. Attitudes about personal finances varied. Some considered the state pension and benefit provision inadequate. Others pointed out that poorly informed choices with regard to employment might have negative financial consequences for retirement without centralised changes. Changed personal circumstances such as divorce or illness might radically diminish one's financial position, so future planning at both a state and individual level was regarded as a necessity. A strand of existing pensioners with assets considered it unfair that those without such assets would receive care if required for free, while they might well be penalised. The seemed a potentially intractable problem.

Universal benefits: Contrary to the dominant approach in ageing policy, older people do not necessarily believe universality to be the best system for delivering benefits. The assumption that 'older people' are more vulnerable to cold weather was felt to be patronising by most people in their 60s. They felt the current system of Winter Fuel Payments does not reflect modern experiences of ageing, which would suggest policy should target such payments, perhaps raising eligibility to those between ages 70-75 in line with disability-free life expectancy. To address inequalities, people receiving income- or health-related benefits could automatically receive Winter Fuel Payments once they reach state pension age.

Housing and independence: Since respondents almost universally expressed great fear at the prospect of moving into residential care, policies and support systems should be developed that allow older people to remain independent and to stay in their own homes for as long as possible. Domiciliary care should be offered rather than early and often unnecessary admission into residential care if they are unable to live on their own. Older people should be encouraged to remain in contact with people of all age groups, sustaining interdependent social networks. Most objected to the unfairness of the current means-tested system that can lead to situations in which the prudent lose their assets in paying for care while those who did not save for their retirement may not need to contribute.

Health and social care: In policy terms, the discriminatory treatment of older people in both the NHS and private provision should be highlighted. Government and health authorities should raise the awareness of doctors who dismiss health problems experienced by older people, regarding them as part of the ageing process, so that they learn to consider them as treatable conditions. It was felt strongly that the system ought to engage with preventative approaches to mental health support, including providing older people with opportunities to remain active and socially engaged.

Dementia: Since most respondents expressed fear of developing dementia in old age, they felt that the government should make research into treatments a priority, whether through state or charitable funding, and raise awareness of discrimination against sufferers.

Carers: Since so many caring for their parents are themselves growing older, they might well be in need of care themselves. It was felt that such older carers currently receive inadequate support and are in need of regular periods of respite.

Active ageing: Given most people saw retirement as a time to remain active and socially engaged, support for voluntary structures such as the U3A should be fostered and provided. Society needs to actively provide increased opportunities for leisure, self-development and physical activity. The axing of state support that made access free for swimmers over 55 was lamented. It was felt critical that policies emerge that provide opportunities for learning and cultural engagement, whether state-funded or simply encouraged, with adult learning opportunities, and sustaining local library and museum services, including mobile libraries. Respondents thought volunteering was an important means for older people to continue to contribute to society, while public spaces and facilities such as leisure centres provided valuable opportunities for intergenerational contact. They believed transport concessions such as the free bus or transport passes were vital to help older people to remain mobile, and economically *and* socially active.

A diversity of service provision to support 'active ageing': Since older subjects are a highly heterogeneous group, a diversity of service provision should be offered since some people would not wish to participate in designated activities for older people. Core services such as libraries and leisure centres should remain available and accessible to older people, as an essential part of supporting active ageing. Segregating service delivery according to age groups can further exclude those already socially isolated.

End of life: Many thought policies should be adopted to ensure the adequacy of care in the final phase of life, avoiding indignities suffered when dying. Some respondents felt strongly thought that euthanasia should be accepted, enabling more control over the manner of death.

Key findings
- People's narrative understanding of ageing is important in determining their experience of ageing.
- There is a relationship between postwar representations of ageing (including fiction) and how ageing is understood, individually and socially.
- New forms of third age (people in their 60s and 70s no longer consider themselves old) and fourth age (people in their later 70s, 80s and 90s are still living full varied lives, despite infirmities) subjectivity have emerged.
- It is important to extend the concept of 'active ageing' beyond physical fitness and wellbeing criteria to include narrative understanding.
- There is a need for new narratives of the life course that enable older people to emerge from the ingrained stereotypes of ageing as social beings in their own right.

Conclusion

Potentially FCMAP offers an innovative model for the in-depth analysis of people's opinions and belief systems in a culture where people are increasingly more guarded about voicing any such values. FCMAP provides an active model demonstrating key aspects of participant democracy. It demonstrates that both researchers and policy-makers concerned with ageing should listen and respond to what is said by older people. Doing so might improve the lives of many, if not most, older people. To achieve this goal society needs to comprehend certain realities that FCMAP's research suggests about the lived experience of citizens as older people, including the need to:

- restore symbolic capital to older people;
- understand the complex processes of social narrative exchanges that shape and modulate our cultural understanding of the experience of ageing in the contemporary period;

- admit the radical ways in which social attitudes towards ageing among older people themselves have changed;
- recognise that narrative tropes of older people may potentially drive policy and demonstrate how they certainly shape cultural norms;
- comprehend that such cultural norms can be interrogated and radicalised;
- use the above to provide a potential platform for rethinking policy and to re-imagine our narratives of ageing and their exchange.

Both FCMAP's theoretical model and its data analysis suggest that cultural and social narrative exchange is a mechanism by which people frame and develop their ideas, but that these cannot effectively be imposed; rather, they emerge from a complex sense of the experiential, the practical and the efficacious. If idealised forms of knowledge and cultural intervention often have unintended consequences, surely it is far better to listen in an open fashion, rather than attempt to prefigure the pattern of opinions expressed in both the data, and therefore the findings and outcomes. Researchers need to allow respondents a space where they might develop their own ideas as autonomously as possible, charting the patterns of social narrative exchange and their relation to a mass of private opinions, the realisation of which is also an essential and cautionary one for both researchers and policy-makers.[3]

Notes

[1] See *New Dynamics of Ageing programme* (www.newdynamics.group.shef.ac.uk).

[2] The Winter 2009 Directive, 'Books and You', drafted by Hubble with MO staff, is available online at www.massobs.org.uk/images/Directives/Winter_2009_Directive.pdf. The earlier directives on ageing that it was designed to complement are the Winter 1992 Directive 'Growing Older' (www.massobs.org.uk/images/Directives/Winter_1992_Directive.pdf) and the Autumn 2006 Directive 'Age' (www.massobs.org.uk/images/Directives/Autumn2006.pdf).

[3] Researchers may wish to further study the FCMAP VRG diaries and associated data that have been archived and are available at both the UK Data Service (see http://reshare.ukdataservice.ac.uk/850580), and in the Special Collections in the library of Brunel University London (https://www.brunel.ac.uk/life/library/Special-Collections/Fiction-and-the-Cultural-Mediation-of-Ageing); the MO material is archived at the Keep, Falmer, Sussex (www.thekeep.info/collections/mass-observation-archive).

References

Anon (2007) *Europe's demographic future: Facts and figures*, European Commission staff working document, Brussels: EU Commission. Available at ec.europa.eu/social/BlobServlet?docId=706&langId=en

Bazalgette, L., Holden, J., Tew, P., Hubble, N. and Morrison, J. (2011) *Coming of age*, London: Demos. Available at www.demos.co.uk/project/coming-of-age

Bennett, T. (2007) 'The work of culture', *Cultural Sociology*, vol 1, no 1, pp 31-47.

Bourdieu, P. (1990) *The logic of practice* (translated by Richard Nice), Cambridge: Polity.

Bourdieu, P. (1993) *The field of cultural production* (translated and introduced by Randal Johnson), Cambridge: Polity.

Bourdieu, P. (1996) *The rules of art: Genesis and structure in the literary field* (translated by Susan Emanuel), Cambridge: Polity.

Bourdieu, P. and Wacquant, L.J.D. (1992) 'The purpose of reflexive sociology (The Chicago Workshop)', in P. Bourdieu and L.J.D. Wacquant, *An invitation to reflexive sociology*, Cambridge: Polity, pp 61-215.

Caracciolo, M. (2011) 'Narrative, embodiment, and cognitive science: Why should we care?', *Project Narrative Website*, 7 November. Available at http://projectnarrative.osu.edu/sites/projectnarrative.osu.edu/files/Caracciolo-PN-Presentation.pdf

Elliott, H. (1997) 'The use of diaries in sociological research on health experience', *Sociological Research Online*, vol 2, no 2. Available at www.socresonline.org.uk/2/2/7.html

Fisher, W.R. (1987) *Communication as narration: Toward a philosophy of reason, value, and action*, Columbia, SC: University of South Carolina Press.

Gubrium, J.F. and Holstein, J.A. (2006) 'Biographical work and the future of the ageing self', in J. Vincent, C. Phillipson and M. Downs (eds) *The futures of old age*, London: Sage, pp 117-25.

Harrisson, T. (1940) 'What is public opinion?', *Political Quarterly*, vol XI, no 42, October, pp 368-83.

Hepworth, M. (2000) *Stories of ageing*, Buckingham: Open University Press.

Holstein, M.B. and Minkler, M. (2007) 'Critical gerontology: Reflections for the 21st century', in M. Bernard and T. Scharf (eds) *Critical perspectives on ageing societies*, Bristol: Policy Press, pp 13-26.

Hubble, N. and Tew, P. (2013) *Ageing narrative and identity: New qualitative social research*, Basingstoke: Palgrave Macmillan.

Ortner, S.B. (2006) *Anthropology and social theory: Culture, power, and the acting subject*, Durham, NC and London: Duke University Press.

Savage, M. (2007) 'Changing social class identities in post-war Britain: Perspectives from mass-observation', *Sociological Research Online*, vol 12, no 3. Available at www.socresonline.org.uk/12/3/6.html

Savage, M. and Burrows, R. (2007) 'The coming crisis of empirical sociology', *Sociology*, vol 41, no 5, pp 885-99.

Sheble, L. and Wildemuth, B. (2009) 'Research diaries', in B. Wildemuth (ed) *Applications of social research methods to questions in information and library science*, Santa Barbara, CA: Libraries Unlimited, pp 211-21. Draft version cited available at http://laurasheble.web.unc.edu/files/2012/07/DRAFT_sheble-Wildemuth_research-diaries.pdf

Stevenson, R. (2005) *The Oxford English Literary History, Volume 12. 1960–2000. The Last of England?*, Oxford: Oxford University Press.

Tew, P. (2007) *The contemporary British novel* (revised 2nd edn), London: Continuum.

Tew, P., Tolan, F. and Wilson, L. (2008) *Writers talk: Conversations with contemporary British novelists*, London: Continuum.

Vaneigem, R. (1994) *The revolution of everyday life* (translated by D. Nicholson-Smith), London: Rebel Press/Left Bank Books.

Waugh, P. (1995) *Harvest of the sixties: English literature and its background 1960-90*, Oxford: Opus.

FOURTEEN

Narrative representations of the self: encounters with contemporary visual art

Andrew Newman and Anna Goulding

Introduction

How and why older people create narrative identities in response to encounters with contemporary visual art is explored using the results from 'Contemporary visual art and identity construction – Well-being among older people', a 28-month study (May 2009-October 2011) that examined the responses of 38 older people who were taken to three contemporary visual art galleries in North East England, UK. Participants visited the galleries in pre-existing groups – a writers' group, an older person's advocacy organisation, a film club for the over-60s, a charity providing activities for older men and a group from a sheltered accommodation unit. Baseline interviews provided background information about participants including their engagement with art and culture, the art forms that they preferred, as well as general demographic information, such as marital status, social networks, education and employment history. The groups visited galleries three times over the duration of the project – each visit included a guided tour, and then participants discussed their impressions and reflected on what they had seen in focus groups.

The project's overall aim was to determine how older adults consume contemporary visual art as content for identity construction practices, and how that relates to wellbeing. This chapter explores the influence of encounters with contemporary visual art on the construction of older persons' narrative identities, and how this involves the process of positioning in respect to wider societal meta-narratives, specifically those to do with age, class and gender.

Theoretical framework

This section provides an introduction to the theory that has been used to support the analysis of the data. It starts with a description of narrative identities and then considers the role of meta-narratives in identity formation. Following this is an account of how negative meta-narratives of ageing may influence the self-construct of people in later life.

Recent approaches to understanding identity (De Fina and Georgakopoulou, 2012) emphasise its social nature and its narrative component. As McAdams (1993, p 5) states:

> Identity is a life story. A life story is a personal myth that an individual begins working on in late adolescence and young adulthood in order to provide his or her life with a purpose.

A useful way of analysing narrative is provided by Hammack (2011), who suggests that narrative exists on two separate but interrelated levels of analysis. First, individuals use narrative to make sense of the world around them and in order to do this they draw on meta-narratives (variously described as discourses, master-narratives or scenarios) that they are exposed to in order to construct a narrative identity for themselves. These narratives that individuals construct then serve as 'motivational forces for particular sets of actions' (Hammack, 2011, p 313) that are designed to support that particular narrative, or life story, as expressed within, or influenced by, a particular social context.

Individuals use meta-narratives in order to position themselves in relation to events that they feel have helped to define them (De Fina and Georgakopoulou, 2012). De Fina and Georgakopoulou note that, 'rather than being positioned in a deterministic way by out-there structures, speakers actively and agentively select, resist and revisit positions' (2012, p 163). People are motivated to construct narrative identities, or self-presentations, in order to communicate positive images of themselves or to address negative views that they might feel that others have about them.

The second level of analysis, described by Hammack (2011), concerns meta-narratives or a storyline that is viewed as compulsory by members of a group to the extent that it is integrated into a personal narrative. Such meta-narratives can be identified as being associated with 'gender, race, nationality, class and sexual identity' (p 313), and it is often assumed that they take on essentialist characteristics. The individual might view themselves as being assigned positions in relation to these meta-narratives rather than being part of the process through which those meta-narratives are being constructed. Individual narrative identities of age and ageing are expected to be inflected by meta-narratives associated with the categories of gender, class or ethnicity.

Meta-narratives that have become associated with older people have been explored in a study by Fealy et al (2012) that considered how the Irish Government's decision to remove automatic entitlement to health and welfare services for those over 70 was presented in newspapers. Older people were referred to with collective nouns or phrases such as 'the pensioners' or 'the retired' (p 90), implying a level of homogeneity among the older population and ignoring its diversity. The authors identified five distinct identity types that were presented:

- victims
- frail, infirm and vulnerable
- radicalised citizens on the march
- the deserving old, and
- the undeserving old.

Here narratives were used for political ends – to influence the debate on how the needs of older people can be addressed within the context of a difficult financial national situation. Murray et al (2014, p 79) note that younger people are generally cast as 'agents of change, of life creators while older people are cast as passive recipients of care.' Nonetheless, it is important to emphasise that narratives are not fixed and political needs can help to construct or modify existing narratives (Phelan, 2011).

From a study that focused on representations of ageing in UK women's magazines aimed at the over-35 age group, Soden (2012, p 85) identified what she described as three myths of ageing that are presented as 'normal' and 'natural' in conversation:

- Ageing is a decline scenario: it involves both mental and physical decline.
- Age is synonymous with loss of power: sexual, economic and social.
- Ageing must be resisted.

These meta-narratives were not questioned and were incorporated into narratives of ageing presented by this media.

Meta-narratives that privilege young people might be seen as a threat to the self-construct of older people. The result of this can be seen in attempts by older people to distance themselves, individually, from the category of 'old' (Hurd, 1999). In a comparative study of age identities between Germany and the US, Westerhof et al (2003) found that 'Americans and Germans tend to feel younger than their actual ages' indicating the presence of negative cultural meaning of old age in both countries' (p 378), and that the 'need to identify with younger ages is more strongly felt in American than German culture' (p 379). Alarmingly, the significance of these stereotypes or meta-narratives on older people has been shown to be physiological. Levy et al (2002), from a study of 660 people aged 50 and older, suggests that some younger people automatically accept as true the negative stereotypes or meta-narratives associated with age, and by the time they become relevant, they have been internalised. The study revealed that those who maintained a positive self-perception of ageing (measured up to 23 years earlier) tended to live longer. The expected increase in life expectancy was 7.5 years after age, gender, socioeconomic status, loneliness and functional health were controlled for.

The role of the artworks in prompting discussion of wider meta-narratives and how they are used in constructing more individual or group/community narratives of participants is explored below. Importantly, this chapter attempts to determine the purposes that a particular narrative might serve.

Data and methodologies

Mishler (1995) provides three different approaches to using narrative theory as a methodology. This chapter uses the third approach presented (p 90), which concentrates on the following:

- contexts and consequences
- narrativisation of experience
- cognition, memory, self
- narrative and culture
- myths, rituals, performance
- storytelling in interactional and institutional contexts
- the politics of narrative
- power conflict and resistance.

An account of narrative analysis used in ageing studies is provided by Phoenix et al (2010), who provide a theoretical basis for this type of research and a typology of approaches.

We adopted a qualitative approach for the analysis as it enabled us to identify how encounters with contemporary visual art influenced the respondent's construction of personal narratives (Silverman, 2006).

Participants

Some of the groups of older people were pre-existing while other groups came together specifically for this research, although their members already belonged to a common organisation. For example, the sheltered accommodation group members lived in the same place and knew each other, but they had not come together for activities before they volunteered to take part in the study. The recruitment process involved the research team making an appointment to talk to the groups where the purpose of the research and the practicalities of the research project were explained and people were asked to volunteer. Participants were then subsequently contacted to arrange baseline interviews. Contacts were made with local black and minority ethnic groups (BME), but a Muslim women's group and a Jewish group were unwilling and/or unable to commit. Other BME groups such as a local Chinese Association and a further education group for people who did not speak English as a first language were involved, but due to delays, participants only made one visit. It was decided not to recruit people with dementia, and ethical approval was applied for and received from Newcastle University, Newcastle upon Tyne, UK, on that basis. This chapter focuses on the 38 older people who made three visits to galleries.

Data collection

There were seven data collection points for each group during the research project and five groups with between six and nine members in each. For the baseline data, one-to-one interviews or group interviews were offered. Baseline interviews addressed a range of topics including participants' social and family relationships/networks, housing/neighbourhood, previous occupations, educational histories, interests, voting practices, general perceptions about ageing and attitudes towards contemporary visual art.

Each group visited three exhibitions over the lifetime of the project, the final one being chosen by the respondents. A description of the venues and shows attended is provided in the Appendix at the end of this chapter. The groups were taken to the gallery by taxi or mini-bus, given lunch and then given a guided tour around the exhibition by a curator or education officer. Focus groups were then used to record responses to the experience of the visits. Two members of the research team were present during the focus groups, with one being a moderator and the other observing and making notes. The stimuli for the discussion were the artworks and the gallery within which it was displayed. The moderator initiated the discussion by asking participants what they had thought of the exhibition, and then the group members discussed the exhibition and venue among themselves, responding to comments that others in the group made. Participants responded to what they had seen and heard without a structure being imposed by the moderator.

The focus groups were of between 30 and 120 minutes' duration, and were digitally recorded and then transcribed. This resulted in 69 transcripts that were then coded using the NVivo 9 software designed to help manage qualitative data (www.qsrinternational.com). Codes were derived from close reading of the transcripts and informed by the literature on narrative identities, particularly that related to older people. Inferences about respondents' use of the artworks to construct personal narrative identities were derived from the interpretations they placed on the artworks and the themes chosen for discussion.

Groups recruited to the project

Sheltered accommodation group, Gateshead, Tyne and Wear: This group consisted of seven women aged 62 to 90 who live in sheltered accommodation in Gateshead, Tyne and Wear. They had lived locally before taking up residence. All of the group, apart from two, were over 68; of the younger ones, a 64-year-old had a learning disability and a 62-year-old was deaf and had recently been widowed. All apart from the 62-year-old (who had been a nurse) had left school aged 14 or 15 and had gone into employment immediately, working in occupations such as cook, factory worker, punch card operator and sales person. This group visited the BALTIC Centre for Contemporary Art to see 'Parrworld' and 'A Needle Woman' (12 November 2009), the Shipley Art Gallery to see 'Knitted Lives' (9 March 2010), and the Northern Gallery for Contemporary Art to see 'Systematic' (15 June 2010).

Writers' group, Sunderland, Tyne and Wear: This group, formed in 1986, consisted of six women aged 64 to 87, five of whom were over 72. One member had 'O' and 'A' levels, while the others had left school without qualifications at age 14 or 15. Three returned to formal education, with one obtaining a degree at the age of 62. Occupations included cook, cleaner, shop worker, nurse, social worker, probation officer, housewife, secretary and factory worker. This group visited the Northern Gallery for Contemporary Art to see 'Rank' (17 June 2009), the BALTIC Centre for Contemporary Art to see 'Parrworld' and 'A Needle Woman' (26 November 2009), and the Great North Museum: Hancock (24 March 2010).

Group recruited from an advocacy organisation for older people, Gateshead, Tyne and Wear: This group consisted of nine individuals, six females and three males, who ranged in age from 63 to 83. Three were aged 63- 64, while six were aged between 79 and 83. Occupations included cook, civil servant, teacher, cabaret singer, private industry worker, dental nurse, shop manager and university researcher. Educational qualifications obtained ranged from none to a PhD. This group visited the BALTIC Centre for Contemporary Art to see 'Parrworld' and 'A Needle Woman' (26 November 2009), the Northern Gallery for Contemporary Art to see the show by Semiconductor (10 March 2010), and Belsay Hall, Castle and Gardens to see 'Extraordinary Measures' (12 May 2010).

Group recruited from a daytime film club for the over-60s in Newcastle upon Tyne, Tyne and Wear (henceforth called the 'film group'): This group contained three females and four males, who ranged in age from 61 to 65. Occupations included primary school teacher, chartered engineer, social worker, occupational psychologist and someone who had had a supervisory job at a local brewery. All, apart from the former brewery worker, were educated to degree level, with the primary school teacher returning to education and qualifying as a teacher after leaving school at 16. This group visited the Northern Gallery for Contemporary Art to see the show by Semiconductor (23 March 2010), the BALTIC Centre for Contemporary Art to see a show by Jenny Holzer (13 May 2010), and a show by Anselm Kiefer (14 October 2010). Three people from the group (one female and two males) also visited a show on the representation of older women that was organised by the NDA project 'Look At Me!' entitled, 'Look at Me! Images of Women and Ageing' held at the Workstation, Sheffield, UK on 15 March 2011.

Men's group recruited from a 'live at home scheme' (aims to enable members to continue living at home independently while enhancing their quality of life), *Gateshead, Tyne and Wear:* This group consisted of nine men who ranged in age from 62 to 88 (the 62-year-old had a disability and the ages of the others ranged from 72 to 88). Previous occupations included company director, maintenance electrician, clerk, painter and decorator and maintenance fitter for a coalmine. The 62-year-old member of the group had left school with 'O' levels, while the others had left at age 14 or 15 without educational qualifications. This group visited the Northern Gallery for Contemporary Art to see the show by Semiconductor (28 April 2010), the BALTIC Centre for Contemporary Art to see a show by Cornelia Parker (8 September 2010), and the Hatton Gallery to see Hugh Stoneman: 'Master Printer', The Art Fund Archive (3 November 2010).

Analysis

Visual art engagement being used to negotiate identity positions

The following explores how the participants used the experience of visiting the exhibitions to position themselves in relation to the social category of 'old' and the social characteristics that they associated with older people. De Fina and Georgakopoulou (2012, p 172), drawing from Durkheim (1954) and Levi-Strauss (1963), state that social categories are:

> ... moulds provided by culture within which individuals and groups construct oppositions and affiliations, similarities and differences. They are basic to the creation of social meanings in general and to identity in particular.

Respondents distanced themselves from particular characteristics that they associated with 'older people' partially through the act of taking part in the research project, and through visiting art galleries and engaging in other forms of cultural participation in their own time.

A 74-year-old member of the writers' group, who had been a civil servant, stated, after their final visit to the Great North Museum: Hancock:

> 'I mean we are not old, but we have a young outlook and I think you know, sort of realise that you are not catering for the old, you are catering for the older people who are wanting to be stimulated you know, want new ideas brought into their lives, something so they can focus on and feel as though they are still part of society.'

This respondent distances herself from particular characteristics that she appears to associate with older people – that they are passive, uninterested in learning, a burden, and somehow separate or not involved with society. She claims for herself attributes that she feels are more associated with younger people – those of wanting to learn, being productive and playing an active role within society.

Agreement with aspects of negative meta-narratives associated with older people is shown in the following response from an 83-year-old male retired civil servant who was from the advocacy organisation. He states in the final focus group held at Belsay Hall Castle and Gardens, Northumberland:

> 'Well I think because they become immersed in their own life and they have this little sort of narrow alleyway of their life that they are travelling. So in many ways, yes, what you are actually doing is saying to older people, wake up, you know, look for something different in your life.'

This respondent describes older people as 'they', distancing himself from particular characteristics he associates with older people despite being an older person himself. The negative meta-narratives associated with ageing appear to be internalised by many of the research participants and provide a structure for social representations. These take on a prescriptive quality as described by Moscovici (1984, p 9) who states, 'they impose themselves upon us with irresistible force.' When faced with this, the strategy adopted involved respondents distancing themselves from the category 'old' and its negative associations. These results resonate with those of Queniart and Charpentier (2012), who found that the three generations of older women in their study refused to categorise themselves as old.

The respondent quoted immediately above also acknowledges that society is becoming more accepting of older people being active and involved:

> 'It's not just a question now of stick granny in a corner and give her her knitting and tell her to shut up, you know, as it used to happen generations ago. That it is now more acceptable that people of our age will come out and join in to actually want to take part in things. You've got grannies that go abseiling now and do all sorts of weird and wonderful things. So and I think society as a whole is more

able to accept that because we are old it doesn't mean to say our life has come to an end, we are still able to take part.'

For this individual cultural engagement is an important part of a more active and involved life. This could be identified as the development of a positive counter-narrative of more engaged older people that might be seen as a strategy to resist the influence of the more negative ones.

The importance of representing older people as active and enjoying life was emphasised by a member of the film group, a 64-year-old retired engineer, in response to some of the images displayed in the 'Look At Me! Images of Women and Ageing' exhibition (Warren and Richards, 2012):

> 'A bunch of depressives, that's how I would summarise them and none of them were doing anything.... There was none of them painting, working, walking, there were the sort of contrived handstands, I suppose. None of them were actually doing anything. They weren't swimming, playing football, painting, music, art, walking, jumping apart from contrived ones in the studio, it wasn't like an active image of the age group that was there and I think if you looked at that in a 100 years' time you would say "God, that was a depressing period to live in", I would top myself, I'd stick my head in the oven at the age of 60.'

This respondent interpreted the images displayed as supporting negative meta-narratives of older women living passive lives. He feels that a counter-narrative of older people being active would have been a more appropriate topic for the images displayed, and was disappointed by the content. This respondent's approach is political, advocating for a positive image of older people to be displayed.

As can be seen from the responses above, both positive and negative meta-narratives exist at the same time – their relative influence is contingent on the nature of social interaction concerned and how the various meta-narratives at play within that social interaction are understood. The respondents wish to personally distance themselves from the social category of 'old' while at the same time advocating for a more active counter-narrative of older people. Meta-narratives were often the subject of discussion when the characteristics associated with them were not accepted as 'natural' but rather socially derived and so open to challenge.

Art engagement being used to develop an existing narrative identity

Some of the respondents had a life-long narrative identity that incorporated knowledge of various art forms and the process of learning about them. While they were not explicitly reacting to the negative meta-narratives associated with ageing, they might have been doing this implicitly. This was most evident in the responses of the film group and to a lesser extent the group recruited from an advocacy organisation for older people.

A member of the film group, who was 61 years old and had worked at a local brewery, was typical in his arts engagement. He states:

> 'Yes, I like art galleries I mean, when I go on holidays you always pop into the art gallery; I always do, Amsterdam, Paris, places like that. Here I regularly go to the BALTIC because it's ever changing. I go to the Laing Art Gallery.'

This individual makes a point of mentioning that he regularly visits art galleries, both in Newcastle upon Tyne and when he is on holiday. He is self-presenting as someone who is culturally engaged and active.

A number of the respondents were willing to set themselves new challenges that were often in response to life-changing events. A 64-year-old female member of the film group, who had moved back to North East England from Australia after a divorce, was actively exploring new art forms. She states:

> 'I went to the Cheltenham Art Gallery and there was a very small exhibition on surrealist art, Man Ray and Henry Moore and people like that which had been done 40 years before and on the side of that the ad said "Would you like to come to a surrealist writing workshop?" and I thought, "I've got to do that!"'

This represents a willingness to develop an existing narrative identity to incorporate an art form with which she was unfamiliar. The willingness to learn is also illustrated in the following quotation from a 65-year-old former teacher from the film group:

> 'I think what we all have in common is that we still have a curiosity about the world around us, we are not stagnant, that's probably why we signed up for the course. We were still at the cinema, we were looking at stimulating artwork

there in the cinema and we still have a desire to learn and to find out things, and I think once that goes, then that's quite sad.'

Katz (2000, p 144) uses an empirical study to show how older people 'incorporate the professional vocabulary of activity into their stories of retired living', and that the need for activity can become a hegemonic narrative in itself.

The importance of taking up opportunities is illustrated in this quote from an 83-year-old male retired civil servant from the advocacy organisation for older people:

'I am not talking about 60s or getting up to 70s, I'm talking about getting over 70s and to 80, we never got a chance to do what the young ones are doing today, this is our chance now.'

He feels that there are more opportunities available now than when they were younger, and that older people should take advantage of them. Many of the older respondents left school aged 14 or 15 and went directly into work and have enjoyed more leisure time since retirement. It could also be argued that developments in cultural provision such as the abolishment of admission fees for art galleries and museums and grants made available through structures such the National Lottery have changed cultural provision and widened opportunities for access.

Themes from artworks being used to structure previous life experiences

The respondents who did not have a history of arts engagement used themes that they identified in the artworks to identify meta-narratives or aspects of meta-narratives that would be incorporated unconsciously into the construction of a personal life narrative. However, in order to achieve this, the respondents needed to be able to identify themes in the exhibitions, which depended on the nature of the art pieces being viewed. In this situation the meanings created in response to the art pieces in the exhibitions provided a resource to prompt the respondents into constructing a narrative identity. This became more difficult with art that was more avant-garde (Grenfell and Hardy, 2003, 2007), for example, conceptual art, works using digital media, or works that were not naturalistically representative or did not have a clear narrative or use of recognisable symbolism. In such cases, therefore, the personal interpretation provided by the tour was necessary. The following meta-narratives were identified.

The family

Common among the responses from the older women who had lower levels of education and had not worked while they raised their children was the way that encounters with the artworks prompted discussion with a narrative about the nature of family life. Caring for children and other family members was stated as being particularly important. A 64-year-old member of the sheltered accommodation unit noted:

> 'I love being a mother – and looking after me mother, I looked after her as well.'

The 'Parrworld' exhibition at the BALTIC contained posters from the UK Miners' Strike 1984-85 (a labour dispute over the closure of coal mines), which provided themes that were used to engage with a meta-narrative of family. In response to the posters, a 68-year-old member of the Sheltered Accommodation group stated:

> 'With the Miners' Strike it was a situation that my husband was put in because he was a policeman. He was born in a mining village and all his family was miners, his brother was still in the pits, so my husband was on the frontline in the Miners' Strike and it caused a lot of animosity.'

The experience of viewing particular pieces within the exhibition enabled her to recall the Miners' Strike and to place it into a personal context or structure. Within her family were two members on opposing sides, so the wider conflict had played out within her family environment. This disrupted a meta-narrative that views families as stable and cohesive structures, which made it a significant issue to raise.

The place of the respondents in a meta-narrative of family life was also evident in the responses made by this group to the 'Knitted Lives' exhibition held at the Shipley Art Gallery that consisted of a range of knitted everyday objects representing the lives of older women in North East England. A 72-year-old member of the group who was a wheelchair user stated:

'Well my mam [mother], she knitted loads of things and probably stemming from the fact that she had six children and it was cheaper to knit the clothes than it was to actually go out and buy them years and years ago, and then she obviously knitted for the grandchildren.'

Knitting clothes for family members was a normal part of family life and has embedded within it notions of caring appropriately for children and grandchildren. Also implied was a narrative asserting the moral value of stoicism as well as pride in bringing up children in a difficult financial situation. These aspects of a wider meta-narrative of family were considered 'normal' and were therefore unchallenged.

The history of North East England

Responses were also used as part of a resource that allowed participants to create a life narrative that incorporated a sense of the history of North East England. In response to 'Perpetual canon' (2004) by Cornelia Parker, which consisted of crushed wind instruments suspended around a single light bulb, which cast their shadows across the room, a 62-year-old member of the 'live at home' scheme stated:

'What I liked about the idea behind was the brass band and the North East was that the mines are dying off – we don't have them anymore but actually the music still goes on and although there might have been 200 brass bands at the Miners' Gala (see www.durhamminers.org) 20 years ago and there's probably 20 now, it still carries on.'

The meaning of the artwork, as intended by the artist, is not articulated by the discussion. The meaning is seen in terms of what it represents of regional identity, symbolising the loss of traditional industries, such as coal mining, in North East England. To some extent, responses will be conditioned by participants' ages, depending on when events occurred. However, different generations may have a different collective reference point for the same exhibitions.

Class

The writers' group discussed the theme of class after they visited the exhibition entitled 'Rank' at the Northern Gallery for Contemporary Art, Sunderland. In a similar way to the example given above, this group did not discuss the art but used the theme as a prompt for a wider discussion. Members of this group described their political views (they proudly described themselves as working class in the baseline interviews) and the reasons for them in a discussion that ranged widely over their life course experiences. A 73-year-old female who had obtained a university degree when she was 40 and had gone on to become a probation officer, stated:

> 'Social conditions have improved as well with the National Health Service coming into being. It meant that the lower working classes as "they" liked to refer to them, the "undeserving poor" as they used to refer to them, "they" had access then to doctors and hospitals. At one time you had to be on a doctor's panel before you could be seen, and pay every month, but with the free medical treatment and better housing and better conditions with drainage and everything ... the working classes have improved in that way because they didn't have access to these things before – that the upper class had – but now, you know, they have got good living conditions now, so that's helped. It used to be "us" and "them" but now it's sort of blended in now, but that's thanks to the various Acts, Education Acts and Health Acts.'

The narrative identity being constructed was very important to these respondents' sense of self that incorporated the working-class communities with which they identified.

Wider meta-narratives associated with family, gender, regional identity and class, all inflected by age, were incorporated into personal narratives prompted by encounters with the artworks. Unlike in the responses detailed in the first part of this section, the narratives and characteristics associated with them were not contested by those in the groups concerned, and were easily and naturally adopted. However, while there was less discussion as to whether the characteristics associated with particular narratives were correct or not, political choices were being made as to the nature of the stories that were constructed. It might be theorised that the reason why these particular meanings were created was the respondents' need to align themselves with particular underlying meta-narratives that they felt were accepted and important within the social group. The negotiation and sharing of these stories within a particular context also creates a community narrative, bonding the group together (Murray, 2002). Associated with the underlying meta-narratives were various social roles (for example, to do with the family) and moral positions (for example, class) (Harré and Moghaddam, 2003), which were unquestioned and claimed by the respondents.

Policy and practice implications

The above analysis demonstrates how the respondents used the encounters with contemporary visual art to negotiate identity positions in relation to meta-narratives associated with ageing. The respondents tended to reject the characteristics that they associated with the category 'old' that they had internalised and at the same time privileged a more positive counter-narrative. Some used the experience to develop an existing narrative identity associated with arts engagement, while others identified aspects of meta-narratives in encounters with the artworks, such as family and class, which they incorporated into their constructed life narratives.

The main implication of this work is that arts/cultural policy needs to be rethought with more emphasis on the consumption of art rather than its production. Arts policy documents, such as the Arts Council England's strategic plan (2010), focus on the production of the artistic experience by artists and galleries, and assume that the meanings created are consumed unproblematically (Newman, 2013). The consequence of this is that little attention is given to visitors and the roles art plays in the construction of narrative identities. For some of the respondents art is incorporated into a lifelong narrative identity that was deepened by the visits. However, for others without existing arts engagement, themes identified in the art were nothing to do with the meanings the artists intended to convey, yet were still important for the negotiation of narrative identities.

The above demonstrates one of the ways that engagement with art might support wellbeing among older people by providing resources through which past, current and future selves might be negotiated (Sabat and Harré, 1992). This supports Chapman's (2005) understanding of wellbeing in older people as them being able to construct multiple selves in an open-ended way. Some of the respondents seem to be doing this in response to life transitions, such as divorce or retirement, but for the majority it appeared to be a normal response to the social context within which they found themselves. This also appeared a very straightforward process for the respondents, all of whom demonstrated narrative intelligence, as understood by Randall (1999). Some of the meta-narratives (particularly those associated with older people) were actively challenged while others were unrecognised and incorporated into a personal narrative identity. This also provides a way of understanding cultural value (Crossick and Kaszynska, 2014), which is important in a policy environment that privileges measurable outputs and as a result can misunderstand the true value of engaging with arts and culture.

A further implication is that it provides galleries with ways of understanding how older people, particularly those without a history of arts engagement, respond to the artworks that they show. This provides guidance for interpretative strategies and the sorts of information provided to visitors. It also enables them to make a stronger case to funding bodies (such as the Heritage Lottery Fund), being able to articulate the wider social value of proposed arts-based activities, particularly those designed for older people either in the gallery or in a community setting.

It was indicated by a number of the respondents that in order to remain active and to engage with arts and culture there was a need for a level of wealth and to be sufficiently physically healthy. As noted by Chapman (2005, p 14), the process of 'ongoing negotiation of selves occurs amid diminishing levels of resources.'

A 64-year-old member of the film group stated:

> 'I think my age group, really, the two fundamental things are having a reasonable amount of money and being healthy, those are the two basic prerequisites. You can waffle on as much as you like about the arts or politics or whatever you like, but if you haven't got those two prerequisites – and reasonable housing that goes with it. I worked abroad a lot so I've got quite a lot of capital built up, own a house, no mortgage that sort of stuff so financially I'm hardly a billionaire but I'm OK, you know, but that would be irrelevant if I wasn't healthy as well, which I am really.'

The importance of keeping physically fit was an important theme for those in the film group (who were mainly retired professional people) – most engaged in exercise, either swimming or attending a gym. This was often for enjoyment but mainly to ensure that they could continue to do the things that that they wanted for as long as possible. This implies that the basics of life such as sufficient income, good housing and good health need to be prioritised in policy terms. Without this it is difficult to ensure the general wellbeing of older people that cultural engagement might contribute to.

None of the respondents demonstrated narrative foreclosure, as described by Bohlmeijer et al (2011), where an individual might feel that their life is over, and no new interpretations of the past are possible and no future change conceivable. However, this might be a consequence of the data set as respondents volunteered to take part in the research and so were not, by definition, in this position.

Key findings
- Participants use the experience of visiting exhibitions in galleries to position themselves in relation to wider societal narratives such as perceptions that older people have little to offer society and are a burden.
- Some participants use the experience to support an existing narrative identity of them as being culturally engaged. They also advocate that older people take up new opportunities which were now available to them.
- Identified themes from the artworks were used to explore and structure previous life experiences for those who have little history of arts engagement. Themes identified from the art works include the family, regional history and class.
- The work illustrates how engagement with art supports wellbeing through providing the resources through which past, current and future selves are negotiated and this process often was undertaken in response to transitions such as retirement.
- It is suggested that galleries take more account of the ways that art is consumed by older people and develop interpretative strategies that respond to their needs.

Conclusions

The respondents use the meanings they created through encounters with contemporary visual art to construct a personal narrative identity. This consisted of a number of interconnected elements – first, a conscious negotiated engagement with meta-narratives, such as those associated with older people and second, an unconscious adoption of aspects of meta-narratives, for example, to do with the family. This unconscious use of aspects of meta-narratives in the formation of a personal narrative identity is no less political than the conscious rejection of the more negative meta-narratives associated with older people. The social group that participants visited exhibitions with as part of a programme, and their accepted behavioural norms, seemed responsible for many of the processes involved. This has implications for cultural policy and gallery practice in terms of taking into account and understanding participants' existing communities as integral to the experience of a visit. However, cultural engagement is viewed as secondary to the need to be financially secure and to be in good health.

References

Arts Council England (2010) *Achieving great art for everyone a strategic framework for the arts*, London: Gavin Martin Colournet Ltd.

Bohlmeijer, E., Westerhof, G., Randall, W., Tromp, T. and Kenyon, G. (2011) 'Narrative foreclosure in later life: Preliminary considerations for a new sensitizing concept', *Journal of Aging Studies*, vol 25, pp 364-70.

Chapman, S. (2005) 'Theorizing about aging well: Constructing a narrative', *Canadian Journal of Aging*, vol 24, no 1, pp 9-18.

Crossick, G. and Kaszynska, P. (2014) 'Under construction: Towards a framework for cultural value', *Cultural Trends*, vol 23, no 2, pp 120-31.

De Fina, A. and Georgakopoulou, A. (2012) *Analyzing narrative, discourse and sociolinguistic perspectives*, Cambridge: Cambridge University Press.

Durkheim, E. (1954) *The elementary forms of religious life*, London: Allen & Unwin.

Fealy, G., McNamara, M., Treacy, M. and Lyons, I. (2012) 'Constructing ageing and age identities: A case study of newspaper discourses', *Ageing and Society*, vol 32, no 1, pp 85-102.

Grenfell, M. and Hardy, C. (2007) *Art rules, Pierre Bourdieu and the visual arts*, Oxford: Berg.

Grenfell, M. and Hardy, C. (2003) 'Field manoeuvres: Bourdieu and the Young British Artists', *Space and Culture*, vol 6, pp 19-34.

Hammack, P. (2011) 'Narrative and the politics of meaning', *Narrative Inquiry*, vol 21, no 2, pp 311-18.

Harré, R. and Moghaddam, F. (eds) (2003) *The self and others: Positioning individuals and groups in personal, political, and cultural contexts*, Westport, CT: Praeger.

Hurd, L. (1999) '"WE'RE NOT OLD!" Older women's negotiation of aging and oldness', *Journal of Aging Studies*, vol 13, no 4, pp 419-39.

Katz, S. (2000) 'Busy bodies, activity, aging, and the management of everyday life', *Journal of Aging Studies*, vol 14, no 2, pp 135-52.

Levi-Strauss, C. (1963) 'The structural study of myth', in *Structural anthropology*, New York: Basic Publishers, pp 206-31.

Levy, B., Slade, M., Kunkel, S. and Kasl, S. (2002) 'Longevity increased by positive self-perceptions of aging', *Journal of Personality and Social Psychology*, vol 83, no 2, pp 261-70.

McAdams, D. (1993) *The stories we live by: Personal myths and the making of the self*, New York: William Morrow & Company.

Mishler, E. (1995) 'Models of narrative analysis: A typology', *Journal of Narrative and Life History*, vol 5, no 2, pp 87-123.

Moscovici, S. (1984) 'The phenomenon of social representations', in R. Farr and S. Moscovici (eds) *Social representations*, Cambridge: Cambridge University Press, pp 3-69.

Murray, M. (2002) 'Connecting narrative and social representation theory in health research', *Social Science Information*, vol 41, no 4, pp 653-73.

Murray, M., Amigoni, D., Bernard, M., Goulding, A., Newman, A., Ricketts, M., et al (2014) 'Understanding and transforming ageing through the arts', in A. Walker (ed) *New science of ageing*, Bristol: Policy Press, pp 77-112.

Newman, A. (2013) 'Imagining the social impact of museums and galleries: Interrogating cultural policy through an empirical study', *International Journal of Cultural Policy*, vol 19, no 1, pp 120-37.

Phelan, A. (2011) 'Socially constructing older people: Examining discourses which can shape nurses' understanding and practice', *Journal of Advanced Nursing*, vol 67, no 4, pp 893-903.

Phoenix, C., Smith, B. and Sparkes, A. (2010) 'Narrative analysis in aging studies: A typology for consideration', *Journal of Aging Studies*, vol 24, pp 1-11.

Queniart, A. and Charpentier, M. (2012) 'Older women and their representations of old age: A qualitative analysis', *Ageing and Society*, vol 32, no 6, pp 983-1007.

Randall, W. (1999) 'Narrative intelligence and the novelty of our lives', *Journal of Aging Studies*, vol 13, no 1, pp 11-28.

Sabat, S. and Harré, R. (1992) 'The construction and deconstruction of self in Alzheimer's disease', *Ageing and Society*, vol 12, no 4, pp 443-61.

Silverman, D. (ed) (2006) *Qualitative research: Theory, method and practice*, London: Sage Publications.

Soden, S. (2012) 'Redefining cultural roles in older age: Grandmothering as an extension of motherhood', in V. Ylanne (ed) *Representing ageing: Images and identities*, New York: Palgrave Macmillan, pp 84-99.

Warren, L. and Richards, N. (2012) '"I don't see many images of myself coming back at myself": Representations of women and ageing', in V. Ylanne (ed) *Representing ageing: Images and identities*, New York: Palgrave Macmillan, pp 149-68.

Westerhof, G., Barrett, A. and Steverink, N. (2003) 'Forever young? A comparison of age identities in the United States and Germany', *Research on Aging*, vol 25, no 4, pp 366-83.

Appendix: The venues and shows visited by the groups

Northern Gallery for Contemporary Art, Sunderland, Tyne and Wear

- 'Rank, picturing the social order', explored inequality in society.
- 'Semiconductor' are Brighton-based artists Ruth Jarman and Joe Gerhardt who explore scientific knowledge through video.
- 'Heliocentric' is a three-screen installation that uses time-lapse photography and astronomical tracking to plot the sun's trajectory across a series of landscapes.
- 'Systematic' by Chad McCail explores how 'society produces and fails to produce "normal" individuals who accept its rules.'

BALTIC Centre for Contemporary Art, Gateshead, Tyne and Wear

- 'Parrworld' was produced by photographer Martin Parr, and consisted of a collection of photographs and assorted objects documenting historical and political moments and second, an exhibition entitled 'Luxury', showing the different ways in which people display their wealth.
- 'A Needle Woman' by the Korean artist Kimsooja. Consisting of eight simultaneous videos, it documents the artist as she stands motionless in the crowded streets of Lagos, Mexico City, Cairo, New York, Delhi, Tokyo, Shanghai and London.
- Jenny Holzer used electronic text to explore themes such as authorship, power, hope, despair, need and longing.
- Cornelia Parker transforms familiar everyday objects, interrogating the meanings society gives to them.
- Anselm Kiefer is interested in myth, history, theology, philosophy and literature, and his work consists of painting, sculpture and installation.

Shipley Art Gallery, Gateshead, Tyne and Wear

- 'Knitted Lives' consists of a range of knitted everyday objects, such as a shopping trolley—produced by 32 older women from the region.

Belsay Hall, Castle and Gardens, Northumberland

- 'Extraordinary Measures' is a collection of artworks on the theme of scale.

Great North Museum: Hancock, Newcastle upon Tyne, Tyne and Wear

This museum was chosen for a visit by the writers' group from Sunderland. It shows mixed collections, for example, world cultures, natural history, archaeology and geology.

FIFTEEN

The place of theatre in representations of ageing

Miriam Bernard, David Amigoni, Ruth Basten,
Lucy Munro, Michael Murray, Jackie Reynolds,
Jill Rezzano and Michelle Rickett

Prologue

The interdisciplinary 'Ages and Stages' project, funded initially under the New Dynamics of Ageing (NDA) programme, has evolved into a continuing collaboration between Keele University and the New Vic Theatre, Newcastle-under-Lyme. The first 'Ages and Stages' project (2009–12) examined historical representations of ageing within the Vic's ground-breaking documentaries and docudramas (produced between 1964 and 1995), and explored the contemporary recollections and experiences of older people who are, or have been, associated with the theatre in different ways. Archival and interview material was drawn together to create the 'Ages and Stages' exhibition and a new, hour-long, documentary drama, 'Our Age, Our Stage'. Between 2012 and 2013, further funds were secured from the Arts and Humanities Research Council (AHRC) follow-on scheme to focus on translational work, and we were subsequently awarded two additional grants by the AHRC under their Cultural Value Project. In this chapter we concentrate on the first three-year project; readers interested in following through what we have done subsequently are invited to visit the 'Ages and Stages' and 'Live Age Festival' websites (www.keele.ac.uk/agesandstages and www.liveagefestival.co.uk).

Act One: Setting the scene

Social and critical gerontologists, as well as literary and cultural scholars, are increasingly interested in the artistic engagement of older people, and in how the arts may construct, perpetuate or challenge stereotypical views of old age and existing models of the ageing process (Gullette, 1997, 2004, 2011; Basting, 1998, 2009; Small, 2007; Lipscomb and Marshall, 2010; Mangan, 2013). While recent reviews (Cutler, 2009; Castora-Binkley et al, 2010; Mental Health Foundation, 2011; Noice et al, 2014) affirm the value of older people's engagement in cultural activities, they also point to a lack of research on theatre and drama more specifically. This is despite the fact that, as Lipscomb (2012) argues, theatre provides us with an untapped potential for interdisciplinary collaborations and investigations; it is a cultural arena in which both ageing and older people are highly visible as audience members, participants, characters and increasingly, as performers (Bernard and Munro, 2015).

In terms of representations, there is a long tradition of theatre drawing heavily on stereotypes of older people and on deficit models of the ageing process, extending back to early Greek tragedies (Charney, 2005; Robson, 2009). In addition, there have been shifting fashions in respect of whether actors can or cannot play certain ages on stage. As Mangan (2013, p 45) notes, today's actors receive far less training in 'how to act old' than they once did, although some notable theatre productions have sought to engage directly with the process of ageing and to question realist approaches to theatrical age. These include the Bristol Old Vic's 'Juliet and her Romeo' and Fevered Sleep's/the Young Vic's 'On Ageing', both performed in 2010.

An allied development has been the remarkable growth of what has come to be called 'senior theatre' (Basting, 1998; Vorenberg, 1999). Anne Basting charts the evolution of this movement in her path-breaking book, *The stages of age*, and her critique in this, and subsequent writings (Basting, 1998, 2000, 2009), echoes and parallels the work of Margaret Morganroth Gullette (1997, 2004, 2011) around the cultural aspects of ageing and ageism, with both sharing a desire to integrate performance studies and performance theory with gerontological debates. By 2011, there were over 800 senior theatre groups in North America (Vorenberg, 2011), mostly amateur in nature, but often linked with community theatres. In the UK, too, community-based theatre, rooted in oral traditions and often connected to the growth of socially and politically aware theatre, is the basis of much contemporary drama work with older people. Pam Schweitzer's (2007) development of reminiscence theatre with older people is perhaps the best known example of this heritage. Interestingly, too, in the context of our own project, Schweitzer (2007, p 15) acknowledges the influence on her work of what came to be dubbed the 'Stoke method': the verbatim documentary drama techniques developed by the late Peter Cheeseman during his 36 years as artistic director at the Victoria and New Vic

Theatres (1962-98). As we shall see, his 11 social documentaries and five docudramas were the basis for one of the three main strands of the 'Ages and Stages' project.

Yet, we still know comparatively little about what participation in theatre and theatre-making means to older people and what benefits they derive from it. Such evidence as we do have comes from a combination of practitioner knowledge and experience, from existing small-scale evaluations and research projects, and from some academic research. Practitioners on both sides of the Atlantic have shown that theatre and drama work have demonstrable social, physical and emotional benefits (Basting, 1998, 2009; Schweitzer, 2007, 2010; Vorenberg, 2011); they also have positive effects on intergenerational relations and on the wider community (Schweitzer, 2007; Cutler, 2009; Magic Me, 2009). Academic research in the UK further demonstrates how working with older people through drama activities enhances intergenerational learning (Hafford-Letchfield et al, 2010); helps create positive impressions among children of older people as active and fun (Johnson, 2011); and, for older people, enhances their skills and learning ability, improves confidence and self-esteem and supports the development of new social connections and friendships (Pyman and Rugg, 2006). In North America, research carried out by Tony and Helga Noice and their colleagues over the last 25 years (see Noice and Noice, 2008, 2013; Noice et al, 1999, 2004), leads them to conclude that studies on theatre and drama produce 'converging evidence of cognitive/affective benefits' and 'present a fairly cohesive picture compared with those of other art forms' (Noice et al, 2014, p 750). As Mangan (2013, p 169) observes, their work 'gives good experimental and empirical reason to think what many have long suspected: that acting is good for you.'

Finally, it is important to make mention of the policy context against which our study took place. In the run-up to start of the project, it was evident that government policy was beginning to recognise positive links between the arts, health and wellbeing (DCLG, 2006; DCMS, 2006; Bunting, 2007; DH/ACE, 2007). There were also important national and local policy initiatives related to 'an ageing society' (HM Government, 2005, 2009; Staffordshire County Council, 2007; Stoke-on-Trent City Council, 2007) which were of potential relevance to what we were planning to do. However, it was notable that these two policy arenas – the arts and ageing – were yet to be brought into one field of engagement: the role of the arts in 'active ageing' or in effecting cultural change was, and still is, neglected, despite calls from organisations such as the Baring Foundation (Cutler, 2009, 2013) and the Mental Health Foundation (2011), which affirm the value of participation in the arts for older people, and point out that this is often overlooked in policy and service provision.

With this as a backcloth, the initial 'Ages and Stages' project sought to undertake a detailed case study of the place of one particular theatre – the Victoria/New Victoria Theatre in North Staffordshire – in the lives of older people. The project aimed to explore:

- How age and ageing have been constructed, represented and understood in the theatre's social documentaries from the 1960s to the present day.
- The part the theatre has played in constructing individual and community identities and creating and preserving community memory.
- The relationship between older people's involvement in the theatre and continuing social engagement in later life.
- The practical and policy implications of our findings.

Act Two: The project takes shape

'Ages and Stages' was based in the Potteries, North Staffordshire, an area with a long history of heavy industry (ceramics, coal, steel and tyre manufacture) that, over the past 50 years, has undergone considerable social and economic change and decline. These changes have had marked effects on the expectations and opportunities of the area's residents, and local cultural institutions – not least the Victoria Theatre (now the New Vic Theatre) – have both reflected and reconstructed these changes. Working in partnership with local older people, with the theatre and with its archive housed at Staffordshire University, we brought together an interdisciplinary research team with backgrounds in social gerontology, cultural theory and history, social and health psychology, social anthropology and theatre studies to jointly organise the research programme around three interrelated strands: historical representations; recollections and contemporary representations; and performing and re-presenting ageing.

Strand 1: Historical representations

As noted earlier, the Victoria Theatre pioneered a distinctive form of social documentary under artistic director Peter Cheeseman (Elvgren, 1974; Rowell and Jackson, 1984; Schweitzer, 2007). It is also an important theatre-in-the round and, when it moved to its current premises in 1986, was Europe's first purpose-built theatre of this kind. The social documentaries draw on print, manuscript and oral source materials to chart social, economic and political changes in the Potteries. Between them, they reflect the community's self-image at various points in the area's history, and illustrate the roles and positions of different generations within the community. Much of this historical material is housed in the archive that contains not only scripts, programmes, photographs, audio recordings, correspondence and an extensive collection of reviews and press cuttings, but also the original research materials on which the documentaries were based. This includes newspaper reports and a remarkable collection of taped interviews with members of the community, many of whom were older people. For our purposes, these older members of the community were thus an important source for the theatre's documentaries: their testimonies and life stories woven into broader narratives, and preserved in the archive.

Strand 2: Recollections and contemporary representations

As well as investigating the archive and studying the social documentaries, the project explored the recollections and experiences of older people who are, or have been, associated with the theatre in different ways. In order to do this, we undertook 79 individual or couple interviews (93 people in total) with 29 longstanding audience members; 26 current or former theatre volunteers; 23 theatre employees and actors who continue to live in the area; and 15 people who were sources for some of the original documentaries. Guided by a loosely constructed interview schedule, participants told us how they had come to be involved with the theatre, what part it had played – and continues to play – in their lives, and what recollections and involvements they had had with the documentaries. In addition, we held 10 group interviews involving 51 people (two each with audience members and sources, and three each with volunteers and employees). These focused on three emerging themes – ageing, intergenerational relationships, and the place of the theatre in the community and in individual lives – and discussions were stimulated by using (anonymised) quotations from individual interviews. All interviews (both individual and group) lasted for between one and two hours on average, and all were digitally recorded, transcribed and analysed using NVivo. Alongside the interviews, our research associate carried out participant observation with New Vic volunteers for several months, exploring their continuing social and creative engagement in later life. In the reporting of our findings, pseudonyms have been given to all participants.

Strand 3: Performing and re-presenting ageing

Building on work begun in 2004 (Harding, 2005), our intention in the final part of the project was to recruit an intergenerational group of participants to work with us on a new social documentary and an associated exhibition, drawing on the findings and materials from the archival and interview work. In the event, 25 people volunteered to take part: 16 older people (aged 59-92) who had been interviewed earlier in the project and 9 'senior' members (aged 16-19) of the New Vic Youth Theatre. Through a series of regular workshops held at the New Vic between September 2011 and May 2012, the material was honed into a one-hour documentary, 'Our Age, Our Stage', under the directorship of the Vic's Head of Education and research team member, Jill Rezzano. An intensive two-week rehearsal period in June was followed by four performances to the local council, at a school, a college and a retirement community. At the conclusion of the tour in July, 'Our Age, Our Stage' played to a capacity audience on the theatre's main stage, attended by participants' families and friends, members of the project's Advisory Group, and delegates to the British Society of Gerontology's annual conference being hosted at Keele University. In total, over 700 people saw the productions across the two weeks and engaged in discussions with us and the group members after each performance.

Alongside 'Our Age, Our Stage', some of the 25 participants worked with us to put together the associated 'Ages and Stages' exhibition. While it had always been our intention to hold an exhibition, what we had failed to realise at the time we submitted the original research proposal was that 2012 would mark the 50th anniversary of both the theatre and Keele University. This was a happily serendipitous and evocative moment for an exhibition charting and celebrating the theatre's work and recalling its place in the lives and histories of the people of the Potteries. The theatre's designer envisaged the exhibition as a 'visual scrapbook', starting with the archive and a timeline of the key productions out of which the memorabilia people had saved over the years would 'explode'. This chimed with our earlier experiences of interviewing people, many of whom spontaneously shared physical memorabilia with us, part of their 'personal archives'. In addition, we held a 'bringing-in-day' on one Saturday in May 2012 from which we were able to select additional materials to be included. Those who brought memorabilia that day were filmed talking about their objects and about what the theatre meant in their lives; a DVD of these recollections played throughout the exhibition which ran for a month from 25 June to 20 July 2012.

Not surprisingly, these three strands yielded a rich and complex set of data that we worked on – and continue to work on – collaboratively and individually within, and across, disciplines. It is difficult to do justice here to the complex and multilayered nature of these analyses so, for the purposes of this chapter, we simply focus on findings around two key themes: the place of the theatre in people's lives, and understandings of ageing and later life. Other themes and perspectives, for example, around narratives and ageing, representations, the perspectives of volunteers, intergenerational relations, specific documentaries or the policy dimensions of our work, form the basis of papers and chapters already published or in press and in preparation, as well as a doctoral thesis (Amigoni, 2013; Basten, 2014; Murray et al, 2014; Bernard and Munro, 2015; Bernard et al, 2015).

Act Three: Theatre and ageing

A theatre such as the Vic, which has been at the heart of its community for 50 years, was recalled in many and varied ways by participants and through examination of materials in the archive. Although the theatre was obviously a 'young' institution when it was established in the early 1960s, its artistic director Peter Cheeseman believed passionately that theatre had, as he put it, a responsibility to take the place of 'old men' and to 'show people the past of their community' (Elvgren, 1974). A number of the documentaries return to the Potteries' 19th-century foundations as a large-scale industrial community, while others feature events which were within living memory such as the 1910 formation of Stoke-on-Trent (depicted in 'Six Into One' [1968]), the incorporation of the North Staffordshire Railway into the London, Midland and Scottish Railway in 1921 (depicted in 'The Knotty' [1966]), and the Second World War (depicted in 'Hands Up: For You the War is Ended!' [1971]). Some of the most famous documentaries depict industrial disputes, notably 'Fight for Shelton Bar!' (1974), which focused on the struggle to save the North Staffordshire steel works, 'The Dirty Hill' (1990) concerning the community's outcry against British Coal's plan for open-cast mining on Berryhill, Stoke-on-Trent, and 'Nice Girls' (1994), which portrayed the protest against pit closures mounted by members of the North Staffs Miners' Wives Action Group. The theatre and the documentaries therefore lie at the intersection between individual and family histories, and the trajectories of changing and declining local industries.

The documentaries played an important role in bringing together different groups of people, both in the process of their creation – which brought theatre employees into contact with people working in different local industries – and in the staging of them, which attracted diverse audiences to the Vic. For newcomers to the Potteries, the documentaries could help people settle in; for local people who had family connections to the industries portrayed, they helped them to feel more bonded with the theatre, as these two audience members comment:

> 'As a newcomer to Stoke, that sort of helped root you into the local community in a way, as you'd learned about it … they kind of earthed you in Stoke in a way, so you understood something about the culture and the background of Stoke.' (Patricia Oakes)

> 'I think the particularly interesting thing was that they'd gone out and actually spoken to local people about their experiences and then out of that created the plays … that was bonding with the community but also celebrating what this area had been all about, you know, the various occupations and experiences people had.' (Emily Parker)

The intimacy of the theatre, both in its original venue (a converted former cinema in Stoke) and within the current purpose-built theatre (opened in 1986 in Newcastle-under-Lyme), was important to the older people we interviewed. The theatre-in-the-round format meant that people were literally and metaphorically 'close to' the action on stage and they valued the sense of being part of the life of the theatre. Those who had been sources for some of the original documentaries spoke about being valued and recognised when they went to the theatre, while audience members and volunteers feel welcomed and part of a shared community of theatre-goers and supporters:

> 'There's this sort of sense that you are all coming in here together and you are all part of the same thing.' (Michael Hall, audience member)

'I can't think of many times I've been here and I've not seen
somebody that I know from somewhere. It's just lovely isn't
it?' (Diana Holmes, volunteer)

Many people we interviewed described the theatre as 'homely', 'like
a home from home', 'like going home' and 'feeling like home', and
the metaphor of the theatre as 'family' was especially common. For
volunteers and audience members, the theatre was – and still is – a
familiar and comfortable place, while former and current employees,
many of whom moved to the Potteries as young people but then
stayed and made their lives in the area, spoke about the family nature
of the theatre. This sense of family was related to Peter Cheeseman's
vision of a permanent company rooted in the area and, as one former
actor told us, "You're a family, you were part of a family that stretched
decades" (John Carter).

Here, too, is another former actor, vividly recalling his first
impressions of arriving in the Potteries and becoming part of the
community and the 'Vic family':

'So I arrived at Stoke-on-Trent and it was winter and
there was snow on the ground at Stoke-on-Trent station. I
thought "Oh no what is this?"… I had digs in Etruria for a
couple of nights and I was looking out on to the pot banks
and I thought "Oh I can't stay here." I'd been in London for
10 years or more and I thought "No I can't stay", and then
… I walked down Hartshill Road. That's where we all met
and then things began to get better and the lovely thing, I
suppose it's still the same, is the atmosphere, and you had a
very communal atmosphere.' (Thomas Cook, former actor)

What was particularly striking was that even employees who had
left the theatre many decades before we interviewed them, or who
had only been there for a comparatively short period, felt that their
involvement had had a disproportionate and formative effect on their
lives. They spoke about the Vic introducing them to a creative world:
about it opening up lifelong creative pathways and about learning to be
part of a team and taking the values they had been imbued with into
other areas of their lives. This social identity, although talked about
in very positive ways, could also have its downsides. Actors and other
employees felt a great sense of obligation to the theatre and, especially
in the early days, it was taken for granted that everyone would work
very long hours and weeks. However, one woman left because she

worked such long hours that she barely saw her children, while former actor, John Carter, speaks here about feeling increasingly exhausted:

> 'In the early days when I was younger, acting, loved it, great, fantastic. But then as I got older, it became much more difficult. I think in the end I'd played that many parts that I'd burnt myself out really, and creativeness had gone out of it…. I was on this slow journey to a nervous breakdown, but you don't know it at the time because the discipline is so strong, that you just keep … and you don't want to let anybody down.'

Although this working 'family' can be supportive and affirming, it can potentially be oppressive and constraining as well. John's quote above also raises questions about whether, and how, ageing and growing older might take its toll on people.

In both individual and group interviews, participants responded in varying and contrasting ways to this issue. For some actors and employees, growing older was coupled with diminishing physical capabilities: theatre was spoken of as "being a young person's business" (Kathleen Davies, designer), and people measured what they were able to do now, physically, against how they had been when they were younger. In one group interview, designer Kathleen Davies spoke about how, when she started working at the Vic, she would think nothing of sprinting round the drum (the circular corridor underneath the seating), but went on to say:

> 'I reckon it's got bigger that circle, now! It's definitely further! So physically … it is quite a physically demanding job … when I was young … I was bringing my energy then and my ability to work long hours and all those things that you've got when you're in your 20s and 30s, and I haven't really got those anymore. If I had to do an all-nighter now it would do me in completely, I'd be no use at all…. I can't sprint up and down stairs endlessly anymore.'

In similar vein, here is Paul Evans, a former stage manager, talking about his awareness of physical limitations on his capabilities:

> 'You just picked up certain things because you needed to do the job…. I've never really thought about it, I just went on … until the muscles started packing up. The last time I did

a lighting demonstration I was 20 foot up in the air, at the tallest bit, with my last group of first years, and I thought, "I can't get this lantern back on the bar!".... I'd reached out probably further than I should … but I wasn't doing it every day … and I thought "Oh! What do I do now?" And sheer adrenalin I think got it back on the bar and I thought "I've got to be careful", and that's the point where you think, "Well there are some things I sensibly shouldn't do anymore 'cos they're just going to rip bits in my body".'

Although not so prevalent, corresponding views were expressed by some audience members and volunteers: age-related hearing loss, for example, diminished people's enjoyment of the theatre; even with hearing aids, the theatre-in-the-round format is difficult because actors will inevitably have their backs to the audience. Overwhelmingly, however, those we interviewed tended to speak about growing older and their involvement with the Vic in terms of the opportunities for continued creativity, the new challenges it presented them with, and the important role it plays in key transitions in people's lives such as retirement and bereavement. For women in particular, bereavement and the need to connect or reconnect with others had often provided the spur to their volunteering, as encapsulated here by Victoria Mason:

'My interest was as a result of bereavement, and the lifeline that it gave to me, which was greatly needed at the time. Still is. So that's really how I came to be involved.'

In this respect, volunteering can offer a new beginning during a time of transition, sometimes deepening, but inevitably changing, a previous involvement, or sometimes providing a totally new experience. Many interviewees talked vividly about becoming 'entangled' or 'caught up' in the life of the theatre in retirement: with more time and (in some cases) money, they could renew their interest in theatre or discover a creative side to their lives, perhaps for the first time:

'In my retirement the Vic theatre has been one of the important things in my life.... I think the arts in general really, since I've retired and I've got the time, I am more interested in the arts and the theatre.' (Diana Holmes, volunteer)

In this sense, the theatre provides a forum for widening people's experiences. Indeed, expansive metaphors about 'broadening horizons', 'widening outlooks' and 'entering new worlds' were frequently used. Interviewees talked about the challenges, new knowledge and new skills they had acquired and, as this audio-describer comments, its value lies in the fact that "It's still developing us, and that's what's so great" (Alice Hancock). Audience members also talk about the stimulation that the theatre provides, as captured in this exchange:

> EMMA MARSH: '... I find when I get home, after I've been to the theatre, that I can't go straight to bed! It's, you know ... it's still there in your head and I have to sit and have a drink and watch a little bit of television. Whereas watching television at night, I fall asleep!'
> ANNA GREEN: 'I think it gives you knowledge as well.'
> EMMA MARSH: 'It's better for your brain isn't it?'
> ANNA GREEN: 'I really think it gives you a lot of knowledge as well, coming to the theatre. I mean, you learn things that you've gone all your life and not really gone into in depth, they've all been surface, and now you can really come here, see something, think about it and you think, "Oh gosh, I shall have to look that up", and then you read about it.'

However, ageing and growing older is a complex and multifaceted experience: for some, it has proved positive, while others find themselves encountering age-based discrimination. In one group discussion about ageing and theatre, Janet Barber – who was still acting professionally – finds herself caught between the expectation and the reality:

> 'I think ... as long as you can still remember the lines as an actor you can still carry on older than you would in other [professions]. Having said that, I've just been turned down for a job for somebody younger. I mean I was told that, "No, we've gone for somebody younger".'

We also came across other interviewees who seemed to be willing to internalise the decline narrative of ageing, sometimes using age-related stereotypes to explain their withdrawal from engagement with theatre and talking in terms of being 'past it', 'too long in the tooth' or 'losing their grip'. Terry Rogers, an audience member who had also been active as an amateur director, told us:

> '… I think oldies standing in the way, not a good idea. So you back out and you watch things from a distance.… I gave up directing because I realised that age was, you know, you'd got to be really on top and I couldn't fool myself any longer that I'd got a grip on everything.'

By contrast, others spoke convincingly about how ageing had brought a reassessment of their capabilities and a realisation that they probably had different things to offer now. Here is designer Kathleen Davies again, in one of the group interviews:

> 'Hopefully I've still got other things to offer now.… I think experience and confidence and maybe a different sort of resourcefulness. Maybe the resources that I'm drawing on in myself are different to the ones I was drawing on then, you know, because what I was drawing on then, a lot of it was energy and enthusiasm and, you know, that kind of crazy optimism that you've got, you know, "We can do anything!" Nowadays I wouldn't necessarily think we can do anything, but I think I would, well I hope, I think I probably work with designers better than I used to do.'

As noted earlier, the interviews provided much of the raw material from which the script for 'Our Age, Our Stage' was crafted; excerpts were also used during devising workshops to provoke further debate and discussion. In particular, some of the quotations about ageing and creativity were used in a 'value line exercise' led by facilitator and artistic director Jill Rezzano. Participants were asked to demonstrate their agreement or disagreement by standing close to Jill (if they agreed) or further back (if they disagreed). Quotations used included: 'my age would never stop me doing something creative'; 'if something sounds interesting, I'll take a risk, I'll get involved'; and, echoing Terry Rogers' contention above about 'oldies' not standing in the way: 'there comes a time when you have to step aside'.

The quotation about 'stepping aside' provoked the most diverse responses: some participants reiterated that age does indeed bring (physical) limitations that necessitate stepping aside; others passionately refuted this, one person even going so far as to remove himself completely from the workshop room to stand outside the double glass doors, telling us "I won't step aside until I'm pushed aside." A former actor/director who stood in the middle of the room (neither agreeing nor disagreeing) suggested that it might be possible "to step aside, but maybe step forward into another area." These lively debates about ageing were subsequently translated into a key scene that appears about two-thirds of the way through the performance piece, and in which both older and younger performers argue heatedly with each other (Rezzano, 2012, pp 26-7):

> OLIVIA WOOD: 'You said earlier that working in theatre was all you wanted to do, is that still the case?'
>
> JOHN CARTER: 'You see theatre's a young person's game.'
>
> ADAM BROWN: 'No, no, no!'
>
> JOHN CARTER: 'It is! Professionally, you get tired.'
>
> WILLIAM BATES: 'For me, creativity is just part of me, it's what I've always done, it's just part of....'
>
> CHARLIE ROBINSON: 'Life. Everyone has something to contribute.'
>
> JULIA NIXON: 'I think if you're involved in this kind of activity, ageing means less to you.'
>
> JOHN REYNOLDS: 'Yes, but I know people are still being creative and publishers etc don't want to know.'
>
> JULIA NIXON: 'Sorry, I didn't understand how age would stop you being creative, how would age stop you being creative?'
>
> JOHN REYNOLDS: 'We don't look good on book covers and programmes!'
>
> CHARLIE ROBINSON: 'Okay, but anyone, regardless of age, can contribute to theatre; acting, creating, I'm sure everyone in this room has it in them. I don't think it ever leaves you.'
>
> JOHN CARTER: 'But I don't want to do it anymore.'
>
> CHARLIE ROBINSON: 'Look at David Jason; he's one of the best actors I've ever seen.'
>
> JOHN CARTER: 'It's not whether people are good or not, it's a psychological thing, about energy and all the rest of it. Just because David Jason is still doing it and picking up million pound cheques is neither here nor there!'
>
> THOMAS SALT: 'There comes a time when you have to step aside.'
>
> ALICE HANCOCK: 'I don't mind stepping aside, I just don't want to be told to step aside.'

WILLIAM BATES: 'I wouldn't step aside for anyone, this is my time. Your best years are when you're doing something that you're passionate about.'

JOHN CARTER: 'I'll let others do it. Step aside from what I did but step forward into a new area: new passions.'

In the end then, there are, of course, no simple or straightforward answers to the questions about what ageing is or is not like, and what is or is not possible as one grows older. What the project and the new social documentary did do, however, was to celebrate the theatre's 50-year existence, begin to open up debates and discussions about ageing itself with diverse audiences and, through a methodology that mirrored the theatre practices developed by Peter Cheeseman, bring this kind of research-based theatre practice (or performative social science) 'full circle' (Basten, 2014).

Key findings

- It is important to challenge stereotypes that creativity declines/ceases in old age.
- There are connections between identity, belonging, wellbeing, self-esteem and self-confidence, and they can be enhanced through theatre and drama.
- Participation is important – through volunteering and involvement in creative activities – particularly at times of transition and bereavement.
- Theatre and drama have a role to play as a medium for the inclusion of older and younger people.
- There are positive health outcomes and a sense of wellbeing for both older and younger participants, as well as practical and policy implications for community cohesion.
- Policy agendas on 'arts, health and wellbeing' should be joined up with those addressing the needs of an 'ageing society'.

Epilogue

Although we have not been able to go into depth about all aspects of the project, the findings presented in this chapter, together with other outputs, demonstrate at least half a dozen key points. First, in keeping with existing research and scholarship, 'Ages and Stages' clearly shows the importance of continuing to challenge stereotypes that creativity declines or ceases in old age. Second, all three strands of our work highlight close connections between identity, belonging, wellbeing, self-esteem and self-confidence, and how these can be enhanced through theatre and drama. Third, the project affirms yet again the benefits of participation and engagement, in this instance through volunteering and involvement in creative activities, particularly at times of transition and bereavement. Fourth, the intergenerational nature of the last strand of our project emphasises the role that theatre and drama can play as a medium for the inclusion of both older and younger people. Fifth, although 'Ages and Stages' was not designed specifically to explore health benefits, older and younger participants spontaneously associated their involvement with a range of positive health outcomes. Finally, the project points to the necessity of joining up policy agendas on 'arts, health and wellbeing' with those addressing the needs of 'an ageing society' if we are to move away from an entirely problem-oriented and deficit model of what ageing and old age can be like.

We have also been fortunate to secure further grants to enable us to set in motion a number of the practical, academic and policy-related recommendations arising from our initial three years. This has included extending our research into a critical review of the literature and into an exploration of the cultural value of theatre-making with older people (see Crossick and Kaszynska, 2016). In addition, we have been able to use and re-use our findings and research materials to underpin other translational activities. First, instead of having to disband the 'Ages and Stages' group at the end of the project, it has now been transformed into the Ages and Stages Theatre Company. The company continue to meet for regular workshops at the theatre, and have worked with us on subsequent projects to develop, devise and tour new and different kinds of performance pieces. Some have again involved members of the Youth Theatre (aged 13-19) and some have been in response to invitations from other theatres such as the Royal Exchange in Manchester and West Yorkshire Playhouse in Leeds. A key feature of the company is that it enables older people to participate in other aspects of theatre-making should they not wish to perform on stage: this has included facilitating discussions at performances, participating with members of the research team at conferences and other events, and co-facilitating workshops for practitioners and policy-makers. In the years since the initial project ended, membership has been renewed, refreshed and expanded; the company is now an independent community group hosted at the New Vic under Jill Rezzano's artistic direction, and has elected co-chairs, co-secretaries and co-treasurers.

Second, we have been able to test out whether the kinds of creative research and drama-based techniques employed during the last strand of the project might have wider applicability. In 2013, we developed a pilot six-session interprofessional training course for which we had nearly 60 applications for the 12 available places. In the end, we accepted 18 participants onto the course drawn from arts organisations, the voluntary sector, local government, health and social services, and housing. Freelancers and volunteers were included as well as paid professionals from organisations. The group ranged in age from 20 to 72 and came from as far afield as Manchester, Wolverhampton and Herefordshire. Although a number of participants were experienced in working with young people, older people or drama, they were all inexperienced in using intergenerational drama within their practice. Themes and issues covered on the course included ageing, drama and creativity; stereotyping; intergenerational relationships; and intergenerational drama in practice. Three sessions involved invited speakers and members of the Ages and Stages Theatre Company, and participants attended a performance by the company, entitled 'Happy Returns', at one of a number of regional venues. The evaluation shows improved age awareness, increased confidence in facilitating activities, adaptations to participants' own practice using the tools and techniques learned on the course, and indications of learning being cascaded to other colleagues (Reynolds, 2013).

Third, in terms of wider policy and practice-related recommendations, we were also able to initiate discussions with local policy-makers and representatives from a range of organisations (for example, community arts organisations; over-50s groups; both local universities; cultural venues; and the health and social care sectors) about the potential for holding a Creative Age Festival in Stoke-on-Trent and North Staffordshire. Following an initial scoping meeting in 2013 attended by 20 participants, a working group of arts and older people's organisations came together to put on the first pilot 'Live Age Festival' in 2014. Timed to coincide with UK Older People's Day on 1 October, the Festival celebrates the artistic and creative talents of older people who are also involved at every level including planning, leading activities, participating, performing, and evaluating the events. Subsequent Festivals have expanded in scope and content and now take place in a variety of cultural and community venues across North Staffordshire. An important element of the Festival is the Live Age Symposium that features inspirational speakers and offers exciting opportunities for researchers, practitioners, the general public and anyone interested in late life creativity to share knowledge and experiences. Evaluation reports for each Festival – together with films, photographs and details of all the activities to date – can be found on the Festival's website (www.liveagefestival.co.uk).

Beyond these practical and policy-related outcomes of our work, we conclude by suggesting that the value of an interdisciplinary project of this nature lies also in the avenues it opens up for further ageing research. As the project progressed, and especially during the final strand when we were devising our own documentary production from the research materials gathered earlier, we were increasingly reminded of the potential of theatre as a provocation: not only as a creative medium for representing and performing the past and present, but also as a forum for raising questions and imagining the future. Echoing Lipscomb's (2012, p 131) contention that 'this branch of the arts remains woefully under-researched and under-theorised', there is much more that could be done to examine the place of theatre in the lives of older people including analyses of plays, scripts and characters; evaluations of the benefits of engagement in senior and intergenerational theatre groups; comparative studies of theatre and other art forms; the use of theatre to tackle and raise awareness of pressing issues such as age discrimination in policy and practice; and critical examinations of the disjuncture between arts and ageing policies (Bernard and Munro, 2015).

The 'Ages and Stages' project attempted to take up the challenge of articulating what the engagement of older people in theatre-making adds to their lives beyond a focus on the therapeutic and health aspects. In so doing, we hoped to capture the 'transformative' power of theatre (Basting, 1998) by confronting stereotypes that creativity declines or ceases in old age, by celebrating the ground-breaking role the New Vic Theatre has played in the local community, and by exploring ways in which theatre could capture the creative potential of older people and promote intergenerational exchange in the future. The extent to which the objectives we set ourselves were achieved is probably not for us to judge; what we do know is that we were privileged to have been part of a project which challenged all of us (researchers, performers and participants) to see behind and beyond conventional views of what ageing and old age might be like.

Acknowledgments

The 'Ages and Stages' project was funded originally under the UK's NDA programme (project number RES-356-25-0005), and the research team were ably supported throughout by Tracey Harrison, project administrator. We are grateful to everyone who took part in the project and so generously shared their views and experiences with us, and for the help and advice of our Advisory Group.

References

Amigoni, D. (2013) 'Active ageing in the community: Laughing at/ thinking about Victorian senescence in Arnold Bennett's *The old wives' tale* and its theatrical afterlife', in K. Boehm, A. Farkas and A.-J. Zwierlein (eds) *Interdisciplinary perspectives on aging in nineteenth-century culture*, New York: Routledge, pp 181-96.

Basten, R. (2014) 'The circle of life: Narrative, performativity and ageing in Peter Cheeseman's documentary dramas "Fight for Shelton Bar!" and "Nice Girls"', Unpublished PhD thesis, Keele: Keele University.

Basting, A. (1998) *The stages of age*, Michigan, MI: University of Michigan Press.

Basting, A. (2000) 'Performance studies and age', in T.R. Cole, R. Kastenbaum and R.E. Ray (eds) *Handbook of the humanities and aging*, New York: Springer, pp 258-71.

Basting, A. (2009) *Forget memory: Creating better lives for people with dementia*, Baltimore, MD: Johns Hopkins University Press.

Bernard, M. and Munro, L. (2015) 'Theatre and ageing', in J. Twigg and W. Martin (eds) *Routledge handbook of cultural gerontology*, Abingdon: Routledge, pp 61-8.

Bernard, M., Rickett, M., Amigoni, D., Munro, L., Murray, M. and Rezzano, J. (2015) '*Ages and Stages*: The place of theatre in the lives of older people', *Ageing and Society*, vol 35, no 6, pp 1119-45. Available at http://dx.doi.org/10.1017/S0144686X14000038

Bunting, C. (2007) *Public value and the arts in England: Discussion and conclusions of the arts debate*, London: Arts Council England.

Castora-Binkley, M., Noelker, L., Prohaska, T. and Satariano, W. (2010) 'Impact of arts participation on health outcomes for older adults', *Journal of Aging, Humanities, and the Arts*, vol 4, pp 352-67.

Charney, M. (ed) (2005) *Comedy: A geographic and historical guide*, Westport, CT: Praeger Publishers.

Crossick, G. and Kaszynska, P. (2016) *Understanding the value of arts and culture: The AHRC Cultural Value Project*, Swindon: Arts and Humanities Research Council.

Cutler, D. (2009) *Ageing artfully: Older people and professional participatory arts in the UK*, London: The Baring Foundation.

Cutler, D. (2013) *Local authorities + older people + arts = a creative combination*, London: The Baring Foundation.

DCLG (Department for Communities and Local Government) (2006) *Strong and prosperous communities*, White Paper, London: DCLG.

DCMS (Department for Culture, Media and Sport) (2006) *Taking Part Survey: Provisional headline findings on engagement, future engagement and non-engagement in cultural and sporting activities*. Available at http://webarchive.nationalarchives.gov.uk//http://www.culture.gov.uk/reference_library/publications/3556.aspx

DH (Department of Health)/ACE (Arts Council England) (2007) *A prospectus for arts and health*. Available at www.artscouncil.org.uk/publication_archive/a-prospectus-for-arts-and-health/

Elvgren, Jr, G.A. (1974) 'Documentary theatre at Stoke-on-Trent', *Educational Theatre Journal*, vol 26, pp 86-98.

Gullette, M.M. (1997) *Declining to decline: Cultural combat and the politics of midlife*, Charlottesville, VA: University Press of Virginia.

Gullette, M.M. (2004) *Aged by culture*, Chicago, IL: University of Chicago Press.

Gullette, M.M. (2011) *Agewise: Fighting the new ageism in America*, Chicago, IL: University of Chicago Press.

Hafford-Letchfield, T., Couchman, W., Webster, M. and Avery P. (2010) 'A drama project about older people's intimacy and sexuality', *Educational Gerontology*, vol 36, no 7, pp 604-21.

Harding, S. (2005) 'Stages: Evaluation of an intergenerational drama', Unpublished report.

HM Government (2005) *Opportunity age: Meeting the challenges of ageing in the 21st century*, London: HM Government.

HM Government (2009) *Building a society for all ages*, London: HM Government.

Johnson, R. (2011) *'On Ageing' case study: Evaluation report*, London: Fevered Sleep.

Lipscomb, V.B. (2012) '"The play's the thing": Theatre as a scholarly meeting ground in age studies', *International Journal of Ageing and Later Life*, vol 7, no 2, pp 117-41.

Lipscomb, V.B. and Marshall, L. (eds) (2010) *Staging age: The performance of age in theatre, dance, and film*, New York: Palgrave.

Magic Me (2009) *Our generations: Report on a three year programme of intergenerational arts projects in Tower Hamlets, East London April 2006-June 2009*, London: Magic Me.

Mangan, M. (2013) *Staging ageing: Theatre, performance and the narrative of decline*, Bristol: Intellect.

Mental Health Foundation (2011) *An evidence review of the impact of participatory arts on older people*, Edinburgh: Mental Health Foundation.

Murray, M., Amigoni, D., Bernard, M., Goulding, A., Munro, L., Newman, A., et al (2014) 'Understanding and transforming ageing through the arts', in A. Walker (ed) *The new science of ageing*, Bristol: Policy Press, pp 77–112.

Noice, H. and Noice, T. (2008) 'An arts intervention for older adults living in subsidized retirement homes', *Aging, Neuropsychology, and Cognition*, vol 16, no 1, pp 56–79.

Noice, H. and Noice, T. (2013) 'Extending the reach of an evidence-based theatrical intervention', *Experimental Aging Research*, vol 39, pp 398–418.

Noice, H., Noice, T. and Staines, G. (2004) 'A short-term intervention to enhance cognitive and affective functioning in older adults', *Journal of Aging and Health*, vol 16, pp 1–24.

Noice, T., Noice, H. and Kramer, A.F. (2014) 'Participatory arts for older adults: A review of benefits and challenges', *The Gerontologist*, vol 54, no 5, pp 741–53.

Noice, H., Noice, T., Perrig-Chiello, P. and Perrig, W. (1999) 'Improving memory in older adults by instructing them in professional actors' learning strategies', *Applied Cognitive Psychology*, vol 13, pp 315–28.

Pyman, T. and Rugg, S. (2006) 'Participating in a community theatre production: A dramatherapeutic perspective', *International Journal of Therapy and Rehabilitation*, vol 13, no 12, pp 562–71.

Reynolds, J. (2013) *Ageing, drama and creativity: Inter-professional training course evaluation report*, Ages and Stages Project. Available at www.keele.ac.uk/agesandstages/outputs/

Rezzano, J. (2012) 'Our Age, Our Stage', Unpublished script.

Robson, J. (2009) *Aristophanes: An introduction*, Bristol: Bristol Classical Press.

Rowell, G. and Jackson, A. (1984) *The repertory movement: A history of regional theatre in Britain*, Cambridge: Cambridge University Press.

Schweitzer, P. (2007) *Reminiscence theatre: Making theatre from memories*, London: Jessica Kingsley Publishers.

Schweitzer, P. (2010) 'Experience shared and valued: Creative development of personal and community memory', in J. Bornat and J. Tetley (eds) *Oral history and ageing*, London: Centre for Policy on Ageing/Open University, pp 57–77.

Small, H. (2007) *The long life*, Oxford: Oxford University Press.

Staffordshire County Council (2007) *Ageing with opportunity in Staffordshire*, Stafford: Staffordshire County Council.

Stoke-on-Trent City Council (2007) *Ageing well, living well: 10-year plan*, Stoke-on-Trent: Stoke-on-Trent City Council.

Vorenberg, B.L. (1999) *Senior theatre connections: The first directory of senior theatre performing groups, professionals and resources*, Portland, OR: ArtAge Publications.

Vorenberg, B.L. (2011) 'The new senior theatre survey: A reflection of what's happening in community theatres', *AACT Spotlight*, November/December. Available at www.seniortheatre.com/A_New_Senior_Theatre_Survey_article.pdf

SIXTEEN

Conclusion

Alan Walker

As with Volume 1 this Conclusion is devoted mainly to a summary of the key findings from the New Dynamics of Ageing (NDA) projects represented by the chapters herein. It also provides an opportunity to review the contribution made by the NDA programme to ageing research, which follows the key findings. The first book in this NDA series, *The new science of ageing*, contained thematic syntheses of all of the research conducted by the programme, written by multidisciplinary teams of NDA researchers. Thus the three volumes together provide a comprehensive picture of the NDA programme: the first one synthesising the programme into its main themes and the other two providing detailed insights into each project, together with summaries of their main findings. Readers wanting even more details are requested to follow up the references cited in all three volumes and to visit the NDA website at www.newdynamics.group.shef.ac.uk

Key findings

As in Volume 1, this section summarises the key findings from each of the projects reported on in the earlier chapters. Again, fuller details can be found on the NDA website (see above).

Chapter Two: Sleep and autonomy in later life: the SomnIA project

- Good sleep is a pre-requisite for older people's wellbeing and ability to engage fully in daytime activities, whether living in their own homes or in a care home.
- Older men and women would rather not go to their doctor for help with poor sleep because they expect to sleep less well as they age, and believe they may be prescribed sleeping medication.
- Care home routines, staffing levels and care practices influence both the sleep and night-time experience of care home residents.

- Residential care homes have low levels of artificial lighting. Artificial light supplementation in communal areas can increase the time that care home residents spend under brighter light conditions without producing adverse effects.
- Sensitively designed new technology has much potential to support sleep in older people. Four prototypes developed were musical pillows, automatic bedroom lighting, an illuminated tray for easy access to items at night, and a portable hearing aid.

Chapter Three: Negotiating unfamiliar environments

- The meaning of space is important: cognitive maps are constructed through more than just physical and built environments. Emotional spaces are pertinent for older people.
- The hidden 'unseen' landscape beyond the immediate vision forms part of people's perception of the area.
- Neighbourhood environment walkability (how pedestrian-friendly the environment is) is a significant determinant of 'ageing in place'.
- Buildings and landmarks are important and helpful markers in unfamiliar environments.
- Designing outdoor spaces that are pleasant and easily walkable as well as routes that are navigable is important in making the environment less worrisome.

Chapter Four: Financial elder abuse

- Financial abuse of people with dementia or declining cognitive and physical functioning is of growing concern.
- It is equally important to protect professionals and carers from unfair allegations of financial abuse as it is to safeguard the assets of vulnerable older people.
- There is little comparative evaluation of the efficiency of safeguarding procedures in different authorities, and no evidence base underpinning the effectiveness of decision-making in cases of suspected abuse. A major gap in policy exists in understanding the long-term effects of financial abuse on victims.
- Multi-agency procedures have only a limited focus on financial abuse with the consequence that it features as secondary in importance to other forms of abuse.

Chapter Five: Maintaining dignity and independence

- Focusing on the day-to-day, participants view their struggles with illness and increasing disability as a fact of life that requires a great deal of perseverance to deal with.
- Not surprisingly, the loss of independence or self-reliance is hard for people to accept, and seen by most as inevitably leading to a loss of dignity.
- Not wanting to be a burden but having to accept a growing reliance on others is a complex task facing older people, and their identity and dignity are bound up in this.
- Participants frequently spoke in terms reflecting the shifting and precarious nature of life. Typical expressions were: "At the moment I'm still able to cook my own food" and "As long as we're able to manage, we'll stay living where we are." These convey the instability of their current circumstances and the prospect of further change ahead. Needing help from strangers with personal, bodily care is often dreaded: "The very thought of having somebody washing me, you know", said May. Most find that personal care is not as bad in reality as expected, but this depends on how the help is given.

Chapter Six: Families and caring in South Asian communities

- The onset of 'old age' is not linked to a specific age such as 65 or 70, but by key 'life events' such as the marriage of their children or the birth of (grand)children that involve changes in family roles and responsibilities.
- Family networks are very strong and locally focused. Ties back to Bangladesh and Pakistan were weakening over time. New global links were being established as their children moved to Europe and other countries. These highly complex and interlocking sets of family/social networks have implications for both expectation and provision of care and support.
- Strong links with the local community are the norm, and these provide vital resources in coping with growing old in a foreign land, give a focus for social engagement and provide support in times of celebration (weddings) or stress (bereavement).
- Expectations of their children providing care for old age are strong and 'state' care services viewed as only to be used as a last resort. However, some participants are uncertain if their expectations will be realised in the future, and others are ambivalent about having such expectations of their children.

Chapter Seven: Understanding immunesenescence

- One-third of older hip fracture patients develop new onset depression within six weeks after hip fracture.
- Hip fracture patients who develop depression have significantly poorer physical function, for example, walking speed, at both six weeks and six months after surgery, and poorer balance at week six.
- There is an increase in the stress hormone cortisol, an immune suppressor, and a decrease in the immune-enhancing hormone, dehydroepiandrosterone sulphate (DHEAS), leading to an increase in the cortisol:DHEAS ratio in depressed hip fracture patients compared with non-depressed patients or healthy controls.
- Patients with higher depression scores have a higher cortisol:DHEAS ratio.
- Slower walking speed is related to a higher cortisol:DHEAS ratio in the depressed group, suggesting that this hormonal imbalance might contribute to the reduced physical function in these patients.
- An Indian Punjabi group of hip fracture patients report being more affected by their hip fracture, perceiving that the treatment had helped their hip fracture far less, with significantly more emotional distress resulting from their hip fracture than the UK Caucasian patients.

Chapter Eight: Towards understanding the biological drivers of cell ageing

- Cell senescence is likely to underlie many age-related deleterious changes seen in the body.
- A novel molecular tool has been developed to selectively remove a key anti-ageing protein from cells. Loss of this protein results in early onset of many of the signs and diseases of normal ageing, together with highly premature cellular senescence.
- The new molecular tool responds to a small chemical switch that allows tight regulation of the protein in cells. This should enhance the progress of biochemical research on cell senescence in the lab.
- As cells age, they express elevated levels of DNA damage response proteins and various other stress response factors. Cellular stress and stress-signalling are therefore likely to be involved in driving cellular senescence.
- A potential anti-ageing drug, rapamycin, significantly affects the rate of onset of senescence – that is, the trajectory of cell senescence can be modulated using a clinically licensed drug.

Chapter Nine: NANA: a tale of ageing and technology

- Older people are happy to use new technology in their own homes.
- Older people are comfortable recording what they eat and drink on a daily basis.
- Older people are prepared to record their mood on a daily basis.
- Older people will complete cognitive measures on a daily basis.
- Older people will record their physical activity and function using new technology.

Chapter Ten: Combating malnutrition in hospitals

- A novel prototype for food provision and the nutritional management of older hospital patients has been developed in a multidisciplinary iterative process involving users and stakeholders.
- The prototype was informed by ethnography that identified the core factors contributing to malnutrition as: inefficient and inflexible food ordering/provision systems; poor mealtime ambience; lack of required assistance at mealtimes; poor monitoring of patient nutritional intake; and lack of accountability for nutritional care.
- The involvement of designers, and the integration of design methods and approaches with more traditional social science methods, enhances user and stakeholder engagement and optimises project outcomes.
- An iterative development and participative co-design process facilitates user engagement and innovative design approaches make ideas and opportunities tangible through mock-ups and prototyping methods.
- To address an identified need for smaller nutrient-dense foods for ward-level food provision, a range of mini-meals were developed including nutrient-enriched biscuits, ice cream, savoury sauces, soups and cakes.

Chapter Eleven: Migration and nutrition

- High levels of obesity were found among Bangladeshi mothers and daughters living in Cardiff, which are associated with frequent consumption of high fat savoury and sweet foods and low levels of physical activity.
- Low levels of physical function are common among Bangladeshi mothers living in Cardiff, which are associated with low physical activity levels and increased risk for frailty.

311

- Bangladeshi mothers and daughters living in Cardiff report poorer health status than their counterparts in Bangladesh.
- The exchange of health and nutrition knowledge is dynamic and spans across generations and countries through a range of mediums, including word of mouth, the internet, formal education and health professionals.
- There is a need for health promotion and public health campaigns and materials tailored for the Bangladeshi community that actively engages them, uses oral Sylheti information, and provides health and social care services designed to meet the diverse needs of this increasingly ageing population.

Chapter Twelve: Representing self – representing ageing

- Women in their 50s to 60s feel more pressure from media and advertising imagery compared with participants in their 80 to 90s.
- Eighty-eight per cent of visitors to the project exhibitions want to see more images of older women, like those created through the project, displayed in public.
- Participants captured various experiences from continued public involvement, friendships and fun to fears of increasing limitations and invisibility. Images challenged stereotypes such as the 'grumpy old woman' and reflected rarely represented grief and loss.
- Participants want to see more images of 'ordinary' older women who are still 'making a contribution'.
- Images produced by participants show that women experience ageing at the site of the body, for example, in the form of wrinkles and greying hair.
- Participatory visual methods give women a sense of solidarity and ownership of the research process, impacting on wellbeing and a feeling of public validation.

Chapter Thirteen: Ageing, fiction, narrative exchange and everyday life

- People's narrative understanding of ageing is important in determining their experience of ageing.
- There is a relationship between postwar representations of ageing (including fiction) and how ageing is understood, individually and socially.
- New forms of third age (people in their 60s and 70s no longer consider themselves old) and fourth age (people in their later 70s,

80s and 90s are still living full varied lives, despite infirmities) subjectivity have emerged.

- It is important to extend the concept of 'active ageing' beyond physical fitness and wellbeing criteria to include narrative understanding.
- There is a need for new narratives of the life course that enable older people to emerge from the ingrained stereotypes of ageing as social beings in their own right.

Chapter Fourteen: Narrative representations of the self: encounters with contemporary visual art

- Participants created meanings through engaging with contemporary visual artworks that were used for identity maintenance and revision purposes. This could aid transitions in later life such as bereavement, moving into sheltered accommodation and adjusting to declines in health.
- Older people introduced to contemporary art increase their knowledge and understanding of contemporary art after only three visits.
- Older people already engaged with cultural activities see such opportunities as a way of learning and keeping mentally stimulated, and relate this to maintaining wellbeing.
- Practical barriers to participation were identified including access to venues, transport and a misconception that entrance fees are required. Small fonts on labels are difficult to read.
- Psychosocial barriers to participation include a perception that art galleries are run by an elite. Complicated language on interpretation panels make some participants feel that they are not intelligent enough to understand the art. Being given a tour by an education officer or curator is cited as an effective way to access the art.

Chapter Fifteen: The place of theatre in representations of ageing

- It is important to challenge stereotypes that creativity declines/ ceases in old age.
- There are connections between identity, belonging, wellbeing, self-esteem and self-confidence, and they can be enhanced through theatre and drama.
- Participation is important – through volunteering and involvement in creative activities, particularly at times of transition and bereavement.

- Theatre and drama have a role to play as a medium for the inclusion of older and younger people.
- There are positive health outcomes and a sense of wellbeing for both older and younger participants, with practical and policy implications for community cohesion.
- Policy agendas on 'arts, health and wellbeing' need to be joined up with those addressing the needs of an 'ageing society'.

Contribution of the NDA programme

The very broad compass of the programme and its generation of important findings in many varied aspects of the changing dynamics of ageing is obvious from the summaries provided above and in Volume 1. It is reasonable to ask, however, what lasting contribution the programme has made to ageing research and beyond. According to my assessment there are 10 main contributions that the programme can claim:

Multidisciplinarity: The programme pushed back the boundaries of multidisciplinarity in ageing research by its inclusive disciplinary approach that embraced a wide spectrum, from biology to arts and humanities. This has left very solid foundations on which to develop even closer sharing of methods and approaches. In particular, ageing research will benefit from further combinations of biological and social sciences and a bigger push for *inter*disciplinarity.

Arts and humanities: The NDA programme left a fledgling arts and humanities and ageing research community that needs to be nurtured and developed (see Chapters Twelve to Fifteen).

Biology of ageing: The small number of projects with a biological focus made major advances, particularly with regard to cell senescence, cardiovascular ageing and immunology. In the latter case the combination of biological and social science expertise led to path-breaking research on the inhibiting role of depression following hip fracture and how to overcome it (Chapter Seven).

Longitudinal data analyses: The NDA programme's work on longitudinal cohorts also produced some path-breaking research and none more so than that uncovering associations between childhood deprivation and poor health in later life (Volume 1, Chapter Four). This research is at the forefront of efforts to improve the quality of later life and limit unnecessary health spending, and demands further support.

Representations of ageing and old age: The programme's research on representations of later life in theatre, fiction and visual arts, coupled with the extraordinary explosion of creativity by older women in the 'Representing self – representing ageing' project (Chapter Twelve), constituted the most powerful rejection thus far of misleading and false cultural stereotypes of old age.

Research methods: The programme made a substantial contribution to methods in ageing research – from visual arts techniques, to drama, to the linking of cohort data sets, to the creation of virtual representation. There is a deep and very rich pool of experience for others to dip into, replicate and develop further.

Design and ICTs: The NDA programme produced important new insights into how design and ICTs can be employed successfully to improve quality of life, for example, in the hospital and care settings (Chapters Nine and Ten), in the active third age (Volume 1, Chapter Ten), and for those with continence difficulties (Volume 1, Chapter Eleven). There is also a toolkit of ideas about how to sustain internet usage (Volume 1, Chapter Nine).

Nutrition in later life: The three NDA projects devoted to this issue leave an important legacy of understanding about the social, cultural and psychological role of food in older people's lives, including cross-culturally and the place where it is prepared (Chapters Nine to Eleven; Volume 1, Chapter Thirteen).

Economic development and ageing: The two NDA projects that looked at developing countries provided new insights into ageing and wellbeing in a development context, including the first comprehensive inquiry into the crucial role older people play in the family and wider economies, again demolishing stereotypes of passivity in old age.

Theory building: Last, but not least, the programme made substantial varied contributions to the theoretical basis of gerontology. Examples include bridging biology and social sciences in conceptualising the life course (Walker, 2014, 2018); understanding place and particular places in older people's lives (Chapters Three and Fifteen; Volume 1, Chapters Seven, Eight and Thirteen); the role of neoliberalism in structuring the lives of the poorest older people (Volume 1, Chapter Sixteen); new insights into gender representations (Chapter Twelve) and ethnicity and ageing (Chapters Six and Eleven); and clearer conceptions of dignity and independence (Chapter Five) and identity construction (Chapters Twelve and Fourteen).

In addition to these academic advances the NDA programme made many contributions to policy and practice, as well as to new products in prototype and drugs ready for trial, full details of which can be found on the NDA website.

Despite observing the principle of scientific rigour, a programme director-cum-editor is bound to have a partial take on the issue of contribution. Ideally this assessment would be qualified by a more detached one. As it happens, four Research Councils (AHRC, BBSRC, EPSRC and ESRC) commissioned an independent evaluation of the NDA programme by a team from Aston and Surrey Universities, the results of which were published as this book went to press (see Holland et al, 2017). While the evaluation team did not examine the NDA's contributions to specific aspects of ageing research, it did comment on the overall contribution to the field:

> That the NDA programme had an influence that was greater than the sum of its parts is an understatement. There is a range of evidence to suggest that the programme organisation had an enduring influence on science in ageing related research in addition to the direct achievement of individual project objectives. For example, its influence on integrative European research strategies (notably the European Road Map for Ageing Research) still resonates today, as does its part in the development of multidisciplinary working. (Holland et al, 2017, p 6)

The evaluation went further to commend the open and inclusive organisation of the programme as the foundation of its academic success:

> This was a ground-breaking research programme that owed as much to the overall programme "addons" as to the individual project and programme research funding. The ECR workshops and facilitation to attend European FLARE [Future Leaders of Ageing Research in Europe] meetings, the NDA conferences, support for policy links,

the organisation of the Older People's Reference Group (OPRG) to enable the involvement of older people, and the international networking were all facilitated by the Director and his team. (Holland et al, 2017, p 6)

The independent evaluation also echoed my own observations in the Programme Director's final report and in the introduction to the first book in this series (Walker, 2014), which praised the UK Research Councils for enabling cross-disciplinary working:

Funding for multidisciplinary programmes is essential for complex societal and health challenges such as ageing. Multidisciplinary and indeed holistic thinking are essential, and this understanding has been crucial in developing the way forward in international research. The coherent working of the research councils was crucial in enabling this. (Holland et al, 2017, p 6)

The evaluation also appraised the contribution of the NDA programme to capacity building in ageing research, and concluded that it was significant and lasting:

The capacity building capability of the programme was commendable. We identified and mapped 54 early career researchers' career development to date. The majority, 74%, had remained in academic work but when the job roles for those who had left academic work were considered, we determined that the NDA programme had benefited 92.6% of those who had taken part. (Holland et al, 2017, p 5)

Finally, in terms of the scientific quality and academic impact of the programme, the independent evaluation found that:

- To date the programme had produced 135 peer-reviewed articles, with a significant scientific impact in a range of fields.
- Over 75 per cent of the papers achieved a Multi-methods Appraisal Tool (MMAT) rating over 3★ for methodological assessment, while 57 per cent achieved a 3★ or higher quality appraisal rating, and 19.5 per cent received the highest mark of 4★, although 13 of the 35 projects produced no papers in the time span that were rated as 4★.

- The programme clearly achieved 3★ and 4★ rated research, both in terms of methodological quality and overall scientific quality, including internationally excellent and world leading research, with some clearly providing important step-changes and major influence on a research theme or field.
- Over 80 per cent of the papers had been cited internationally.

Final words

It is reassuring to have one's inevitably partial assessment of the academic quality and value of the NDA programme confirmed by independent evaluators employing sophisticated techniques. (An earlier evaluation of the programme's non-academic impact had identified a wide range of ways in which it had influenced policy and practice in particular; see National Development Team, 2015.) There is little doubt that, as well as many important contributions to different aspects of ageing research and wider impacts, the foundations have been laid for further major investments towards significant step-changes in our understanding of ageing and therefore in our capacity to respond to it successfully. If such investments are forthcoming I would concentrate research on large multidisciplinary collaborations (the NDA Collaborative Research Projects, see Chapter One), and shift the focus from old age to ageing. The specific aim would be to examine the multiple pathways to later life and especially the intersectional inequalities (gender, social class, ethnicity and so on) that play a major role in determining old age outcomes and indeed, whether old age is, in fact, attainable at all. Capacity building would need to be central to such a programme of research, particularly in multidisciplinary working, and also the involvement of key stakeholders such as older people. However, to maximise the impact of a life course-focused programme of research, a multigenerational approach should be encouraged. For their part, both funders and universities need to reflect on how they can sustain impact potential after the end of projects and programmes:

> We spoke to many committed, persistent and inspirational researchers over the course of this evaluation. They were clearly giving their all, often without any funding and little support from their institutions, to ensure their work makes a difference to older people, as well as to policy, practice and product development. (National Development Team, 2015, p 7)

References

Holland, C., Griffiths, H., Nabrey, I., Tritter, J. and Gwyther, H. (2017) *Academic evaluation of the New Dynamics of Ageing Programme*, Aston: Aston University, Aston Research Centre for Healthy Ageing.

National Development Team (2015) *Evaluation of the impact of the New Dynamics of Ageing Research Programme*, Swindon: Economic and Social Research Council.

Walker, A. (ed) (2014) *The new science of ageing*, Bristol: Policy Press.

Walker, A. (2018) 'Why the UK needs a social policy on ageing', *Journal of Social Policy*, vol 47, no 2, pp 253-73.

Index

Note: Page numbers in *italics* refer to figures or tables.

W

Werner syndrome (WS) 137–8
Westerhof, G. 266
WinDiets dietary analysis software 168,
    169
Winter Fuel Payments 257
women ageing *see* representing self –
    representing ageing (RSRA)
working in later life 256
WRN 137–8
  reduction of 139–40, 142–3

Z

Zhong, J. 36